ASIAN AMERICAN PLAYS
for a NEW GENERATION

ASIAN AMERICAN PLAYS

for a NEW GENERATION

Edited by

JOSEPHINE LEE, DON EITEL,
AND R. A. SHIOMI

TEMPLE UNIVERSITY PRESS ⊤ PHILADELPHIA

12/11 S got me 4 Xmas

6/12 Read Ching Chong, I lk 7 How to Succeed

TEMPLE UNIVERSITY PRESS
Philadelphia, Pennsylvania 19122
www.temple.edu/tempress

Copyright © 2011 by Temple University
All rights reserved
Published 2011

Library of Congress Cataloging-in-Publication Data

Asian American plays for a new generation / edited by Josephine Lee, Don Eitel, and R. A. Shiomi.
    p. cm.
  Includes bibliographical references.
  ISBN 978-1-4399-0515-9 (cloth : alk. paper) — ISBN 978-1-4399-0516-6 (pbk. : alk. paper) — ISBN 978-1-4399-0517-3 (e-book)
1. American drama—Asian American authors. 2. American drama—20th century. 3. American drama—21st century. 4. Asian Americans—Drama. I. Lee, Josephine, 1960– II. Eitel, Don, 1975– III. Shiomi, R. A., 1947–
  PS628.A85A885 2011
  812'.54080895073—dc22

                                                            2010042421

♾ The paper used in this publication meets the requirements of the American National Standard for Information Sciences—Permanence of Paper for Printed Library Materials, ANSI Z39.48—1992

Printed in the United States of America

2 4 6 8 9 7 5 3

CONTENTS

A

ASIAN AMERICAN PLAYS
for a NEW GENERATION

Introduction

JOSEPHINE LEE *prof AA Stud ∪ Minn*

> Tam (*as a Bible Belt preacher*): Born? No! Crashed! Not born.
> Stamped! Not born! Created! Not born. No more born than the
> heaven and earth. No more born than nylon or acrylic. For I am a
> Chinaman! A miracle synthetic!
>
> **Frank Chin,** *The Chickencoop Chinaman*

*No. Ex Lee's Man, hot wife
is written by Ailsabet
not @
Asian
at all
John*

One might well ask whether "Asian American plays" are more than a collection of works that just "happen" to be written by Asian Americans. What follows by way of introduction are some reflections that argue for more than just this casual connection. My argument is that "Asian American plays" first and foremost comment on the distinctive relationship between racial and theatrical performance. Thus, drama, while often thought of as a subset of literature more generally, really deserves its own space for discussion, as it references theatrical enactment—the live encounter of performers and audiences in a particular time and place and the perception of individual and collective bodies.

In May Lee-Yang's *Sia(b)*, a young Hmong woman, her mouth and tongue undulating over each significant syllable, gives the audience a lesson on how to say her name. Sun Mee Chomet's *Asiamnesia* opens with a re-creation of the 1834 display of a real "Chinese lady" (Afong Moy) at the American Museum in New York. Lauren Yee's *Ching Chong Chinaman* features a spectacular tap-dancing sequence that sparks a furtive love affair in the laundry room. Through the staging of specific instances of human expression and encounter, these plays provide a focused way to examine more generally the cultural politics of racial perception and interaction. In this way, Asian American plays, such as the seven collected here, present a unique opportunity to think about how racial issues are engaged through physical contact, bodily labor, and fleshly desire, as well as through the more standard elements of plot, setting, characterization, staging, music, and action.

At the same time, we ought to be careful not to assume that plays simply *represent* Asian Americans, simply showing a re-creation of real-life experience. Rather, theater is both presentational and representational; it might "hold the mirror up to nature," to use Hamlet's famous expression, but it also creates experiences unique to the stage. Thus, the versions of racial behavior and interaction shown here are clearly *plays*, driven by theatrical devices as much as by social agendas. From the intimacy of the one-man show of *Indian Cowboy* to *Walleye Kid*'s nod to Broadway glitz to the history lessons given by *Happy Valley* and *Bahala Na*, these plays highlight both the possibilities of imaginative staging and the day-to-day workings of what Michael Omi and Howard Winant have called "racial etiquette" off the stage.[1]

Reading plays teaches important lessons about what it means to think about race. Carefully analyzing the work of theater production, rather than just enjoying the fruits of theatrical design, rehearsal, and production, exposes a certain kind of artifice that teaches us something about the construction of social performance more generally; just looking at acting reminds us how we labor to manufacture and sustain our own various social identities. This is particularly relevant in the case of Asian American identity, which is notoriously unstable. To quote Tam Lum, the protagonist of Frank Chin's play *Chickencoop Chinaman*, "Chinamen are made, not born."[2] Asian American theater highlights the work it takes to "make" an "Asian American"—to formulate this single racial category out of so many distinct ethnic, generational, class, gender, religious, cultural, and political attributes. But just as it exposes the fallacies of lumping so many different people together, theater presents the possibility of productive collaboration. While theater shows how people certainly do not act alike, being together in the theater does give opportunities for them to act together. Theater not only presents visions of offstage relationships and communities; it actually creates its own human bonds and interactions in both rehearsal and production. Thus, it has the potential to forge alliances, to rally individuals to collective action, or to create a more modest sense of connection.

This has long been the case with Asian American theaters and plays. From the collaborative work of such Asian American theater companies as East West Players in Los Angeles, Pan Asian Repertory Theatre and Ma-Yi Theatre in New York, and Mu Performing Arts in the Twin Cities to a host of less formal collectives, such as Slant, Peeling the Banana, and Here and Now, the making of theater has provided an important starting point for building relationships, raising political awareness, and creating active communities. Public performance has been of particular value for Asian Americans, who have been called the "invisible minority." Asian American plays provide correctives to this invisibility.

1. See Michael Omi and Howard Winant, *Racial Formation: From the 1960s to the 1990s* (New York: Routledge, 1986), 62.
2. Frank Chin, *The Chickencoop Chinaman and The Year of the Dragon* (Seattle: University of Washington Press, 1981), 6.

The 1990s saw a number of new anthologies of Asian American drama, begin-
ning with Misha Berson's *Between Worlds: Contemporary Asian-American Plays*
(1990). Collections edited by Roberto Uno (*Unbroken Thread: An Anthology of
Plays by Asian American Women* [1993]), Velina Hasu Houston (*The Politics of
Life: Four Plays by Asian American Women* [1993] and *But Still, Like Air, I'll
Rise: New Asian American Plays* [1997]), Brian Nelson (*Asian American Drama:
Nine Plays from the Multiethnic Landscape* [1997]), and Alvin Eng (*Tokens? The
NYC Asian American Experience on Stage* [1999]) were also published during
that decade, signaling a boom in the production, as well as in the publication,
of Asian American plays.

Asian American plays have won Tony and Obie awards, met with critical success, and perhaps most important, moved a generation of audiences
to think, to feel, and to act. We now have easy access to multiple plays and
theater pieces by individual playwrights such as Ping Chong, Edward Saka-
moto, Dan Kwong, Young Jean Lee, and Chay Yew, to add to earlier volumes
of works by Frank Chin, Philip Kan Gotanda, and David Henry Hwang. Some
have chosen to jettison the capacious and in many ways unwieldy term "Asian
American" in favor of a more specific ethnic designation, such as Filipino and
Filipino American works produced by New York's Ma-Yi Theatre Company;
Savage Stage, edited by Joi Barrios-Leblanc (2006); and Esther Kim Lee's
Seven Contemporary Plays from the Korean Diaspora in the Americas (2011).
Other playwrights eschew racial or ethnic labels entirely, fearing that these
might limit or marginalize their work. Is marking drama as "Asian American"
no longer necessary, or is it even detrimental in this so-called post-racial society? In what ways might the rubric "Asian American" still be viable, albeit in
need of reformatting?

Several decades have passed since the first successes of Asian American
playwrights and the appearance of these earlier anthologies, and it seems high
time to address these questions anew. This collection includes seven plays
that touch, entertain, and move us to think about the contemporary present of
Asian Americans. These particular plays were not included in this anthology
on the basis of their broad commercial success; though they have been warmly
received by audiences and critics lucky enough to catch their runs, the plays in
this collection for the most part have had limited circulation. Nor can we make
claims for their radical aesthetics, although these works are certainly theatri-
cally engaging, in turns funny, poignant, funky, clever, strange, and chilling.
These works were chosen for their ability to pressure readers into questioning
current assumptions about racial identities marked as Asian American. Their
inclusion in this collection does not mean that they hold the mirror up to some
quintessential experience. With their singular stories and distinctive characterizations, these plays defy the charge to represent homogenous identities even
while they comment profoundly on cultural and national affiliation.

At first glance, what these works present as "Asian American" may not seem
so surprising. One immediately finds in these plays some of those preoccupa-

tions familiar to Asian American literature, film, and plays written since the 1970s. They tackle issues of immigration and migration; problems of marginalization, racism, and stereotyping; and crises of identity. They eloquently stage generational tensions, angry parents, disaffected children, enigmatic grandmothers, and buried family histories. They tell stories of transnational ties and ethnic and pan-ethnic communities, and they express anxiety over adaptation, assimilation, and upward mobility.

Yet in major ways, these plays also depart for territory hitherto unexplored. Just looking at some of their settings—for instance, the Minnesota landscape of *Walleye Kid*—shows us that we are no longer in the locales that defined earlier versions of Asian America. Location is essential here, and this collection moves us away both from California as the central locus of Asian America and from New York as the mecca of American theater. One characteristic that may strike us most is that many of these plays feature characters who find themselves alone, whether by choice or by compunction. Whether the character is an actor seeking the perfect role, an adoptee looking for roots, a gay man examining his ambivalence about fatherhood, or a dying matriarch journeying into her past, he or she experiences a profound sense of isolation, undertakes voyages of reinvention, or is singled out for punishment.

The sense of singularity and disenfranchisement is intimately tied up with where these plays come from. If we compare this anthology with earlier collections of Asian American drama, we notice that the sites of writing and production for many plays previously published were either in California or New York. Skimming through these earlier volumes produces an intense sense of connection; actions take place in Chinatown, a South Asian restaurant, a Japanese American internment camp, referencing well-established Asian American communities and settings. In repeated references to older Asian American theater companies, such as East West Players or the theater scenes of New York, the sensation of connection and community is magnified. In contrast, these plays originated in the Twin Cities of Minneapolis and St. Paul—metropolitan areas, to be sure, but still viewed as provincial, regional, or even, to borrow a phrase, a "vast banana wasteland" where Asian America is concerned.[3]

I first encountered these plays by attending productions and staged readings at Mu Performing Arts, Mixed Blood Theatre, and Dreamland Arts. Through the intimacy of these smaller theater spaces and communities, and the revelations that these plays presented to their relatively young audiences—many of them my own college students and first-time theatergoers—it became clear to me that what I was seeing was substantively different from my other experiences of Asian American theater in New York or on the West Coast. The Twin Cities area is home to an active and vibrant theater community, with reportedly more theater seats per capita than any other U.S. locale other than New York

3. William Wei, *The Asian American Movement* (Philadelphia: Temple University Press, 1992), 11–12, 29.

City. With well-established regional arts venues such as the Guthrie Theater, the Playwright's Center, the Children's Theatre Company, and Penumbra Theatre, as well as a host of smaller companies and collectives, Minneapolis and St. Paul make a hospitable home for new theatrical writing and production. The racial climate, however, is somewhat more uncertain. The populations of the Twin Cities are diverse compared with those of outlying areas but remain mostly white. Concentrations of relatively new migration—Hmong families from refugee camps in Thailand, young adults and children adopted from Korea and China into white families—join with individual Asian Americans who have come to the Twin Cities for work, education, family, or less predictable reasons. While Asian American activists have been hard at work in the Twin Cities for decades, a sense of pan-ethnic community and solidarity still seems tentative at times, and Asian American studies, if the subject exists at all, is still fairly new at colleges and universities such as the University of Minnesota.

Asian American theater artists often find their foothold here through Mu Performing Arts, established in 1992 by R. A. (Rick) Shiomi, Dong-il Lee, Diane Espaldon, and Martha Johnson. Mu's productions have been as varied in content and form as their performers and audiences, including low-budget readings of new works, taiko drumming, stagings of Shakespeare and Sondheim, and partnerships with the Guthrie Theater on plays by the Tony Award–winning playwright David Henry Hwang. Mu makes eclectic choices, reflecting a dynamic and sometimes uncertain understanding of what "Asian American theater" is all about.

Asian American concerns may at times seem old hat in places such as California. The demographics of the West Coast point directly toward a future in which the United States has no single racial majority. There, well-established Chinese American, Japanese American, and Filipino communities are continually joined by sizable waves of immigrants from Southeast Asia, India, Korea, and Taiwan. Here in the Twin Cities, it means something quite different to perform Asian America. The prevailing sensibility that Minnesota is "white" is belied by the large concentrations of Hmong and Korean adoptees, both constituencies fairly new to claiming "Asian American" identity. What is produced by way of theater registers these distinctions. Mu's first production, *Mask Dance*, featured the stories of young Korean adoptees raised in Minnesota. This focus on adoptees, many of whom grew up as the only non-white individuals in their rural communities, departs radically from an understanding of Asian American stories as centered on immigrant families.

These differences in the imagining of "Asian America" cannot be dismissed as just a set of quaint regional distinctions. Titling a play *Walleye Kid* has relevance beyond associating transracial adoption with a notably Minnesotan fish; it emphasizes the prominence of the adoptee in refiguring what "Asian American" is. Racial isolation is an experience familiar to many in the Midwest, so much so that it should be thought of as a paradigmatic rather than a peripheral part of Asian American experience. Moving away from a bicoastal Asian

America suggests more broadly how Asian American experience never has had a real center. Instead, it is a mass of changing relationships among often quite disparate individuals and groups, whose sense of self, community, and home must be renegotiated time and again. Thus, far from being odd, the sense of dislocation and isolation experienced by Asian adoptees in the Midwest serves as a reminder that many experience their racial, ethnic, and cultural identities in ways that are far different from those in traditional ethnic enclaves and the larger urban centers of California and New York.

This set of plays more broadly confirms that "Asian America" must be imagined differently, and it does so sometimes seriously, sometimes irreverently. There is both humor and freshness in this writing, which may have to do with the focus of these characterizations on adolescents and young adults. This reminds us that Asian America has a conspicuously young face. Asian Americans not only are the fastest growing racial group in the United States but also, according to data from the 2004 U.S. Census, had a median age of thirty-five, about five years under that of non-Hispanic whites. The lines between "Asian" and "Asian American," native-born and newcomer, citizen, permanent resident, and visitor are often blurred; about half of foreign-born Asians are relative newcomers, having arrived in the United States since 1990. Judging identity and affiliation through culture and language are also tricky; although about 77 percent of Asians speak a language other than English at home, about 63 percent of Asians age five and older speak only English or speak English fluently.[4] These changing demographics and attitudes force a constant reassessment of how categorizations of race, ethnicity, national affiliation, and culture work.

A number of other themes run through this volume and connect these works. An interest in reclaiming Asian and Asian American history remains a strong concern here, as it does in much of Asian American drama more generally. Whether whimsically presented, with characters led toward the past by a giant fish (*Walleye Kid*), or gathered for an evening of drunken celebration (*Asiamnesia*) or more somberly brought to light through the family secrets and stories of *Bahala Na* and *Sia(b)*, the past intrudes on the present in unpredictable and sometimes violently disruptive ways. There are a number of reasons that, even after several decades of excavation, Asian American histories are still not more broadly known. Asian Americans go unnoticed in many conversations about race that are still centered on a black–white divide. The trauma of war, immigration, and dislocation creates rifts and lapses in the transmission of family stories, and life in the United States stresses reinvention and cultivates amnesia. These particular stories—of the Korean War, of Chinese plantation labor and Japanese military occupation in the Philippines, of Asian American female performers, of Hmong participation in the "Secret War" in

---

4. U.S. Census Bureau, "The American Community—Asians: 2004," American Community Survey Report, February 2007.

Laos—are even less familiar to American audiences than those of Japanese internment or Chinese railroad workers. If plays such as *Indian Cowboy* and *Happy Valley* show characters subjected to the formative political and social events of the present, others stress that contemporary Asian American life is equally in thrall to the past. The significance of the past is paramount, and its revelation becomes a consistently forceful action within these plays. Nonetheless, their telling of history is by no means straightforward; historical facts are fragmented, contested, and misremembered, and the movements they trace are left unresolved.

These plays take for granted that the familial, experiential, and imaginative connections of Asia and the United States are multidirectional; no longer can "Asian American" be viewed as a one-way ticket from Asia to the United States and degrees of straight-line assimilation. Rather, it comprises multiple journeys from different sites. The plays' characters draw on distinctive ethnic, cultural, and religious affiliations, identifying themselves first as Hmong, Zoroastrian, Korean adoptee—and only peripherally as "Asian American." Their relationships provide a window into a much broader set of contemporary mappings of Asia to America. Through these plays we see the legacies of multiple imperialisms—European, Japanese, American—on Asian and Pacific peoples. Other moments register the global economies and new patterns of labor migration that have redefined Asian America. *Walleye Kid*'s little orphan Annie travels through the traumatic past of the Korean War and the politics of transnational adoption. The Hmong family in *Sia(b)* feels the effects of the Central Intelligence Agency's "secret war" in Laos a generation later. *Bahala Na* traces a family history linking Chinese labor migration, Japanese colonialism, and gay sexuality in the United States and the Philippines. *Happy Valley* depicts relationships between Hong Kong Chinese, Mainland Chinese, and Filipina domestic servants as shaped by the larger upheavals during Hong Kong's reversion to Chinese rule. In *Asiamnesia*, an Asian American actress becomes the new "it" girl for moviegoers in Korea as well as in the United States. In *Ching Chong Chinaman*, a Chinese American family indentures a servant from China, and videogames bring the world closer together.

These treatments of history, migration, transnationality, and colonialism point toward another prominent aspect of these plays: their probing of the uneasy racial positioning of Asian Americans and how the modern state manages and regulates visibility. We see a particular familiarity with the model-minority stereotype so often ascribed to Asian Americans since the 1960s and 1970s. The model minority presents an enhanced and colorized version of the quintessential American rags-to-riches story, simultaneously affirming the compliant docility of immigrant labor and managing anxieties about racism and colonialism. The success story of Vietnamese refugee children, for instance, not only marvels at the resilience of exceptional children but also alleviates guilt about U.S. military involvement and blames the poverty of the "non-model" minorities—African Americans and Latinos—on their presumed unwillingness to work. Michael Omi has summarized and questioned the contradictory arguments that Asian Americans are far from being disadvantaged or underrepresented and that selected social and economic indicators show them as having achieved parity with whites with respect to income and levels of education.[5] Omi addresses the split within Asian American communities between the poverty levels of certain groups (notably Southeast Asian, such as Hmong and Cambodian, refugee groups) and those who have moved into positions of relative affluence and influence (such as Chinese and Japanese communities). He also stresses the continued presence of stereotypes and racism in American life that continue to belie the status of Asian Americans as "honorary whites." Yet progressive Asian American activists are nonetheless haunted by the fear of Asian Americans' becoming the "racial bourgeoisie," as Mari Matsuda puts it:

> If white, as it has been historically, is the top of the racial hierarchy in America, and black, historically, is the bottom, will yellow assume the place of the racial middle? The role of the racial middle is a critical one. It can reinforce white supremacy if the middle deludes itself into thinking it can be just like white if it tries hard enough. Conversely, the middle can dismantle white supremacy if it refuses to be the middle, if it refuses to buy into racial hierarchy, and if it refuses to abandon communities of black and brown people, choosing instead to forge alliances with them.[6]

Omi and Matsuda articulate the need to redefine "Asian American" as a term that is more about consciousness and political solidarity than about biological or cultural similarity. Matsuda points out the extent to which "issues do define us," emphasizing how "Asian American" encompasses a strong wish for a politics of affiliation and activism as well as a racial category being imposed by the state.

In many ways the characters in these plays express a longing, however guarded, for some form of racial or ethnic community. At the same time, these plays are distinctive in their wariness toward reproducing the clichés of minority oppression and a crisis of identity caught "between worlds." In Lauren Yee's *Ching Chong Chinaman*, the teenage Desdemona laments that she will not get into an Ivy League school: "I'm an Asian American female with a 2340 and a 4.42 GPA at an elite public high school. That's like the worst thing in the world. Nobody's gonna want me." To counter this, she manufactures a past that includes a host of clichés of racial struggle and identity crisis, making note

5. Michael Omi, "Asian-Americans: The Unbearable Whiteness of Being?" *Chronicle of Higher Education* 55, no. 5 (September 26, 2008): B56.
6. Mari J. Matsuda, "We Will Not Be Used: Are Asian-Americans the Racial Bourgeoisie?" in *Where Is Your Body? And Other Essays on Race, Gender, and the Law*, ed. Mari J. Matsuda (Boston: Beacon Press, 1996), 149–159.

of the successful formulas of "teen marriage, drug abuse, adultery, concubine, suicide, disfigurement, drowning" borrowed from *The Joy Luck Club.* Yee's scathing parody sharply pinpoints a contradiction in seeing Asian Americans as racially oppressed and identifies how such ethnic identities are packaged and marketed, managed as performances of melodrama and victimization. Desdemona is not exceptional in claiming a certain image of otherness to make herself distinctive, to get ahead. At the same time, what happens to the real subjects of oppression, brutality, trauma, and violence if their pain is co-opted and transformed into cliché? Even more pointedly in *Sia(b)*, May Lee-Yang points out a porn site featuring "Hmong Hotties" that carries the caption "The Hmong in America: A Story of Tragedy and Hope," echoing the humanitarian impulse of racial uplift: "We hope that Hmonghotties.com will help you better understand the Hmong people in the United States, and the tragic events that brought them here." On this, she comments: "I just love how even an aspiring porn site has to provide some background education on the Hmong culture as though you can't look at my boobs unless you know how my people came to the United States."

Ching Chong Chinaman features a not-so-gentle parody of Asian American solidarity, pan-ethnicity, and ethnic "roots," questioning both the commercialization of multiculturalism and the obsolescence of old-school racial pride. Much less funny are the violent hate crimes, detainment, and interrogation that affect South Asians depicted in the pre- and post-9/11 world of *Indian Cowboy.* In snide and more somber ways, these plays complicate any paradigmatic sense of who Asian Americans actually are, where they live, how they got there, and where they are going. These characters are complicated and conflicted beings whose responses and actions do not easily peg them as heroic social reformers or as tragic victims of racism. These plays are far from "post-racial"; instead, they make new uses of the ever more complicated vocabularies of racial behavior and identity. What we find are not characterizations of "authentic" Asian Americans that somehow can replace the tired clichés of the yellow peril and Madame Butterfly but, rather, multiple questionings of Asian Americans as they are imagined as moving into and between various roles—never simply oppressed subalterns, activists, victims, perpetrators, radical feminists, closet chauvinists but sometimes all of these and more.

In closing this Introduction, I return to the importance of looking at these works as plays rather than novels or memoirs, and I encourage even casual readers to imagine their production and, whenever possible, to read them aloud with others. Live performance gives these issues vitality, immediacy, and impact, emphasizing the material and visceral ways that we experience them. The small details of the everyday—conversations, food, clothing, gestures of love and loathing—bring the perceptions, effects, and consequences of being Asian American closer to home. These plays also affirm the collaborative and public nature of theater making; not only do the plays depict different kinds of Asian American communities, testing the notion of the "ethnic enclave," but they also gesture toward new interactions and relationships that are formed through the very act of performing plays. What is "Asian American" is actively relational—the forming of identity happens in contact with others, never in an isolated way. The different dimensions of theater practice—casting, development, directing, acting, production, marketing, reception—illustrate how these interconnections substantively matter. Audiences must confront live actors who may or may not affirm their expectations of racial, ethnic, or cultural identity. Performers must rehearse and perform together, working toward a unified artistic vision that often tests their own preconceptions of how others can or should perform. The messy facts of human contact—both displayed visibly and more covertly informing each production—are routinely part and parcel of theater practice. A sense of camaraderie and common mission can be created through theater, encouraging racial and ethnic solidarity, but theater is also the place of conflict, uneasy negotiation, and even violence. Thus, the significance of race, ethnicity, and culture is changed by how Asian Americans come together to make theater as writers, producers, performers, audience members. Ultimately, I hope that this volume provides multiple occasions for engaging directly and actively with Asian American issues through performance, for coming together rather than standing aloof.

1

Indian Cowboy

ZARAAWAR MISTRY

INTRODUCTION, *by Josephine Lee*

Indian Cowboy premiered at Mixed Blood Theatre in Minneapolis from January 27, 2006, to February 12, 2006. Commissioned by Jack Reuler and Mixed Blood Theatre, with development of the script supported by the Jerome Foundation, the play was performed by Zaraawar Mistry and created in collaboration with Kathleen Sullivan, with original music composed and performed by Keith Lee.

Indian Cowboy follows the life of the actor Gayomar Katrak from his adoption by a Parsi family of three brothers and a sister in Hyderabad, India, to his trials and tribulations as an actor in the United States. It is a touchstone of a particular moment; Zaraawar Mistry lightly satirizes immigrant fantasies of American culture as well as New Age fascination with India, yuppies, method acting, and high-tech modernization. The play belies the hopes inherent in both multiculturalism and cross-ethnic casting. In a sense, Gayomar, named after the Zoroastrian version of Adam, becomes "Guy," an everyman whose crisis of identity makes us ponder the various choices and temptations American culture offers to hopeful arrivals. Yet his story, full of quirky details, is also highly distinctive, reminding us of the limits of ethnic, racial, religious, or national identity. Transnational, Zoroastrian, adopted, and an actor, Guy does not fit easily into tidy boxes such as "Indian," "South Asian," or "Asian American." Cast in a

Illustration: Zaraawar Mistry in *Indian Cowboy*.
(Photograph by Ann Marsden, courtesy of Mixed Blood Theatre.)

range of roles, as "Mediterranean, or Iranian, or Puerto Rican or Alien," Guy's ethnically ambiguous appearance at first makes him an undistinguished figure among others in the American mosaic. But as the play moves toward its resolution, he is again marked as the enemy and other, reminding us of the continuing salience of race in a post-9/11 world.

It is important to note that this play was first produced as a one-man show; in these productions Mistry used only minimal props and lighting, marvelously transforming himself through his voice, expression, and movement to capture distinctive characters and situations. In embodying Guy's journey from Hyderabad to the United States and back again, Mistry became our anchor through time, space, and imagination, suggesting how, in the performance of story, even ordinary lives might be granted meaning and magic.

———————

STORYTELLER: It was Christmas Day, some forty years ago, on the outskirts of the city of Hyderabad in southern India. The sun had just set, and the sky was orange blue. Three Parsi brothers, Fali, Mehli, and Soli, were driving home after a long trip into the countryside to visit their old aunt Soonamai at her orphanage, when they stopped for a rest by the side of the road under a large banyan tree. During the day, the banyan would have been witness to the bustling of travelers, vendors, and monkeys, but now it stood silent and still. On the distant horizon, a small group of villagers were slowly leading their cattle home, oblivious to the giant satellite dish that stood staring into space by the headquarters of Hindustan Telecommunications.

It had been an unusually hot day. The brothers got out of the car, walked over to a clump of bushes, unbuttoned their trousers and . . . Ah! A gentle breeze washed their streams in helix patterns over the dusty earth. Standing there in their white pants and white shirts with rolled-up sleeves, with their slicked-back black hair and pencil-thin mustaches, Fali, Mehli, and Soli looked like three young Clark Gables.

(A baby cries.)

MEHLI: What's that?
STORYTELLER: Mehli, the middle brother, was the first to notice that there was a naked baby lying in the bushes.
MEHLI: Oh my goodness! I hope I didn't do it on him.
SOLI: You must have. He's frowning at you.
STORYTELLER: Soli, the youngest, was a soap salesman.
SOLI: Hello, cutie. He looks just like the poster baby for Johnson's Soap!
FALI: Don't be ridiculous. And stop gawking, you two. That baby needs our help.

STORYTELLER: Fali, the first-born, gently picked up the baby.

FALI: What's a baby boy doing here? Left for us by some unwilling mother, I suppose.

MEHLI: For us?

STORYTELLER: Said Mehli, in the middle.

MEHLI: What are we going to do with a baby? It will bring us nothing but trouble. We must report it to the police.

FALI: And what are the police going to do with him? Put him in some orphanage.

SOLI: Why don't we just leave him there?

STORYTELLER: Suggested Soli.

SOLI: Maybe the mother will come back.

STORYTELLER: But Fali, who was in the film business, liked movies with happy endings.

FALI: We'll give him to Nergish. This boy is for her. Arey, che-chey, he's doing it on me. Take him, Mehli. Take him.

STORYTELLER: Mehli took the baby boy and carefully wrapped him in his sweaty white shirt. The brothers went home to their little sister, and Soli said . . .

SOLI: Merry Christmas, Nergish.

STORYTELLER: And Nergish, who badly wanted a child but knew she would never marry, began to weep . . .

NERGISH: Life works in mysterious ways. He looks just like the poster baby for Johnson's soap!

STORYTELLER: And that's how I entered into the lives of the Katrak family of Hyderabad. Nergish Katrak became my mother, and Fali, Mehli, and Soli my three uncles. They told everyone they knew that I'd been adopted from Aunt Soonamai's orphanage, but they always told me, with a great deal of love, that I'd been found—by a narrow little stream.

But what should they name me?

FALI : I think he should be called Farokh, after papa.

SOLI : Farokh? That's a Parsi name. Maybe he should have a Hindu name, like Vishnu, or Shiva.

MEHLI : What about something to reflect that we found him on Christmas Day? Like, Joseph. We could call him Joe.

NERGISH: Enough, you three. Enough.

STORYTELLER: My mother was a small woman—but she had a big presence.

NERGISH: I have consulted with Babu Nath.

STORYTELLER: Babu Nath was a local wise man.

NERGISH: We know the baby was abandoned because it's most probably illegitimate. But Babu Nath has told me that . . . this boy has a special gift.

MEHLI: Gift? What kind of gift?

SOLI: Everyone has a special gift.

FALI: That Babu Nath is nothing but a fraud!

NERGISH: Therefore, Babu Nath said, to honor this gift, we should name him with a "guh" sound. Guh, guh.

SOLI: How about Ganesh?

FALI: I like Gusti.

MEHLI: Is anyone opposed to Gilbert?

NERGISH: Enough you three, enough! I want to name him Gayomar.

STORYTELLER: Ganesh, Gusti, Gilbert, Gayomar. The Katraks eventually named me Gayomar, after the first man, the Adam, of Zoroastrian mythology. Katrak means tailor. The Parsis, Zoroastrians who emigrated from Iran to India in the tenth century, often took new family names based on their profession, although none of the Katraks were tailors anymore—their grandfather had been the last one. In Hyderabad, I knew Parsi families with last names like Chenai, because they had an export business to China, there was a Bankwalla (literally, "bank-person," "Bankwalla," or "banker"), Batliwalla (bottle-person, whose business was collecting old glass bottles—for recycling). There was even a soft drink vendor in town named Soda-batli-opener-wala. Parsis are known to be somewhat eccentric, and the Katraks were well ahead of the competition; being the peculiar menagerie that we were, our surname could easily have been Cuckoowalla.

Guh, guh, Gayomar. No one ever called me that. I was always known as Gayo, until I went to America, where I became Guy, which my mother didn't like one bit, because in Hindi Guy means . . .

NERGISH: Are you a cow? I don't know why you let people call you such a stupid name! Guy. Moo.

STORYTELLER: I went to America because . . . at sixteen, I fell in love—with America, land of the free, land of opportunity. America had equality and justice—for all. America had put a man on the moon. America had Hollywood and Broadway. And fast cars, on freeways with exit ramps. America had Velveeta and Tang.

GAYO: Ma, I finally know what I want to be.

NERGISH: You do? Let me guess. First you were going to be an explorer, then a magician, and then you wanted to join the circus. Now I suppose you'd like to be . . . a cowboy?

GAYO: No, Ma. I'm going to be all of those things. I'm going to be an actor.

NERGISH: Have you lost your brains?

GAYO: And I'd like to study acting in America.

NERGISH: America? You're out of your marbles. I'm sure Babu Nath will have something to say about this.

STORYTELLER: In spite of all my mother's objections, the stars aligned in my favor, and when I first arrived in America, Behram Baria, a cousin of the Katraks, picked me up at Kennedy airport.

BEHRAM: Acting, huh? That's different.

STORYTELLER: Behram Baria, I'd been told before I left, was "quite a rich man." He'd been part of the first wave of Indians who'd come to America in the late sixties. He'd made his money conducting sightseeing trips for Indian tourists to places like Las Vegas and Disneyland. A large man with a big laugh, Behram looked like a Parsi Elvis Presley, in Elvis's later years. We left the airport in his collector's Cadillac. It felt so low to the ground. In India if you went over one pothole in that car—finished.

BEHRAM: So you want to be an actor. Why not a doctor or an engineer, or even a travel agent? We hear so many stories of young actors ruining their lives, ending up as drug addicts on the streets of New York. Have you seen this movie *Fame*? Wouldn't want such things happening to a nice boy from Hyderabad, huh, Gayo? Of course, one never knows where you might end up, huh? Broadway. Hollywood. The White House! An actor as president! I still can't believe it. Once, OK, but now we've re-elected the son of a gun. Anyway tell me, why the bloody hell do you want to be an actor?

STORYTELLER: I told Behram, "It's the only thing I know how to do." But it wasn't that simple. The fact was I had never been one to say much. When I was little, the Katraks thought I might have a speech problem. Several visits to many doctors and repeated consultations with Babu Nath revealed nothing. Now, my uncle Fali, the oldest one, was the manager of the Empire Cinema in Hyderabad. And thanks to Fali Mama, I'd watched all the movies there for free—everything from *Ben-Hur* to *Benji*. One day, we went to see *The Magnificent Seven*. I loved Yul Brynner with his black cowboy hat, boots, and rifle. When we came home after the movie, I stood in the living room and started talking incessantly—imitating all the characters and describing every scene from it. Dishum. Dishum. And I would do this all the time. The boy who didn't say much once did *Spartacus* in ten minutes. But whoever imagined that I would someday want to be an actor? Nobody we knew did that!

The Empire Cinema was a jewel during the colonial days, which by the time I came around had lost all of its charm. But to us that hardly mattered, because the ramshackle, rat-infested Empire was one of the few movie theaters in town that screened English-language films. Fali Mama loved his job. He and his sidekick, Satya, rode back and forth from the Empire to the train station on his silver Vespa, collecting and delivering boxes of movie reels. Sometimes Fali Mama, wearing a pair of vintage riding goggles, would jump onto his Vespa and say, "Hi yo, Silver, away!"

The year I left Hyderabad, the Empire caught fire and burned to the ground. But until that happened, it was like a second home. I'd sit in the screening room with Satya, who was also the booth operator. He'd stand quietly by himself, chain-smoking filterless cigarettes, a half-smile on his face. I often wondered about Satya. I'd spent countless hours with him, but other than the fact that he was Fali Mama's kind and loyal helper, I didn't know a thing about him. Years later I met another chain-smoking man with a half-smile, who, as it turns out, I didn't know a thing about either.

BEHRAM: Watch where you're driving, bastard! Why don't you go back to your own country? I tell you, Gayo, some of these New Jerseyites drive just like our Hyderabadi auto rickshaw wallahs.

Hey, you're in America now, and nobody here is going to call you Gayo. Let alone Gayomar. From today on you're going to be Guy. You think Americans call me Behram? Forget about it. Everyone calls me Barry. . . . You know, ten years from now I'm going to be able to say, "Guy Katrak? That famous son-of-a-bitch? Arey, I picked him up at the airport the day he stepped foot in America." That's what I love about being a travel agent. Connecting the dots. I used to think about quitting and going into something else, like motels—most of the motels on the East Coast are owned by bloody Indians, you know—but then I'd have to remind myself that I may be a travel agent, yes, but my real business is the pursuit of happiness. I have seen the Grand Canyon fifty bloody times—it's breathtaking and all that and one day you must go there, Gayo—but for me there's nothing better than seeing the look on the face of a grandma from Hyderabad when she poses for a family photo against the backdrop of the sun setting over the South Rim. And all I did was help her to get there. A series of dots, which once connected, led to happiness.

STORYTELLER: It was a little past six o'clock when we pulled into the driveway of Behram Baria's house in Paramus, New Jersey. It was early March. The sun had just set, and the sky was orange blue. Behram, Barry, grabbed my suitcase and headed into the house calling out for his wife—"Freni! Come and meet Guy." I looked around. I was in America. The street was lined with houses upon houses, all fairly similar, with neatly landscaped lawns and two or three cars parked in front. But there was not a single person in sight. I had just come from India. All I could think was, "Where are all the people?"

In fact, it was very quiet and still. There was a strange silence in the air, as if the entire country was holding its breath for its newest arrival, waiting to see what he might do.

I felt as if I was floating. I used to have this dream in which I could spread my arms and rise off the ground. I wasn't a superhero or anything—I couldn't fly fast or save some helpless soul. All I could do was hover, for a few seconds, a few feet over the earth.

The next morning, the Barias put me on a bus—the bus company's name was Bonanza—that would take me to Bradford College in Vermont—I had to enroll in the spring because I'd been denied a visa earlier in the fall. My mother was elated—"I don't want you to go so far away, Gayo"—I'd been very disappointed, but Soli Mama, as always, looked on the bright side; "Try again I say. Let him try again. Gayo is a little like Fali's Vespa in the morning—always has one false start." So a few months later, I applied again, Uncle Soli spoke to someone who knew someone who spoke to someone else's brother at the U.S. Embassy, and I was off to America.

Now I was about begin my undergraduate studies at Bradford. But my real American education had already begun. In the few hours that I spent at Barry Baria's, I discovered the sounds of automatic washing machines, the feel of hard wood floors under my feet, and that peculiar smell of artificial heat. I'd been given a new name and instructed on the pursuit of happiness. And on TV, I learned that the world news could be "brought to you by Bounce."

MEHLI: America. What a country! Go west, young man, go west!

STORYTELLER: Mehli Mama, the middle one, had worked his entire life as a ticket collector for the Indian Railways. "Tickets, please. Thank you." He had traveled up and down the country, and I imagine it was because of the nature of his job, but he always looked like he was on a moving train.

MEHLI: Well, it's almost time for your departure.

STORYTELLER: We were saying good-bye in the front yard of our apartment building in Hyderabad, the day I left for America. The yard was surrounded by a crumbling gray wall, on which I'd sit alone for hours, watching people go by. The street was always crowded, and the traffic, as Uncle Mehli would say, was "complete chaos."

MEHLI: Look at all these people—everybody is going somewhere. And now you are too. Life, Gayo, is a journey. Personally, I don't care if I'm coming or going. Direction is not important. Only movement counts. Your destiny is not a destination. But the problem in India, Gayo, is that everything moves too slowly. India is a country of waiting—for the train to arrive, for the bus to depart, for the cow to get out of the way. You'll like America, Gayo. It's a place where there's no waiting.

STORYTELLER: Mehli Mama had never been out of India. Neither had I, but I absolutely agreed with him. There was no future for me in India—I had to get out. The country was overpopulated and rife with prejudice and corruption. And Hyderabad was a one-horse town.

MEHLI MAMA: You know what I like best about America, Gayo? The roads. In America, the road is like a magic carpet; you want to go somewhere, you get on the road and you go. But I'll tell you honestly, if I ever come to visit you in America, Gayo, I won't be taking Behram Baria's tours to Las Vegas or Disneyland. No, no. You and I will travel along back roads, through small towns. We'll get one of those vans with a kitchen in it, and with cruise control. What a concept, huh, Gayo? You sit, you push a button, and you go. The very best of luck to you, son! Babu Nath said you were born with a gift. I always wondered—what is it? But now I know. You will be an actor.

STORYTELLER: Driving up to Bradford on a clean, comfortable Bonanza bus, with the snow-covered countryside around, the wide blue sky up above, and the smooth American highway underneath me, I felt like I was indeed gliding on a magic carpet, with cruise control.

My first few months in America were like living in a dream. Bradford was so clean; at the post office, people actually waited in line, and at the stores, the cashiers said, "Have a nice day." What more could this boy from Hyderabad want?

WENDY: Everybody, no matter who they are, everybody wants something.

STORYTELLER: Wendy Williams was my first acting teacher.

WENDY: Want is the fundamental principle of character analysis. What do you want? Not you, but your character. What does your character want?

STORYTELLER: Wendy Williams—I learned later that her real name was Judy Schrempf—Wendy was taller than me and had long hair. She was from New York, and was the head of the Theater Department at Bradford. And I had never been in an acting class before; where I came from, there was no such thing—we just put on shows.

WENDY: What do you want? The irony, of course, is that we seldom get what we want. We just get used to taking what we can get. And if we do get what we want, it's often when we no longer want it. That's drama.

STORYTELLER: Wow! In high school, I was useless at any sport, even cricket. In academics, I was just about average. But the one thing I did do was act in plays. Not only in school, but also with Hyderabad's Tattered Curtain Theater Company. I'd done Shakespeare, Beckett, Miller, and even Neil Simon. But studying with Wendy Williams, I realized that I knew nothing about acting. What do you want?

Over the years, Wendy became my mentor. She could be very tough, demanding the best of her students. I studied her as if she were a character and sometimes wondered: What does Wendy Williams want?

WENDY: All the world may be a stage, students, but you are not yet on it. You're still waiting in the wings to make your entrance. If you see yourselves one day standing under the bright lights of the stages of New York City, or on a film set in Hollywood, then when you get your cue, you had better be prepared.

STORYTELLER: Be prepared. That was exactly my mother's mantra. Be prepared. Like a good Boy Scout.

My mother's life was structured around the belief that the world was a very dangerous place, and anybody at anytime could hurt you.

She was the type of person who slept at night with the keys to our third-floor apartment under her pillow, because she'd heard of thieves who would climb up the telephone pole, put a long stick through your open bedroom window, pluck your keys off the dressing table, and break into the house before you could say, "Oh, Dear!" And she was particularly protective of me, her one and only Johnson's Baby.

"Be prepared, baba, you never know what's going to happen to you." That's right. You never know.

NERGISH: Why do you want to be an actor, Gayo? Does the world really need actors? It needs doctors and engineers. Do something in life that will improve the world, baba. Acting is fine for fun. But life is more than fun. It's not a *dishum, dishum* movie.

SOLI: Leave the boy alone, Nergish. Let him do what he wants.

STORYTELLER: Soli Mama, the soap salesman, always took my side. He'd had a rare illness when he was a child, as a result of which one-half of his body, literally right down the middle, had been completely paralyzed. But the other half had become highly animated.

SOLI: Life, Nergish, may not be for fun, but fun is necessary for life. Remember, Gayo has a gift? One day, God willing, he will become rich and famous and make you proud.

STORYTELLER: Of all the Katraks, Uncle Soli was the only one who was religious. And he was ardently so. My mother, on the other hand, had her own religion—Babu Nathism.

NERGISH: I have spoken with Babu Nath. Gayo should be a doctor or an engineer. What you plant, that you reap. Right, baba?

STORYTELLER: My mother lived by aphorisms, although she didn't always get them right.

NERGISH: Besides he should stay in India. This is his country, his home. A rolling stone doesn't gather any grass.

SOLI: But look at him, Nergish. Does he look Indian enough to you? And his Hindi is 100 percent useless. His gift won't be valid over here. Let him try his luck in America. Look what happened to Persis Khambatta; she's in that big new movie, *Star Trek*, shaved head and all . . .

NERGISH: Enough, I say. Enough. None of this acting-facting, America-Shamerica business. It will come to no good.

SAM: Really? Well, you know what they say, Guy: Every hero has to get away from what is familiar, or be confronted with something unfamiliar, in order to find out who he really is.

STORYTELLER: Sam Reese was an aspiring Hollywood screenwriter and a Bradford College alum. Wendy Williams told me to get in touch with him when, during my junior year, I got an opportunity to do an internship in L.A. Sam invited me to go with him on a daylong retreat to the Om Center for Spirituality in North Hollywood, which was a short walk from his house.

SAM: It's pure karma that's led me to you, Guy. I've just begun work on a new screenplay. It's about a young American who goes to India to find his true self. It's called *The First Fire*. I guess it's partly autobiographical. I'm really into India. It's whoa . . . such a spiritual place. I just know I have to go there someday. Come on, the light's green.

STORYTELLER: There were people from all over the world at the center, and everyone had to wear the same flowing white robes—I felt like I was in a Greek drama. Sam and I participated in group discussions on topics such as Reincarnating Your Inner Self and Realigning Your Chaotic Chakras. When people found out I was from India, they wanted to talk to me about yoga and meditation . . . things I knew nothing about. In the evening, there was a gathering, with music and dancing. On the dance floor, bodies swirled around, men dancing with men, women with women. And they weren't exactly dancing; more like trembling and whirling. Sam said it was called "trancing." He asked me to join him.

I'd never danced with a woman before, let alone a man. And I certainly hadn't tranced. Sam was really into it.

SAM: "Bye, Shakti, thanks, I'll see you next week." That was amazing. You know, Guy, after I left Bradford my first job here was moving furniture with a bunch of college kids, and one time we were moving a truckload of stuff for an East Indian woman in the Valley. There was a real peace about her, Guy—in spite of the flurry all around, she was completely still. That is, until one of the moving guys, a real klutz, starts coming out of the house carrying a bunch of boxes, and suddenly the woman comes hurrying out after him, saying, "Be veddy carepul wit tat box." I can't do the accent. Anyway, klutzmeister loses his balance, and the boxes go flying into the air . . . and one of them comes down right into my arms. Whoa. And it's the one she wants. I set the box down carefully, and the woman opens it and takes out all these balls of scrunched up newspaper. But . . . hidden among all that paper is a tiny little glass bottle with some powder in it. I ask her, "Excuse me, but what is that?" And she says, "Dusht." I can't do the accent. It was a handful of dust from her father's village in India. He had died earlier that year. I think that was the moment that changed my life. Anyway, this is the scene with which my screenplay begins. What do you think?

STORYTELLER: I said, "Sam, Is there a part for me in your movie?"

SAM: Hey, I'll write one in. You can be the co-star. Although I have to confess, Guy . . . you don't look East Indian. When I first saw you I thought you must be Cuban or Greek or something. Of course, in Hollywood nobody cares where you're from, as long as you can make them some money. So when you're done at Bradford, are you planning on coming back here? Excellent. I can see it, my friend, *The First Fire* co-starring Guy Katrak. You might think about changing your last name though. You know industry people; they'll say something like, "Katrak? Are you a car or a truck," you know what I mean? Let's see, Ka-truck, Kat-ruck, Kut-ruck, Kut-kar, Ut-kar, At-kar, Aktar. Aktar? Actor. Guy Actor! Ah . . . never mind. So, Guy, tell me, uh, tell me about India.

STORYTELLER: I told Sam all that I knew, and didn't know, about India. We became good friends. And later, Guy Katrak actually became Guy Aktar, named, like many Parsis, after my profession! Sam did go to India, and he had a wonderful time. In Hyderabad, he met my family and started his. Then . . . we lost touch.

Sam was one of many Americans I met over the years who said they'd always wanted to go to India. Not to live there, just to visit. And those who had been there said they couldn't wait to go back. When I lived in India, so many people I knew wanted to go to America, to live there, not just to visit. And most of us who went, stayed, and returned to India only to visit. Except people like me—who wasn't yet ready to go back—and others like Tina Cama, who swore she would never settle in America.

Tina Cama. When I graduated from Bradford I packed the one suit-case that I owned and moved to *New York, New York*—to work at Barry Baria's travel agency at the World Trade Center. The things we do to get that green card. At the same time, I was trying to get work as an actor, and . . . I kept getting cast in these meaningless parts in off-off-off-Broadway plays. Until I finally got a lead role—in a small project being presented by a South Asian theater collective called Manhattan Masala. It was in America that I did my first Indian play—although my part was that of a Palestinian working at a 7–Eleven run by Indians. To the Katraks, however, it was something to celebrate. "Nergish, Gayo has a lead role in a play in New York City." Someone from the cast dragged me to a Diwali party at a university in New Jersey, which is where I met Tina Cama.

I was sitting around with a group of guests who were waiting for the organizers to serve dinner—a couple of students had gone to pick up the order from a restaurant in town and were running an hour late. One of the student hostesses was walking around the room, apologiz-ing to everyone for the delay. "Sorry guys. Indian Standard Time."

A good-looking, sharply dressed man in our group—he was a gradu-ate of the university and a successful software engineer—he was telling us about how rapidly the Indian economy was being transformed in the age of information technology, and that Hyderabad was going to be the next Silicon Valley. I said, "Really? I'm from Hyderabad." And Tina said . . .

TINA: Well that's great. Are you planning to go back?

STORYTELLER: I said, "I don't think so." And she said . . .

TINA: I am definitely going back to India.

STORYTELLER: Tina was wearing a T-shirt with a quote that read, "A woman needs a man like a fish needs a bicycle." She told me later, "It's my uniform for these events. It helps keep you lustful Indian men at bay." Tina had a way of making me shake my head but smile.

TINA: I came to this country because I admired its ideals. America. Just that word meant so much, you know. But from the day I set foot here, all I've seen is the great duplicity of America—it's a country built on the most beautiful expression of freedom and human dignity, but also on this ugly history of discrimination and exploitation. Half the time, I feel like a second-class citizen or something. I came here with my palms like this, but now they're like this. It took leaving India for me to figure out what a great country ours is. As soon as I get my master's, I'm heading home.

ENGINEER: Don't be ungrateful, man.

STORYTELLER: The engineer was dressed in clothes from Ralph Lauren, and he smelled of Brut.

ENGINEER: You come here, benefit from the good life, and then turn around and slam this country? That's not right, man.

TINA: Please don't call me "man." My name is Tina.

STORYTELLER: I looked around to see if the food had arrived.

ENGINEER: Nowadays, people are constantly talking about discrimination, like there's nothing else going on? I don't deny that it exists, but do we really have to make it the focus of our daily lives? Look, I travel all over the world, and I see discrimination around me each and every day. Nobody has the monopoly on discrimination, OK?

Look, you talk about ideals, but let me tell you about reality. No please, let me finish. I'm from a small town where most of the houses didn't even have electricity. I came here for my studies, but I had no idea what an incredible country this really is! Four years after I got my master's, I had my own software development company. Now we've got offices in New York, Hyderabad, and San Fran. Look, don't get me wrong. I love India and I love America—I kiss the ground every time I get off the plane, in both countries. But I couldn't live in India. Things are changing and all that, but talk about discrimination. In India, the Ganga will forever flow through Lord Shiva's hair, you know what I mean? In America, I don't care if you're black, or yellow, or brown, if you really want to do something—just do it. Like Nike, man. I really believe it. I'm living the American dream.

STORYTELLER: Ah! Ah! Suddenly, Tina began to scratch her palms. Then she ran to the drinks table and thrust her hands into a bowl of ice. We hurried over to see if she was OK, but all she kept saying was, "I'm sorry, never mind, I'll be alright." And we just stood there, befuddled. Then, the student hostess announced that the evening's activities were being canceled. "We've just received a phone call. Pramod and Vikram were coming back from the restaurant—when they were attacked by a street gang. They're both in the hospital. The police say it was probably some Dotbusters."

No. Dotbusters was the generic name of anti-South Asian gangs, the dot referring to the bindi that many Indian women wear on their foreheads. Just a few months earlier, a young Indian man had been murdered in the Hoboken area by what was believed to be a gang of Dotbusters.

I spent the rest of the night listening to Tina, sitting in her car, in an empty campus parking lot—which, over the years, became a theme with us; we laughed, cried, fought, and made up in empty campus lots. Tina, a Parsi from Bombay, was doing her master's in neuroscience at the University of Washington in Seattle and was visiting relatives in New Jersey for the weekend.

TINA: My family is very close. So my aunts are always trying to play match-maker. They wanted me to attend this party with the hope that I might meet some nice young Parsi doctor or engineer, perhaps even from Bombay. I can't wait to see the look on their faces when I tell them that I met this Guy, who was a sort of a Parsi struggling actor from Hyderabad.

STORYTELLER: A sort of a Parsi, struggling actor, from Hyderabad! But that did about sum me up. Whatever had happened to my special gift?

This struggling actor eventually packed his suitcase and left New York—for L.A. I had finally gotten my green card—which was actually pink—thank you Barry Baria—and decided it was time to try my hand at TV and film. As Soli Mama would have said, "New York was just your one false start." The day before I left, I called Wendy Williams to say good-bye, and we agreed to meet for a drink.

WENDY: This is the bar where Dylan Thomas drank himself to death. Maybe I'll do the same.

STORYTELLER: Wendy told me, in some detail, about how she'd been made to resign from her position at Bradford because of an alleged incident of sexual harassment.

WENDY: Ahh . . . it's so ridiculous. Thanks for listening, Guy. You've been a comfort. You always were a good listener. Most actors are big talk-ers, but the best ones are good listeners. So you're running off to La La Land? Good luck. Perhaps I should run away too . . . to Hyderabad. What is it like? Forgive me for saying this, but I've never really wanted to go to India; it seems so forbidding. Truth is, I don't even want to go out of New York, let alone America.

America. What's happened to us, Guy? We have nothing to fight about anymore except things like Bill and Monica. It's probably hard for you to understand, Guy, what it means to be an American. More than anything, we believe, that we can make a difference. At least we used to. Why did they pick on me, damn it? Half the teachers at Bradford sleep with their students. Who did you sleep with, Guy? Hmm? Guy. Why don't you go by your real name? Guy-Omar, the first man, it's so evocative, instead of Guy, the Everyman, which is so pedestrian. I'm sorry. Let's take a walk shall we? And get something to eat? If you'd like, there's an Indian restaurant down the street.

GUY: Wendy, for one night, please, I don't want to be thought of as an Indian. Just a person.

WENDY: Of course, Guy, of course. I won't say a word about India.

STORYTELLER: I spent my last night in New York with Wendy Williams. But we didn't eat at the Indian restaurant. We picked up some pizza and a few bottles of wine and walked back to her apartment.

GUY: You know, Wendy, I may not know what it means to be American, but neither do I really know what it means to be Indian. I don't even know what it means to be a Katrak. I don't know what it means to be a Parsi—the priests wouldn't allow it, because I was adopted. Who was I born to? Who are my people? Where do I really belong?

WENDY: Guy. Guy, you poor thing, I do understand. I do.

STORYTELLER: Later, as I lay next to her, I said, "Wendy, I've always wondered, what do you think you really want?"

WENDY: To be loved, silly. What else? And you?

STORYTELLER: When I was a kid, I always wanted to play a cowboy. But if to Parsis I'm not Parsi enough, and to Indians I'm not Indian enough, then it only makes sense that to Americans I'll always be either Mediterranean, or Iranian, or Puerto Rican or Alien.

ANSARI: But you could be from anywhere, that's just the beauty of it.

STORYTELLER: One morning I happened to get into a conversation with a man who introduced himself as Al. This was in Seattle, at the world's first Starbucks. I'd moved to the Northwest to be with Tina, who was still in America, finishing her Ph.D. For me, three lousy years in L.A. were plenty, and I really wanted to be with Tina, . . . "What do you think, Tina, can we give it another try?" . . . and she said . . . So I packed my one suitcase, got into my beat-up Honda Civic, and moved to Seattle. Al was Altab Ansari, who said he was from Pakistan, and thought that I looked Pakistani, "Or perhaps Saudi or Egyptian." I told him a little bit about myself, and we ended up chatting for a long time about movies, acting, cricket, the Parsis he knew in Karachi, and the Ansaris I knew in Hyderabad; no relatives. Al Ansari was a VP with ISC—International Security Consultants.

ANSARI: You've probably never heard of us or seen any ads, Guy, since we don't have any. We don't publicize ourselves too much. We work quietly, under the radar; mum's the word, if you know what I mean? After the bombing of the Federal Building in Oklahoma people are rather concerned about other such things happening here. Did you know that security is one of the biggest businesses in this country? Freedom has a price. And fear is a highly marketable commodity. International Security Consultants does its work based on the concept of "What if?" We have to anticipate threats. We have to be prepared.

STORYTELLER: Be prepared? The Boy Scouts are really onto something. And how on earth did people like Altab Ansari get into the security business—in Seattle? He was obviously very successful; his car keys were for a BMW. Only in America! Maybe America was for people like him and Barry Baria and Mr. Software. For people with guts. Not for false starts like me. Ansari and I exchanged phone numbers and said good-bye. Two weeks later, I got a call from him.

ANSARI: Guy, how would you like to make a little extra pocket money?

STORYTELLER: Al wanted to know if I'd be interested in doing an acting job for him. We met at the Starbucks, got into his BMW, and went for a drive.

ANSARI: Our client is the Top Flight Flying Academy. They've asked us to do an assessment of their admissions process. Here's the scenario, Guy. You are a foreign student, let's say from Saudi, and you're in this country on a student visa. You want to enroll in an aviation-training program at the academy. Our job is to monitor how they handle your application and to see if they follow up thoroughly on the required background checks. If accepted, you will have to go in for a brief interview, which is where the acting comes in, of course. We can pay you whatever you charge for something like this.

GUY: Wait. Wait. Al, I know nothing about Saudi Arabia, and I don't speak a word of Arabic. Why don't I pretend to be from Pakistan, and call myself . . . Imran Khan, like the Pakistani cricketer? That way, if needed, I can fake some Urdu. I know a little bit of the language from growing up in Hyderabad.

And why don't I grow a mustache.

STORYTELLER: But Tina didn't like the idea.

TINA: I don't like mustaches. They make me nervous.

STORYTELLER: I tried to explain the nature of the job: "I can't wear a fake mustache for something like this."

TINA: No. They're slimy. And they're pokey. You can forget about kissing me until the job is done.

STORYTELLER: It wasn't really about the mustache. Tina and I had been on again, off again for years, and now . . . things were going to be off again. "OK. I won't grow a mustache. I'll grow a mustache and a beard."

TINA: Stop it. Please just stop it. You're always playing some role, changing your appearance and pretending to be someone else. Who the hell are *you* Gayomar Katrak? Or should I say Guy Aktar? And you never talk to me . . . half the time I don't even know what you're thinking.

Look at me. Why do you always look away? I'm here, Gayo, here. Here. And where are you? Somewhere here? Ah! Ah! Go get me some ice.

STORYTELLER: Suddenly Tina began to scratch her palms. She had this condition, which, she said, served as a kind of natural early-warning system. She had experienced the same feeling many times before, like the night we met, when the two students were assaulted. She said her palms would first begin to tingle and then itch, and then she would try to ease the itching by scratching her palms, and then little white dots would appear on the surface, as if the nerve endings beneath her skin were shooting sparks through it. And then she knew that something bad was about to happen. I'd always thought itchy palms meant you were going to get a lot of money.

TINA: Will you please get me some ice. It's my thesis defense tomorrow morning. I'm sure Dr. McCollough is going to try and keep me here another year. If he pulls any tricks, he's going to be in for a surprise.

STORYTELLER: Tina's itching palms turned out to be a false alarm. Dr. McCollough was very supportive, and she soon finished her Ph.D.

ANSARI: Congratulations, Guy. Or should I say, Imran. I guess you're all done.

STORYTELLER: Al Ansari called to tell me that my performance as Imran Khan at the Top Flight interview had worked like a charm.

ANSARI: We'll inform them that you're not going to actually enroll—that it was just a test. You don't need to do a thing. Say, Imran, would you be interested in doing something similar? We're testing the security around the Space Needle.

STORYTELLER: Sure. Sure. During the next year, the year Y2K, I did half a dozen security-related acting jobs for Ansari, the best-paying jobs I'd ever had. It was most peculiar. Acting in real life, not on-stage or in front of a camera. Always masquerading as Imran Khan—sometimes as a courier, other times as a street garbage collector, and even a security guard. What was I doing?

Things with Tina, too, went off again, and early one morning, sitting in her car in an empty campus parking lot, we decided to say goodbye. I'm sorry, Tina. I'm sorry I can't tell you who I am. I don't know who I am. I canceled my mail delivery, closed my bank account, took my saved $8,000 in cash, packed my one suitcase, and started driving.

To where? I didn't care. I dubbed my journey the Mehli Mama Memorial Drive. Mehli Uncle had passed away some years before without ever having come to America. So I dedicated my road trip to him. I drove along back roads, through small towns, as he said we would have done. The only thing was my little car didn't have a kitchen in it or even cruise control.

But I did promise myself, "I won't go to Las Vegas or Disneyland."

SAM: You're not going to Disneyland?

STORYTELLER: In L.A., I decided to track down Sam Reese. He insisted that I come over for dinner.

SAM: It's so good to see you. Man, oh man, it's been a long time. Look at you.

STORYTELLER: Sam was now a travel writer for an online magazine.

SAM: Don't ask, but I'm no longer in the movie business. But hey, my India screenplay is done. It's now called *The Last Monsoon.* I've got it here somewhere. Would you like to take a look at it?

STORYTELLER: I told Sam, "Don't ask, but I'm no longer in the acting business. Where is Sunita?"

SAM: China, for work. It's this whole global thing! You've never met her right? Guy, we're going to have a baby. Whoa . . . can you imagine, after all these years? I am going to be dad, at fifty.

STORYTELLER: "Congratulations Sam."

SAM: Oh, come here, come here, you've got to look at this.

STORYTELLER: He led me to his office where on a bookshelf, lined up neatly, were over a hundred little glass bottles with different powders in them.

SAM: As a travel writer, I've gotten to visit a lot of cool places. What do you think is in these bottles? Dust. Now I can do the accent. I scoop some up everywhere I go. This is from the front yard of your apartment building in Hyderabad.

It's OK, Guy. It's OK. Here, sit down. Breathe. Breathe. You're all in knots!

Guy. I can tell that you're feeling low. But listen. You've got to keep going. In America, it's easy to get caught up in the waiting—everywhere you look, people are waiting—to win the lottery, to have their fifteen minutes of fame, to be born again—waiting for their ship to come in, whatever. But you've got to keep going. I learned this in India, my friend. There's only one sure thing about life. There's more to come.

STORYTELLER: Keep going. Keep going.

After I said good-bye to Sam, I headed into the desert. In Nevada, I bought myself a pair of cowboy boots, a black cowboy hat, and a rifle.

One day, I was about a hundred miles west of Phoenix when I heard the news of the attacks on the radio.

I wasn't sure what to do. I was heading for the Grand Canyon, so I thought I'd stay with the plan. But first I called my mother.

NERGISH: Gayo? Where are you, baba? You're nowhere to be found. How many phone calls I've had to make. Are you all right? Tina said you left Seattle. Where are you? I've been trying to call you for weeks.

STORYTELLER: I assured my mother that I was fine and nowhere near New York or D.C.

NERGISH: You're in Phoenix? Gayo, that's where they killed that poor Sikh fellow because he was wearing a turban. I saw it on CNN. Get out of there immediately.

STORYTELLER: I tried to explain that I didn't wear a turban. And that I wasn't in Phoenix, just near it.

NERGISH: You're going to the Grand Canyon? Why are you going to the Grand Canyon, baba?

STORYTELLER: To see the sun set over the South Rim.

NERGISH: I see. Oh Gayo, I know how you must be feeling right now, with things not working out with Tina, and now with this terrible thing going on. But don't worry, son, every dark cloud has a silver trimming.

STORYTELLER: Yes, Ma. And tomorrow is another day.

NERGISH: That's right, baba. Tomorrow is another day. Come home, Gayo. Why don't you come home, baba?

STORYTELLER: It never crossed my mind that that would be my last conversation with her.

When I got close to the Grand Canyon, I found a room at a cheap motel—run by "Friendly Indians," the sign said. Not India Indians but Navajos. As I spoke to the man at the front desk, I caught a glimpse of my face in the mirror. I could easily have passed for one of the nineteen men who had slammed a bunch of planes into the country.

Barry Baria had retired and sold his business, but the travel office I once spent countless hours in had been reduced to rubble. How many nameless people that I saw every day must have . . .

I spent the next few days driving around the Grand Canyon, only returning at night to the Navajo motel. I watched the sun set slowly over the South Rim. I spread out my arms and imagined myself floating above the great chasm in front of me. Late one night, I was looking up at the stars, and when I connected the dots . . . there was a giant celestial finger pointing . . . at me.

It was nearly dawn by the time I returned to the motel. I got out of the car, opened the back door, and reached in to collect my rifle. Suddenly there was bright light shining in my face. I heard someone say, "That's him." I turned around quickly, and slammed my head on the edge of the back door frame. . . .

When I finally went back to India, my uncle Soli came to the airport to pick me up in a taxi. Fali Mama, who now had a car, was supposed to come, but he couldn't get the car to start that morning.

SOLI: It's nice that you're back, Gayo, how long it has been. My, my . . . You should have come at least once to visit, but I'm sure you were very busy, with your plays and movies and everything. Come, come.

STORYTELLER: Soli Mama took me home to see my mother. She lay on a bed in the living room, alive but motionless. When I was young, Soli Mama had a small prayer room in which there were beads and trinkets, candles and incense, and pictures and icons of saints, and gods and goddesses from every faith. Now the entire living room had been transformed into an oversize altar.

GUY: Hello Ma.

SOLI: Gayo, it was too much for her to bear. We hadn't heard from you for so long, not since you spoke to her from Arizona, and no one knew where you were—we even called the Indian Consulate in San Francisco. First she stopped going out of the house, then she stopped talking, and then this. Fali Mama and I tried everything, even Babu Nath—you remember Babu Nath? Now he's more than ninety years old, but he still came all this way to see her. Even he said, "Sorry, there's nothing I can do." So she just lies there, staring at the ceiling. What happened to you, Gayo? We still don't know.

STORYTELLER: How could I explain to him what had happened? How was I to tell him that I had been arrested, detained, and finally sent to a county jail in New Jersey, not far, I later learned, from where I spent my first night in America?

OFFICIAL: Aktar? Why did you change your name? How did you get your green card? Why did you work at the travel agency? Why do you have no address? What were you doing at the Grand Canyon? Why did you have $6,000 in cash on you? Why do you have a rifle? Have you ever had any military training? What have you been doing for the past five months, driving alone around the country? Mike. Could you get me some more ketchup?

What exactly is your religion? What do you think about God? How do you feel about Christians? Do you drink alcohol? Do you eat pig?

STORYTELLER: The questioning went on for days. The authorities wanted to know everything about me. What had I done? What did they want? No one would tell me.

OFFICIAL: Mr. Aktar, do you know a man named Imran Khan?

STORYTELLER: You mean Imran Khan, the Pakistani cricketer? Oh, oh. Imran Khan, Al Ansari, the Top Flight Flying Academy, the planes, Tina's itching palms . . . no, no . . . I told them everything.

They told me that Mr. Altab Ansari didn't work for International Security Consultants. In fact, there was no such company, and there was nobody with that name in the Seattle area. I was held in detention for months, without access to even a telephone. I've never been so afraid, especially of the dogs. And then one day, without any explanation, I was told that I was free to go. . . . I thought, I'm going to fight back; I'm going to get a lawyer—I'm going on Larry King. But instead, I bought a plane ticket to Hyderabad.

Soli Mama wanted to know what had happened. How could I tell him? What would I tell him? I apologized and said that, "It's too difficult to explain." I told him that I wanted to see Babu Nath.

SOLI MAMA: Babu Nath? He has already said that there's nothing he can do for Nergish.

GUY: It's for me.

SOLI MAMA: I see. No problem, son. If you would like to see him, I will stay here with Nergish. Fali will drive you there.

STORYTELLER: Fali Mama, the Lone Ranger, had traded in his silver Vespa for a used car and this time was able to get it to start.

FALI: We're off to see the wizard, the wonderful wizard of Fraud! You're sure you want to see Babu Nath? Look Gayo, how much Hyderabad has changed! They say that it has become the new Silicon Valley. When you were a boy, this was all nothing, just wide, open space. Now there are supermarkets, Internet cafes, big houses, and what not. Where the Empire Cinema used to be is now a call center. You know what that is? Everybody says there are a lot of good actors working there; all Indians pretending to be Americans. You should try for a job. So, Gayo, I hear that Bollywood movies are very popular in America and that soon there will be an Indian musical on Broadway!

STORYTELLER: Yes. Yes. We arrived at Babu Nath's house. It was an enormous mansion. There were more than a hundred people waiting in the courtyard for an audience with him. When it was finally our turn, an assistant led us into the palatial home, which had white marble floors and large TVs in every room. Babu Nath was old and thin, but he sat upright in a leather-armchair, his bright eyes as cloudless as the country sky outside. He didn't speak any English, so Fali Mama told him who we were and served as interpreter.

FALI MAMA: Babu Nath says that he's very sorry, but there's nothing he can do for your mother. Is there anything else you would like to ask him?

STORYTELLER: Tell him that when you found me, Ma had come to see him. He had told her at that time that I had a special gift. I would like to know, if he can remember, what is my gift?

FALI MAMA: Babu Nath says that it was many years ago. But he remembers everything clearly. He says that Nergish had come to him and said that she had received a special gift. You. She wanted to know what to do. He says that he warned Nergish that sometimes a special gift can also be a terrible curse.

STORYTELLER: Then Babu Nath was silent. His eyelids drooped. He'd fallen asleep. The assistant indicated that our visit was over. Fali Mama gave him an envelope. He opened it and looked inside.

Fali Mama, he's lying. He just made that up. You're lying. You made that up, you bastard! He's a liar and a cheat! He's not a healer. He's not a wise man. He's a fraud. How many other people have you lied to, you fraud?

I kept shouting at him, until Fali Mama and the assistant. . . . They dragged me outside, shoved me into the car and we drove off.

FALI MAMA: I warned you, Gayo, Babu Nath is a complete fraud. He is the one who is a terrible curse. I went along with all of this only because your mother is so devoted to him. But I must admit that, today, I think he was telling the truth. Maybe Nergish is the one who . . . Chah!

So what happened to you in America, Gayo? You still haven't told us. Still the boy who doesn't say much. You know, sometimes you have to be your own wise man. When I was young, I used to think that everything one needed to know about life could be found in the movies. So every time I ran into a tricky situation all I had to do was ask myself, "If this were a movie, what would I do, in order for the plot to evolve and make for a good ending?" I saw life as an epic film, in which I was the leading man. Then several years ago, maybe it was midlife or whatever, I became very depressed and began to see my life as a big box-office flop. This was just after the Empire burned down. But then one day, I woke up, and phutt, since then everything has been A-OK. You see, Gayo, I realized that my life is indeed a fantastic Oscar-caliber movie. It's just that I'm not the hero. I'm an extra.

Look, look, there's your banyan tree. We must have been busy talking on the way to Babu Nath's and I forgot to point it out.

STORYTELLER: We stopped by the banyan tree and got out of the car. The sun had just set, and the sky was orange blue. At this time of the day, in years gone by, the banyan would have stood alone, silent and still. But now the place was filled with the bustling of shoppers and vendors. Streetlamps illuminated every corner, and the bushes where the Katrak boys had found me were long gone, replaced by a multiplex theater whose neon marquee advertised the latest Bollywood blockbusters.

Here I was, back in India, the country of my birth. But what would I do in India? And I didn't want to return to America. Where did I belong? If my life were a movie, how would the plot evolve to make for a good ending? . . .

(He goes upstage and then re-enters the light as a cowboy.)

You kept asking me "What happened to you, Gayo? What happened?" Now you know, beginning with the day that you found me. This was the only way I knew how to tell you, through this play, I suppose, which I've just performed here in our living room, for you. For you, Soli Mama; for you, Fali Mama; and for you, Ma—I know you will get better. I know you've heard every word. I'm surprised you didn't suddenly sit up and say, "You should have listened to me. I told you so."

I want you to know that I am sorry. I left here with one suitcase and returned twenty years later with a pair of boots and a cowboy hat. Someday I might go back to America. Yes, maybe the first time was just my one false start.

But whether I do or do not, it doesn't matter. Not anymore. My destiny is not a destination. It doesn't matter to me now where I live or to whom I was born, if I have a gift or a curse, whether I am Gayomar Katrak or Guy Aktar. It doesn't matter. Because now I think I finally might be prepared. I think I know where I belong. It is . . . here. Here. Here. Here.

(He floats up into the air, and hovers, for a few moments, a few feet above the stage.)

END OF PLAY

2

Walleye Kid: The Musical

MUSIC *and* LYRICS: KURT MIYASHIRO

BOOK: R. A. SHIOMI *and* SUNDRAYA KASE

INTRODUCTION, *by Josephine Lee*

Walleye Kid: The Musical was first produced by Mu Performing Arts and presented at Mixed Blood Theatre in Minneapolis from March 11, 2005, to March 27, 2005, under the direction of Jon Cranney. A revised version, directed by Jon Cranney, was presented at the Ordway Center's McKnight Theater from January 18, 2007, to February 3, 2007.

After the Korean War ended in 1953, approximately 110,000 children were adopted from South Korea, with about 75,000 children going to the United States and the rest to such places as Canada, Australia, the Netherlands, Scandinavian countries, and Great Britain. In the 1980s, more than half of all foreign children adopted in the United States came from Korea. Until 1990, South Korea was the leading source of U.S. adopted children for more than three decades. (In 1991, Romania surpassed Korea.) Significantly, a sizable number of these children were adopted by white families and into nearly all-white communities. The psychologist Richard Lee persuasively describes what he calls the "transracial adoption paradox," a set of contradictory experiences in which Asian adoptees who are raised by white families receive the benefits and privileges of whiteness yet face multiple instances

Illustration: Sarah Ochs in *Walleye Kid: The Musical.*
(Photograph used by permission of John Autey Photography.)

of discrimination and racism.[1] A desire to understand their racial difference and cultural heritage leads some adoptees to travel to Korea to seek out their affinities with their birth culture or to try to find their blood relatives.

Yet Annie of *Walleye Kid* is a figure of fairytale, not a real-life subject. Real experiences, whether incidents of racism in small towns of the United States or the Korean War and its painful aftermath, are mediated through the conventions of the musical stage. *Walleye Kid* has had several incarnations: It was first staged as a play by R. A. Shiomi and Sundraya Kase in 1998, then as a musical with an original score by Kurt Miyashiro in 2004, and finally as this version, revised and revived for a production at the Ordway Center in 2007. It is hard not to glimpse in Annie, who fantasizes about her birth parents and embarks on an adventurous journey accompanied by a faithful non-human companion, the traces of another plucky musical orphan of the same name. Yet *Walleye Kid* is more directly indebted to the Japanese story of Momotaro. Like the Peach Boy, Annie is discovered from a non-human form (walleye) by a couple longing for a child and grows up to embark on a dangerous journey.

ABOUT THE PLAY

SET

The main upstage area has a raised walkway with a backdrop of a Korean landscape that is covered by a poster with Minnesota on it at various times. There are other movable flats and set pieces that can be used to indicate various other locations.

CHARACTERS

CAST OF CHARACTERS (production at Ordway Center for Performing Arts)

CHANGGO DRUMMER	Sangho Kim
OMANI/TEACHER WILSON	Momoko Tanno*
SHAMAN	Sara Ochs
MARY/ENSEMBLE	Janet Hanson
GEORGE/ENSEMBLE	William Gilness*
COACH NELSON/COACH KIM/ENSEMBLE	Marcus Quiniones
AUNT HANNAH/YOON MI/ENSEMBLE	Jennifer Kelley
UNCLE HARLAN/AJISHE/ENSEMBLE	Arnold Felizardo
GROCER OLSEN/SUNG SAY NIM/ENSEMBLE	Sherwin Resurreccion
INGA/AJIMA/ENSEMBLE	Jennifer Weir
ANNIE	Francesca Dawis
DANNY/ENSEMBLE	Tony Williams

---

1. Richard Lee, "The Transracial Adoption Paradox: History, Research, and Counseling Implications of Cultural Socialization," Counseling Psychologist 31 (2003): 711–744.

BETTY/ENSEMBLE	Kira Church
JOHNNY/ENSEMBLE	Dylan Church
ALICE/ENSEMBLE	Danielle Socha
BILLY/ENSEMBLE	Luke Thomley
JANET/ENSEMBLE	Jenny LeDoux

* Member of Actors' Equity Association

ACT ONE

Lights come up on changgo drummer playing softly on upstage walkway. Three dancers wearing traditional Korean mask dance costumes and masks and carrying hang sen enter the downstage area, followed by a young Korean woman in a neutral mask and contemporary clothing, carrying a baby in a basket. As the drummer picks up the beat into a roll, the woman follows the dancers around the stage until they kneel facedown downstage and she kneels upstage center of them. The drummer begins the mask dance song, and the dancers rise and perform the dance. At the end of the dance the dancers exit, leaving the woman and baby. Omani enters upstage left on the walkway.

OPENING LULLABY SONG

(In the middle of the lullaby, Shaman enters and sees them and joins in the singing. Shaman walks slowly around the woman and baby. As Omani sings, the woman tries to leave several times but can't. She touches a small piece of colored cloth, hang sen, that is with the baby.)

OMANI:

> *Rest from your tears,*
> *Rest from sorrows.*
> *Rest from your fears,*
> *Of the troubled years.*
> *Rest now, find release.*
> *Rest from your woes,*
> *Let your suffering cease.*

OMANI:

Let the spirits guard and keep her,

Take her safely 'cross the waters wide.

O-pen arms will soon receive her,

Lavish all their love,

SHAMAN:

Jah jah; ja rah nae ah gi ya

Jah ja ra nae ah gi ya Hah neu reh chun

sah deu ree, Hah neu reh chun sah deu

ree no reh ha neh, Jahl ja rah nae ah gi

And a home pro-vide.
And in time she,
She will re-turn to you,
And she will learn the truth:
You loved her too.
And she'll love you.

ya, um mah pa meh ahn ki uh,
Jahl do jah na na, Nae ah gi ya nae ah
gi ya nae pu meh ahn gi uh suh
jahl jah pah nae ha gi yah
do jah neun ku nah

(*At the end of the song, the woman exits alone in tears, and Shaman picks up the basket and exits as lights crossfade to a spot on Omani on the walkway.*)

OMANI: Long ago, long ago . . . well, maybe not so long ago, a baby was born in Korea . . . and took a magical trip to a land far away called Min-ne-sooo-ta!

(*Lights crossfade downstage to George and Mary in a car in the middle of winter with the sound of the wind howling. Shaman is hidden behind them. Backdrop changes to the Minnesota poster.*)

RADIO VOICE: This is WOOC, and we got ourselves a true Minnesota winter, and that means more snow comin' our way tomorrow! So you better get out ice fishing today, because I heard the fish are biting! And now for a word from our sponsor—

(*George turns off the radio, and the car skids a bit.*)

MARY: Watch out, George, the road is pretty slippery.
GEORGE: I'm doing my best, Mary.
MARY: That's what you always say.
GEORGE: That's what I always do.
MARY: I'm sorry, George . . . for always picking on you . . .
GEORGE: You saved my life more than once.
MARY (*pause*): And I'm sorry about the doctor, too.
GEORGE: No use you being sorry for that. We've done all we can.
MARY: What if we went to another specialist? Maybe they'd tell us we could have a baby.
GEORGE: We been to two already.
MARY: But I feel like it's all my fault.
GEORGE: No use stewing about it, Mary. Let's just get home and sit by the fire.
MARY: I don't want to sit around the house and wonder about things.
GEORGE (*pause*): Then let's head down to the lake and do some fishing. Probably be lots of people out there today.
MARY: Maybe mixing with friends will help us.

(UNDERSCORE *begins with Mary and George's exit, and Shaman rises from behind with baby and exits as well. Music changes to* POLKA MUSIC; *crossfade to lake, which is frozen over. Coach Nelson enters with his bag and puts it down stage right. There's a tinkle of a bell tied to a fishing rod that sits in a bucket center stage with a radio. Coach Nelson checks the fishing rod to find nothing caught and turns off the radio in disgust.* UNDERSCORE *begins as Aunt Hannah and Uncle Harlan enter.*)

AUNT HANNAH: Hi, Coach Nelson.

COACH NELSON: Hi, Mrs. Olafson. Don't it feel great? Freezin' air hitting your lungs!

AUNT HANNAH: What's so great about the cold?

UNCLE HARLAN: Can't ice fish without it, Hannah.

AUNT HANNAH: Why do we keep comin' here?

COACH NELSON: I love the smell of fish guts!

(*Joe Olsen, the Grocer and his wife, Inga, enter.*)

AUNT HANNAH: Volkommen (*Swedish for "hello"*), Joseph!

GROCER OLSEN: Mornin', Mrs. Olafson.

AUNT HANNAH: Good morning, Inga.

INGA: Same to you, dearie.

AUNT HANNAH: Has your mother healed up from her surgery?

GROCER OLSEN: She's healing up just fine.

AUNT HANNAH: You know, she really shouldn't be living alone.

GROCER OLSEN: I tried to move her, but she's stubborn, you know? Norwegians are independent types.

(*Teacher Wilson enters.*)

AUNT HANNAH: Well, I am 100 percent Swedish. My grandfather came over on one of the first boats from Stockholm in 1850.

TEACHER WILSON: That's something my students should know.

COACH NELSON: Forget the classroom stuff, Teach!

UNCLE HARLAN: Swedish, Norwegian, it's all the same over here.

(*George and Mary enter.*)

GROCER OLSEN: Hi there, George, Mary!

GEORGE: Hi, Joe.

INGA: Morning, Mary.

MARY: Hi, Inga. (*To Joe.*) Say, did you get our order for extra bacon?

GROCER OLSEN: Sure did. You usin' it for bait, George?

GEORGE: Just stockin' up, Joe.

GROCER OLSEN: Think you'll catch anything worth keepin'?
COACH NELSON: Maybe the fish of your dreams?
UNCLE HARLAN: Like the one I caught in '62?

GOTTA LET IT GO

GEORGE:
Maybe a walleye,
Maybe trout,
Maybe a pike so big
I can't pull it out.

TEACHER WILSON:
Maybe some crappie . . .

COACH NELSON:
More likely crappy . . .

COMPANY:
What will we find
At the end of the line?

COMPANY A:
Gotta put your line in,

Gotta let it go,

Gotta take your chances,
See what's down below,
It's all we know.

COMPANY B:

Just throw it in

Just let it go

(Dialogue break.)

COACH NELSON: Hey, Teach, I got a new plastic bucket for you to sit on. It's got a big ole bottom on it.
TEACHER WILSON: You should wear it to play hockey.
GROCER OLSEN: If anyone needs extra food, just let me know. I'm ordering from the Cities tomorrow.
UNCLE HARLAN: You better order some perch and say you caught 'em fresh.

(Resume song.)

GROCER OLSEN:
I'll catch the big one,
Biggest you've seen.

COACH NELSON:
>*The biggest fish you've caught*
>*Was one small sardine.*

MARY:
>*Something will happen,*
>*Something grand.*

COMPANY:
>*The future's waiting . . .*
>*Just open your hand.*

COMPANY A:	COMPANY B
Gotta put your line in,	
	Just throw it in
Gotta let it go,	
	Just let it go
Gotta take your chances,	
See what's down below . . .	
Gotta throw out caution,	
	Just throw it out
Throw it to the wind,	
	Throw it away
There's something magical	

COMPANY:
>*About to begin . . .*
>*Just let it in.*

(Dialogue break as kids cross stage.)

BETTY: Hi, Mrs. Gustafson!
MARY: Hi, Betty!
ALICE: Hi, Mary!
BILLY: Got any jellybeans for me?
MARY: Sure do. I always keep some handy for you.

(Mary gives a bag to Billy.)

BETTY: Some for me, too?
MARY: Here's some for all of you to share, OK?
ALICE: You're the best, Mrs. Gustafson!

(Mary looks longingly at kids as they exit.)

AUNT HANNAH: Poor Mary, she sure wants kids.
UNCLE HARLAN: That's none of our business.
AUNT HANNAH: You think it's George's problem?
UNCLE HARLAN: We're here to catch fish, Hannah, not spread rumors.

(*Crossfade to George and Mary in their ice house fishing, after some time.*)

MARY: Can't get a bite, George?
GEORGE: Not a nibble yet, but we just got here.
MARY: Sometimes you're quite an optimist.
GEORGE: Gotta be when it comes to fishing.
MARY: You ever imagine catching a big one?
GEORGE: All the time.
MARY: Maybe if we imagine hard enough, we can get what we want . . .
GEORGE: You want to head back?
MARY: Not yet . . . I'll finish this blanket first.
GEORGE: Who you making that one for?
MARY: Marge Phillips. She's expecting soon . . .
GEORGE: Seems like everyone's expectin' these days . . .
MARY: Yes, it does.

(*Mary freezes as she knits and George sings.*)

PRELUDE TO A FAMILY

GEORGE:
Every day I wait for something more to be,
Just beyond my grasp, beyond the reach of me.
Waiting on the line,
Wishing it was mine,
Hoping to find it here,
Hoping it is near.

(*Back to both Mary and George.*)

MARY: Wouldn't it be wonderful to have our own child?
GEORGE: Let's not talk about that, OK, Mary?
MARY (*hopeful*): I could go to the clinic again . . .
GEORGE: We been through enough with that. . . . Those fertility treatments are so hard on you.
MARY: I don't mind.
GEORGE: We just come from a doctor, and the answer's always the same.
MARY: I know, George. It's just my wishful thinking.

A FAMILY

(Again in isolation George sings.)

GEORGE:

If I had a son I'd teach him what to do,
Everything my father taught me, all I knew.
I'd teach my boy right from wrong,
And how to stand up strong,
Like father, like son
That's what we'd be,
My son and me—
A family.

(Dialogue break as Mary gets up and walks downstage right, and George gets up and goes downstage left.)

MARY: Maybe there's another way to have a child.

GEORGE: By adoption?

MARY: Why not?

GEORGE: That could take five years . . .

MARY: I can't believe that, George . . .

GEORGE: And there aren't many local adoptions, far as I know.

MARY: Does it matter where our baby comes from?

GEORGE: No, I guess not, but . . . there's so many things we don't know about adoption. We'd have to learn a lot.

MARY: Are you afraid of that?

GEORGE: I guess not.

MARY: Couldn't we imagine it, having our own baby?

(In solo as George freezes while fishing, Mary sings second verse of "A Family.")

MARY:

She would be the daughter in my fairytale.
Kind and sweet and gentle as a dove.
She'd be all that I love,
All I think of,
She'd mean so much to me.
Then we would be—
A family.

(George and Mary sing in unison but in separate inner monologues.)

GEORGE and MARY:
> *Our child would be*
> *Everything that we ever could hope or dream.*
> *Smart as they come,*
> *Cute or handsome*
> *Like none,*
> *That's what each blessed child should seem.*

MARY:
> *If it's a he,*
> *What a rascal he'd be.*
> *If it's a she,*
> *What a sweetheart you'd see.*

GEORGE:
> *That would be grand,*
> *Just holding her hand*

MARY:
> *Then we would be—*

GEORGE
> *You, her, and me*

GEORGE and MARY:
> *Then we would be*
> *A family.*

COMPANY A:	COMPANY B:	MARY/GEORGE
Gotta throw your line in		*A family*
Gotta let it go		
Gotta take your chances		*A family*
See what's down below		
Gotta throw out caution		
	Just throw it out	
Throw it to the wind		
	Blow it away	
There's something magical		
about to begin	*about to begin*	
Just pull it		MARY:
In	*Gotta throw out caution*	*Can't let this go*
Just reel it in		
		GEORGE:
	Throw it to the wind	*Our child will let*
		Us be

Something will soon

MARY and
GEORGE:

Begin   *Gotta bring it in*   *A family*

(At the end, they go back to their fishing and knitting.)

MARY: Look, George, couldn't we try something, just one more time?

GEORGE: Every time we talk about kids, we get all worked up and everything. . . . Then it doesn't work out. And that's so hard for us both, right?

MARY: I know that, but—

GEORGE: Maybe Mother Nature is sending us a message, like maybe it's just too late for us, Mary . . .

(Mary goes back to her knitting, and George continues fishing. Mary gets up and walks downstage right while George remains fishing.)

MARY *(to herself)*: It can't be too late for us, George.

GEORGE *(to himself)*: Shouldn't've said that . . .

(Crossfade to spotlight on Mary alone.)

SILENT LISTENER

MARY:

Do You hear me,
Hear my desperate prayer?
Every whisper,
Every plea to You I sigh,
Every longing,
Every hope to You I cry?
Are You out there,
Do You hear me,
Are You listening
Silent Listener of the night?

I have waited,
Longed to hear You speak,
Only silence
Fills the emptiness in me.
All I've longed for,
Every dream my heart could weave,
Now has faded,
Has been traded

For this nightmare I can't leave.
So let me hear You speak,
Hear Your silent voice,
Hear what I have never heard before—
Silent Listener, don't be silent
Anymore.
So let me hear You speak,
Hear Your silent voice,
Hear what I have never heard before—
Silent Listener, don't be silent
Anymore.

(*When Mary finishes, the fishing rod starts bobbing, and Shaman enters as the Walleye followed by a school of little fish. The changgo drums play.*)

GEORGE: Hey, Mary . . . I've got a bite here . . .

(*George and Shaman/Walleye begin to struggle, with* UNDERSCORE.)

MARY: You got one, George?

(*Shaman/Walleye exits stage left.*)

GEORGE: Whoa!!!
MARY: You got a good one?
GEORGE: This is gonna be the best one ever . . .
MARY: Pull it in, George!
GEORGE (*tugging on line*): It's gonna break my line!

JUST PULL IT IN

MARY:
  George, give it line, let it run, play it slowly,
  George, take your time, play it cool, nice and easy,
  George, bring it in, bring it home, that would please me now.

GEORGE:
  It must be a cow.

MARY:
  Bring it in somehow.

  George, don't give up, don't give in, don't surrender,
  Show it who's boss, who's the best, you must send it
  Up from the depths, through the hole, you must make it mine.

GEORGE:
That would just be fine.

MARY:
Keep it on the line.

AUNT HANNAH:
Hey, what's the noise,

TEACHER WILSON:
What's the fuss?

AUNT HANNAH, INGA, and TEACHER WILSON:
What is all this loud commotion about?

UNCLE HARLAN, COACH NELSON, and GROCER OLSEN:
What's it about?

ALL NEIGHBORS and KIDS (BILLY, JANICE, and TINA):
Come on, let's go, let us see what we're missing,
Must be something, no doubt!
Come on, let's go!

COMPANY A:	COMPANY B:	MARY:
Maybe they fell through the ice now they're freezing		
	And they can't get a grip, as they slip,	
and they're wheezing *Out their last desperate cries,* *final shout,* *Won't somebody come to please* *Pull us out?*		
	Please pull us out!	
Hold on tight for dear life.		
	Keep a grip keep a hold	
George just don't let go		*George just* *Make our*
	Just don't give up	*Dreams*
George just don't let go	*George*	*Come true*
		Don't let go
	Don't let go	*Just don't*
	Don't let go	*let go*
	Just don't let go now	*Just bring it* *home*

COMPANY:

> *Don't let this chance slip by you,*
> *It may not come again,*
> *There's nothing that can deny you from your prize,*
> *Gotta let your hopes arise,*
> *Gotta see them through,*
> *Make your dreams come true,*
> *Gotta take a chance,*
> *Make a final stance,*
> *Just reel it in,*
> *Let the fight begin,*
> *You gotta win.*

MARY:

> *George it's a sign, it's time our lives begin.*

(Dialogue resumes.)

AUNT HANNAH: Looks like a big one George.
UNCLE HARLAN: Can't be as big as the one I caught in '62!
GROCER OLSEN: How can you know that?
GEORGE: Whoa, Nellie!!!

(Coach Nelson pops his head in.)

COACH NELSON: Someone call my name?
TEACHER WILSON: What an ego!

(Walleye exits, fishing line goes limp, and music stops. Little fish looks lost.)

MARY: Did it get away?
GEORGE: I don't know . . .
UNCLE: Looks like my record's safe.
COACH: Too bad, George. Coulda, woulda, shoulda, huh?
MARY: Don't give up George
GEORGE: It's gone . . . we lost it . . . Whoa!!!

(Shaman/Walleye comes flying back onto the stage.)

MARY: It's back!
GEORGE: Help me, Mary!

(George and Mary pull together and struggle in tug-of-war with Walleye and the school of fish.)

(Resume song.)

MARY:	COMPANY A:	COMPANY B:
	Don't let the chance	
George, I believe, I know	*slip by you*	
You can do it	*It may not come again*	
I am sure that now	*There's nothing*	*Gotta throw*
You won't lose it	*That can deny you*	*out caution*
George let me help	*from your prize*	*Throw it to*
I'm sure you can use it	*Gotta let your*	*The wind*
Now	*Hopes*	
	Arise	*Gotta see what's*
	Gotta see them through	*waiting*
We can make it	*Make your dreams*	*just before your*
Through this	*come true*	*eyes*
I can help	*Gotta take a chancet*	*Take*
You do it	*Make a final stance*	*a chance*
	Just reel it in	*Make your*
We can bring	*Let the fight begin*	*stance*
It in	*You gotta win*	*and win*

GEORGE *(along with above)*:
   Must be a monster. Must be a prize
   I can't hold on much more
   I need your help to pull it in.

COMPANY:	MARY and GEORGE:
Just pull it in!	*We'll pull it in!*

(Walleye sits down on George's seat.)

EVERYONE: Wow!! What a catch!
MARY: It's bigger than me, George!
UNCLE HARLAN: That is a doozy.
GROCER OLSEN: This one's for Ripley's
GEORGE: I've never seen the likes of one this size!
COACH NELSON: Don't look exactly like a walleye to me.
AUNT HANNAH: Then what the heck is it?

BROADWAY WALLEYE

WALLEYE:
   Well I'm the biggest, baddest fish that you've seen,
   Yeah, I'm the hippest, hottest aquatic queen,

Yeah, I'm the one and only
Fish with a Broadway routine.

FISH SCHOOL:
Well she's a worldly walleye, seafaring kind,
She's been around the world, chic and fully refined,

WALLEYE:
If I were a bird, well I might be a stork,
'Cuz I deliver dreams from Hong Kong to New York.

FISH SCHOOL:
She's the Walleye Queen . . .
Oh, she's the Walleye Queen
She's the Walleye Queen . . .
Oh, she's the Walleye Queen . . .
She's the one and only
Fish with a Broadway routine.

WALLEYE:
Now I have come a long way, and I ain't gonna stay,

FISH SCHOOL:
She's got a mission to fill, and fulfill it she will,

WALLEYE:
I'm a shape-shifting fish, to deliver your wish,
I've got a dream to bring, she's a magical thing.
I'm the Walleye Queen

FISH SCHOOL:
Oh she's the Walleye Queen . . .

WALLEYE:
I'm the the Walleye Queen . . .

FISH SCHOOL:
Oh she's the Walleye Queen . . .
She's the one and only
Fish with a Broadway routine.

WALLEYE:
Now I have come from afar,
An international star.

I'm larger than life,
From a land filled with strife.
And I have brought a prize,
No phony compromise—
A gift from the heart,
A gift I'll impart.

FISH SCHOOL:
    Well she's a worldly walleye, seafaring kind,
    She's been around the world, chic and fully refined,

WALLEYE:
    If I were a bird, well I might be a stork,
    'Cuz I deliver dreams from Hong Kong to New York.
    I'm the Walleye Queen.

FISH SCHOOL:
    Oh, she's the Walleye Queen . . .

WALLEYE:
    I'm the Walleye Queen . . .

FISH SCHOOL:
    Oh she's the Walleye Queen . . .
    She's the one and only
    Fish with a Broadway routine.
    She's the Walleye Queen, Oh Yeah!

(Walleye drops down again, and Fish School exit.)

MARY *(pause)*: Maybe it's a sign of something . . .
GEORGE: Of what?
AUNT HANNAH: Maybe we should put it back.
COACH NELSON: Are you crazy?
AUNT HANNAH: It's kinda un-natural . . . don'tcha think?
MARY *(pause)*: What'll we do?
TEACHER WILSON: Donate it to the school for a science project.
GEORGE: No way. I'm taking this one home.

(As George tries to pick up Shaman/Walleye, it leaps up and wiggles away
as everyone jumps back and then begins to chase Shaman/Walleye around
the stage with UNDERSCORE.*)*

Get my fish!!

GROCER OLSEN: Grab its tail!
COACH NELSON: Don't let it run an end around!
MARY: Be careful please!
TEACHER WILSON: Don't damage it!
UNCLE HARLAN: Don't let it get away!

(UNDERSCORE *as the crowd chases Shaman/Walleye until it tosses a basket into the arms of Mary and exits, followed by everyone else.*)

MARY: George. George? Come back here . . .
GEORGE (*from offstage*): What's wrong?
MARY: I said get back here!

(*The baby in the basket gurgles a few gibberish words. The baby is wrapped in a hang sen. Mary slowly approaches the baby.*)

Oh, my Lord . . . where did you come from?

(*Baby gurgles gibberish back.*)

You're so beautiful . . .

(*George returns.*)

GEORGE: Mary, we lost the walleye! It just took off into the woods! (*Pause as he sees baby.*) Where did that baby come from?
MARY: That walleye left it in my arms.
GEORGE: That's crazy!
MARY: We've been blessed, George . . .

REPRISE: SILENT LISTENER

MARY:
You have heard me
Heard my desperate prayer
Every whisper
Every plea to you I sighed
Every longing
Every hope to you I cried
You were out there
And you heard me
You were listening
Silent Listener of the night.

(*George stops her.*)

GEORGE: Let's not make any hasty decisions. . . . We don't know what's really happening here . . .

MARY: She's here in my arms, and I'm not letting her go . . .

GEORGE: But somebody could've come by and left her here . . .

MARY: If they wanted to give her a loving home . . . then we'll do that, right, George?

GEORGE: But what if we can't keep her?

MARY: Just believe in this, George . . . please . . .

GEORGE: Well . . . maybe you're right . . .

MARY: Don't you love her dark hair and her tan skin?

GEORGE: Yah, it's nice . . . but she doesn't look like she's from around here.

MARY: Does that matter to you?

GEORGE: No, no . . . it's fine with me . . .

MARY: And her eyes, look at her beautiful eyes . . .

GEORGE: Yah . . . uh . . . they sure are . . . now can I hold her for a while?

MARY: Of course . . .

(Mary gives the baby to George.)

GEORGE: Gosh, she's so light . . .

MARY: She's our baby, now, right?

GEORGE: Right, Mary . . .

(The crowd of Aunt Hannah, Uncle Harlan, Coach Nelson, Teacher Wilson, Inga, and Grocer Olsen return.)

UNCLE HARLAN: Haven't seen nothin' like that since '62.

GROCER OLSEN: That was the biggest walleye.

COACH NELSON: We shoulda tackled that fish.

AUNT HANNAH: What's going on?

(They all stop on seeing Mary and George with the baby.)

TEACHER WILSON: What is that??

MARY and GEORGE: She's our baby!

(The group reacts with amazement.)

REPRISE: GOTTA LET IT GO

COMPANY A:	COMPANY B:
Don't let this chance slip by you	
It may not come again	
	Gotta throw out caution
	Throw it to the wind

(UNDERSCORE *for transition from ice fishing on the lake to a summer walk in the town. The kids cross in summer outfits, and Shaman appears as a gardener watering plants at a town fountain. George and Mary enter with the unseen Shaman now watching and commenting from the side. During song, Uncle and Aunt, Teacher and Coach, Inga and Grocer enter in summer outfits and set up.*)

A GREAT DAY

GEORGE: COMPANY:
It's a great day,
just a great day,
Everybody's smiling,
got a nice word to say.
Now it seems like,
it's a dream life.

GEORGE and MARY:
We've got our girl,
we're on top of the world.
Little Annie
How can we
Always be the best
Family

Little baby
It's plain we were
Meant to hold you
To gently mold you
Little Annie
We were meant to be
Little Annie, oh, Little Annie   *Little Annie, oh, Little Annie*
                                          Lillte Annie, oh, Little little Annie

(*Dialogue break.*)

AUNT HANNAH: Did you hear what the social worker said?

UNCLE HARLAN: Is this an official report or another rumor?

AUNT HANNAH: She said she'd never heard of anything so strange in her whole life. But since there was no one else to claim the baby, George and Mary get to keep her!

SHAMAN: For once, the bureaucracy didn't bungle the job.

AUNT HANNAH: But you never know. Somebody could show up ten years from now and claim the child.

INGA: Oh my goodness!

UNCLE HARLAN: You've been watching too many *Cold Case* shows.

SHAMAN: They don't call it the boob tube for nothing.

(Resume song.)

SMALL COMPANY:
> *Little Annie, Annie, you're as cute as they come.*

AUNT HANNAH:
> *But she doesn't look like us,*
> *They don't know where she's from.*

SMALL COMPANY:
> *Little Annie, oh, little Annie.*

SHAMAN:
> *How I'd like to knock some sense into some.*

SMALL COMPANY:
> *Little Annie, Annie, has such pretty black hair.*

AUNT HANNAH:
> *Better keep the sun off her,*
> *Better keep her skin fair.*

SMALL COMPANY:
> *Little Annie, oh, little Annie.*

SHAMAN:
> *Why is skin color something to compare?*

SMALL COMPANY A:	SMALL COMPANY B:
Little Annie, we would like to welcome you,	*we welcome*
Come and be the mascot of our avenue.	*our avenue*
Little Annie, little Annie . . .	

SHAMAN:	SMALL COMPANY:
Oh, how this town	*We love*
needs you.	*you*

(Dialogue break.)

TEACHER WILSON: I know I'll love Annie in my class, and I'm sure she'll be a whiz in math!

COACH NELSON: I'll sign her up for all my teams.

GROCER OLSEN: She'll probably want a part-time job.

TEACHER WILSON: Asian kids are just so smart and responsible.

UNCLE HARLAN: Seems like you got her pegged from the start.

AUNT HANNAH: What's wrong with knowing what's right?

GROCER OLSEN: But what kind of food do I get for her?

COACH NELSON: Whatever it is, you won't find it 'round here!

(Resume song.)

GROCER:	SHAMAN:	INGA:
Now, tell me, what does Annie eat? Name that Asian treat, We'll special order it.		*We'll special order it.*
	How about some pizza	
I will stock some rice,		
		Tofu would be nice.
Some fortune cookies I think would be just fine.		
		That's the best Idea you've had
	Why do we need to draw these lines?	
I'll get you chopsticks for a dime.		

(Dialogue break.)

AUNT HANNAH: You know, I worry about Annie.

UNCLE HARLAN: What now?

AUNT HANNAH: What happens when she grows up?

UNCLE HARLAN: She turns into a teenager.

AUNT HANNAH: But she'll be the only oriental in the whole school!

COACH NELSON: I've got an idea!

TEACHER WILSON: Don't pull a muscle.

COACH NELSON: How about we turn her into the next Kristi Yamaguchi or Michelle Kwan?

UNCLE HARLAN: We got plenty of ice around here.

COACH NELSON: We can build a new arena, 'cause they need to practice year-round.

AUNT HANNAH: That's just going to make her stick out more. Everybody'll be callin' her our oriental ice princess, saying we're takin' that word diversity too far.

(Kids come across, and Danny bumps into Uncle Harlan, dropping his toy pistol. Uncle Harlan makes Danny pick it up and give it to him.)

UNCLE HARLAN: But it kind of makes me sad.
AUNT HANNAH: What now, Harlan?
UNCLE HARLAN: Seeing Annie makes me think of the last war.

(Resume song.)

UNCLE HARLAN:
    Little Annie, Annie
    You remind me of days
    When I was just a young man
    Overseas, in a maze

    Fighting in the Far East
    Till the shooting ceased
    Fighting for our freedom
    I survived at least

    I remem-ber
    Walking through the cities
    I remember how the children
    Were abandoned on the streets
    I remem-ber
    Oh how the children needed love.

(Dialogue part.)

GROCER OLSEN: I have a great idea. I'll give her a job in my store. They're all hard workers, right?
TEACHER WILSON: Sure, that way she can earn money for college.
COACH NELSON: No tellin' what she could do in college sports!
SHAMAN: Might even teach you something new.

(Resume song. The next song section is written in five parts, overlapping. During the song, Annie rides around the stage on a tricycle.)

COMPANY:	SHAMAN:
Little Annie Annie we would	
like to welcome you	
Come and be the mascot	*Little Annie, Little Annie*
on our avenue	*Oh how this town*
Oh how we love you	*needs you*

GEORGE and MARY:	COMPANY A:	SHAMAN:
It's a great day.	*Oh, Little Annie*	*Little Annie,*
Just a great day	*How we love you*	*Little Annie*
Everybody's smiling,	*Oh, Little Annie*	*Oh, how this*
got a good word to say	*How we love you*	*town needs*
And it seems like,	*Oh, Little Annie*	*town needs*
a dream life	*How we love you*	*you*
We got our girl,	*Oh, Little Annie*	
we're on top of the world.	*How we love you*	
Little Annie, we love you	*Oh, Little Annie*	
And we have you	*How we love you*	
A great day!		

COMPANY B (*at same time as above*):
> *Little Annie, oh, Little little Annie*
> *Little Annie, we're glad to welcome you*
> *Be the mascot of our avenue, we're glad to welcome you*
> *Our multicultural you, oh, how we welcome you.*

COMPANY (*spoken*): Hi, Annie!

(*The song ends with Annie on the tricycle downstage center. Transition to George and Mary's house, where the cast is busy setting up the room for a celebration.*)

TEACHER WILSON: Where do these balloons go, Mary?

MARY: Just put them around the room.

AUNT HANNAH: Where's George?

MARY: He's in the kitchen fixing up the cake.

COACH NELSON: I got the present!

TEACHER: I hope it's something worthwhile.

COACH NELSON: Don't worry, Teach. I wouldn't waste our money on something boring like a lab coat.

GROCER OLSEN: But she's good at numbers. Why just yesterday she was counting all the gumdrops in my candy machine.

UNCLE HARLAN: Maybe we should call her the Gumdrop Kid.

AUNT HANNAH: So where is our Walleye Kid?

MARY: Quiet, everyone, here she comes!

(*Annie enters.*)

EVERYONE: Happy Birthday!

ANNIE: Oh boy, presents!

MARY: Oh honey, just a minute . . .

GEORGE: You have to show some patience.
ANNIE: But why? It's my birthday!

THE WALLEYE KID

ANNIE:
> *My mommy says that I should be*

MARY:
> *A little more controlled.*

ANNIE:
> *I need to learn to wait my turn,*
> *And be a bit less bold.*
> *But Daddy says that*

GEORGE:
> *it's OK*

ANNIE:
> *As long as I obey,*
> *'Cuz I'm the Walleye Kid, you see,*
> *And the Walleye Kid is me.*
> *Yes, I'm the Walleye Kid*
> *The Walleye, Walleye Kid*
> *The one and only*
> *Walleye Walleye Kid am I.*

COMPANY:
> *Yes she's the Walleye Kid*
> *The best fish kid is she*
> *'Cuz she's the Walleye,*
> *Walleye, Walleye, Walleye Kid.*

ANNIE:
> *I gotta go, I gotta run,*
> *Can't sit still 'til I'm done.*
> *There's so much that I wanna see,*
> *So much I wanna be.*
> *A fireman, an astronaut,*
> *A scaredy-cat I'm not*
> *'Cuz I'm the Walleye Kid you see,*
> *And the Walleye Kid is me.*

(Annie goes to get the present, but Mary stops her and checks her hands and points to the bathroom. George gets Mary's attention and they exit to get the cake.

(Dialogue after George and Mary exit.)

AUNT HANNAH: I'm just glad school hasn't been so bad for her.
INGA: Yah, sure, you betcha.
COACH NELSON: She'd rather play baseball than do ballet or crochet.
SHAMAN: What if she chose another way?
AUNT HANNAH: I heard it's easier when the kids are under ten.
UNCLE HARLAN: What's that, Hannah?
AUNT HANNAH: When these oriental kids are under ten, it's not so hard.
    But after that, you know, kids start noticing the differences more.

(Resume song as Annie returns with clean hands.)

ANNIE:

COMPANY:
Yes, she's the Walleye Kid
The Walleye, Walleye Kid
The one and only Walleye
Walleye Kid is she

Yes, I'm the Walleye Kid
The Walleye, Walleye Kid
The one and only Walleye
Walleye Kid is me
Yes, I'm the Walleye Kid
The best fish am I
'Cuz I'm the Walleye
Walleye, Walleye, Walleye Kid

Yes she's the Walleye Kid
The best fish kid is she
'Cuz she's the Walleye
Walleye, Walleye Walleye Kid

(At the end of the song, Annie is surrounded by the cast, and George enters with a birthday cake.)

ANNIE: Wow! For me?!
EVERYONE: Make a wish!

(Annie blows out the candles, and all applaud.)

MARY: Now you can open your present!
ANNIE: Yes!

*(Mary hands the box to Annie, who tears it open and then pulls out a
kid's baseball uniform, cap, and glove.)*

Wow, a whole baseball outfit!

COACH NELSON: Ordered it direct from the Cities!

GROCER OLSEN: When you gonna wear it?

ANNIE: At our next game, right, Coach Nelson?

COACH NELSON: You got a week to break that new mitt in.

GEORGE: I'll practice with her.

ANNIE: Thanks, everyone! I love this!

*(UNDERSCORE as Annie changes into her baseball uniform
and set changes to baseball setting.)*

MARY: Will you be at the game, George?

GEORGE: Well, actually, I've got my dental checkup.

MARY: I've got to shop for dinner after work.

GEORGE: Don't worry, I'll try to hurry and catch the end of the game.

*(Danny and the rest of the kids appear to play baseball with Shaman
appearing as the umpire. Annie and Danny toss the bat to see who hits
first. Annie wins and proceeds to the batter's box downstage right while
Danny goes downstage center.)*

HEY, BATTER BATTER

DANNY:

Hey, batter batter, you can't hit this past me,
I got a fastball that nobody can see.
My wicked curveball, or my slider will be
The pitch that strikes you out as I make sports history.

ANNIE:

I'll try my best to score a run once again,
'Cuz though I'm small, I still can hit after all.
Around those bases I will race on and then,
I'll score the winning run, and we'll be second to none.

ANNIE'S TEAM:

Come on home, to a place you belong.

DANNY'S TEAM:

Don't let her home, at the end of this song.

ANNIE'S TEAM:

Come on, come on, we're all depending on you.

DANNY:

If we lose now, we know it just can't be true.

(*Singing ends, but* UNDERSCORE *continues as Danny pitches and Annie hits the ball well and rounds the bases until she slides in at home and Danny tags her too late. Shaman/Umpire waves the safe sign, but Danny ignores her. Johnny, Billy, and Betty are on Danny's team, with Alice and Janet on Annie's team.*)

DANNY: Yer out!
ANNIE: No way! I was safe! The umpire said safe!
DANNY: He didn't see me tag yer knee before you touched home!
ANNIE: Hey, Betty . . . I was safe, right?
BETTY: Well, yeah, I thought so . . .
JOHNNY: Whose side are you on?
BETTY: Well, your side but—
DANNY: So it was close, right?
BETTY: Yeah . . .
ANNIE: But I was safe, right Betty?

(*Resume song.*)

DANNY:

Hey Annie, Annie, don't you try to change her mind.

ANNIE:

I've just a doubt that I was really thrown out.

JOHNNY:

You're just a sneak, just like the wetback kind.

DANNY:

They pulled you out of a fish at the end of the line.

JOHNNY, DANNY, BILLY, and BETTY:

sneaky slant eyes, sneaky sneaky sneaky slant eyes

DANNY:

Hey, Annie, Annie, what if you are a chink?

JOHNNY:

What would you say if that is what we all think?

ALICE:

She's one of us, and she has always been fair.

BILLY:

Then how come her real folks can't be found anywhere?

ANNIE:

I will not play this game with you anymore,
I'll take a walk just like you threw me ball four.

(Annie exits.)

DANNY'S TEAM:

Go on, go home, but you can't just walk away,

DANNY:

You'll hear from us now every step, every day

DANNY'S TEAM:

Go back, go back now to the place you come from,

BILLY:

You're not like us; that's something you can't become.

JOHNNY:

You'll never be American just like me.

DANNY'S TEAM:

You don't belong here in the land of the free.

DANNY:

No matter what you do, or how you behave,

DANNY'S TEAM:

You'll never be at home here, in the land of the free.

(End of song and Annie runs off.)

ALICE: You shouldn't have said that about her family.
DANNY: I was just saying she was out.
JANET: She was safe.
DANNY: Says who?
ALICE and JANET: We do!
DANNY: What you say doesn't matter, hey, guys?

DANNY'S TEAM: Yeah.

ALICE: Come on, Janet.

DANNY: What's your problem?

JANET: You talk too much.

DANNY: What did I do?

JOHNNY: Forget them.

BILLY: Let's play some catch.

(The kids run off, and Annie enters, sits down on a bench brought on by Shaman.)

GEORGE *(offstage)*: Annie? Annie?

(Annie goes to sit downstage left as George enters.)

GEORGE: Annie? *(Sees Annie.)* Sorry I'm late. How'd the game go? Hey, kiddo, what's wrong?

ANNIE: Let's just go home. *(Throws glove down.)* I'm quittin' that dumb league.

GEORGE: OK. *(Silence.)* Want to go and get some ice cream?

ANNIE: Don't you want to know why I am quitting?

GEORGE: Oh, I figure you'll tell me about it when you're ready.

ANNIE: I hate that Danny. He thinks he is sooo great! He's just mad that I'm a better pitcher than he is. He said I was out, but I wasn't out!

(Shaman enters with a broom and begins sweeping floor.)

GEORGE: Sounds like he's a bad sport.

ANNIE *(sarcastically)*: Like that's why he called me sneaky, like I'm a chink.

GEORGE: He called you that?

ANNIE: Yeah, and a wetback!

SHAMAN: I was afraid this would happen.

GEORGE: Well, we should talk this over with your mom.

ANNIE: What's she gonna do?

GEORGE: I don't know. But we'll think of something.

SHAMAN: Maybe it's time

GEORGE: How about that ice cream?

SHAMAN: Not for that.

ANNIE: Let's just go home.

(Annie and George exit and transition to home, where Mom enters and takes broom from Shaman to continue sweeping. Annie enters disgruntled, followed by George.)

MARY: How'd the game go?

ANNIE: Lousy! And the baseball season's over!

MARY: Already?

GEORGE: We've decided to quit the league.

MARY: But why?

ANNIE: Because . . . because . . . because they don't want me playing.

SHAMAN: Let it out, Annie.

MARY: How do you know that?

GEORGE: It's kind of complicated.

ANNIE: They think I'm sneaky and a liar and all that just because . . . because I look different.

MARY: They said that?

GEORGE: I guess they did.

SHAMAN: You know they did!

ANNIE: I'm tired of it, Mom. Tired of their looks and smirks. Why couldn't I just be like you or Dad? Why couldn't you just be my parents?

MARY: Well, I wish you were mine by birth, but that's not important, is it?

ANNIE: Maybe not to you, but the rest of the world is still wondering about it. Danny and Betty and the rest of the kids still talk about it! Everyone still calls me the Walleye Kid because of some dumb story you made up!

MARY: We didn't make up that story, Annie. There was a great walleye, and somehow you landed in my arms the day we almost caught it.

ANNIE: Then where did I come from? And who is my birth mom?

SHAMAN: It's definitely time.

MARY: We don't know, but that never stopped us from loving you. We can deal with this. Let's talk it out.

(*Annie begins singing and Mary speaks back to her.*)

ANNIE GETS MAD

ANNIE:
I don't need your talks.

MARY:
I've felt the same way, too.

ANNIE:
I don't need your thoughts.

MARY:
I'm not saying it's not bad.

ANNIE:

> *I don't need you telling me*
> *It's not bad*
> *So don't get mad*
> *You don't have a clue*
> *Of what goes on.*

MARY:

> *We'll talk to the other parents.*
> *We must all get along.*

ANNIE:

> *I don't need your advice*

MARY:

> *We'll set up some rules*

ANNIE:

> *I don't need your rules*
> *I don't need a mom right now*
> *Telling me how I should feel*
> *Telling me it isn't real*
> *I don't need a mom right now*

MARY:

> *Annie, you need me now more than ever. I'm your mother.*

ANNIE:

> *Sometimes moms don't know that much.*

MARY:

> *Then help me understand.*

ANNIE:

> *Sometimes moms are out of touch*
> *Sometimes moms are not good moms at all.*

MARY:

> *Now Annie, that's enough!*

ANNIE:

> *Give it a rest*
> *Take a time out*
> *Give me a little space.*

MARY:

Annie, it's going to be OK.

ANNIE:

Give me a break
Give me my say
Sometimes things are NOT OK!

(End of song. Annie exits, running to her room.)

GEORGE: What do you think?
MARY: She obviously needs some time alone.
GEORGE: What should we do?
MARY: Take a walk. Get some ice cream.
GEORGE: Yeah, maybe we could talk to some of the neighbors.

(Mary and George exit; transition to Annie
in her room.)

ANNIE: Why me? Why do I have to be stuck here? I wish I could just get back to where I came from. Back to where I belong. Whoever is out there, can't you help me? Oh, Mom and Dad, I don't mean to get mad at you, but somehow, somehow I need something more.

(Annie pulls out a small piece of colored cloth to hold.
It's her hang sen from the basket.)

MAYBE THEN

ANNIE:

I wish I knew the answers,
Wish I knew the truth,
Wish I knew the reason why
You left without a clue.
Maybe then I'd know just why
My heart seems torn in two.

Maybe then
My doubts would be dispelled,
Maybe then
The dreams that I have held
Will still come true,
I'll know you through and through,
And then I'll know me too,

And maybe then
We'll be together once again.

I wouldn't feel rejected,
Neglected or confused.
Wouldn't hear their taunting words
That leave me hurt and bruised.
It would help if I could know
Just why you had to go.

Maybe then
My doubts would be dispelled,
Maybe then
The hopes that I have held
Will still come true,
I'll know you through and through,
And then I'll know me too,
And maybe then
We'll be together once again.

There's so much I should know,
So much I still must learn,
So much beyond each turn,
So much I must discern.
And that is when ...

> (*Annie falls asleep, and Shaman enters as Walleye again. She walks*
> *around Annie and finally taps her on the shoulder. Annie looks up.*)

ANNIE: Hey, where'd you come from? (*Annie looks around, trying to figure out*
how Walleye got there.) Dad? Mom? (*No answer as Annie and the Walleye*
circle each other.)
SHAMAN: They can't hear you.
ANNIE: How come you look like a walleye?
SHAMAN: I'm a shaman, and I can look like whatever I want.
ANNIE: But what do you want with me?
SHAMAN: I heard you singing and thought maybe it was time.
ANNIE: For what?
SHAMAN: What do you want, Annie? More than anything else?
ANNIE: I want to find my birth parents.
SHAMAN: Then follow me.
ANNIE: OK . . .

> (*Annie follows Shaman offstage, and full cast enters up on the walkway.*
> *The whole company joins in on the song.*)

WALLEYE WHALE

COMPANY:

Under the waters of the seven seas,
Under the waters where the fishes breathe,
Beyond the sandy shores and coral reefs
We'll take you back to the home that you seek—
Back to the keys that can set you at ease.
(Just float along to the song of our watery throng.)
Going back to the start of the story,
Going back to the tip of the tail,
Going back to the heart of the matter,
Going past every fin every scale
On your own walleye whale.

(Shaman and Annie enter and do swimming dance around
the stage to music.)

ANNIE:

Across these seas I won't feel out of place.

SHAMAN:

Someday we'll look beyond this thing called race,
Someday we'll find that we're all one of a kind,
And there are far deeper ties that can bind
In our hearts and our minds.

COMPANY:

Going back to the place where it started,

SHAMAN:

Going back to the place it began,

COMPANY:

Going back to the place where we parted.
Going back to find out all that you can
On your walleye sedan.

SHAMAN:

You must learn how to swim with your own two fins,
Even learn how to walk on the water.
Learn to ride every wave, every tide that begins,
But keep an anchor deep inside, deep within,

OMANI and SHAMAN:
> *Where the truth's always been.*

> *(Change in music as Shark enters with his school of sharks and swims around Annie.)*

SHARK:
> *Hey, little kid, you better get out of here,*
> *I don't like folks who'd make fin soup of my rear.*

ANNIE:
> *I don't like that soup, and I'd have to agree,*

LITTLE SHARKS:
> *She's not Chinese?*

ANNIE:
> *The thought of shark fin soup would be a sad destiny.*

SHARK:
> *Believe me, kiddo, that won't happen to me.*

LITTLE SHARKS:
> *No siree!*

SHARK:
> *Chinese, Korean, doesn't matter to me,*
> *You all like sushi and a cup of green tea.*

ANNIE:
> *I don't like seafood that they don't even cook,*
> *Nor do I like kim chee.*

SHARK:
> *Well, you are still just a gook.*

ALL SHARKS:
> *Go on, get out, we don't want you anymore,*

SHARK:
> *It's nothing personal, as I've said before.*

LITTLE SHARKS:
> *Go on, get out, there's nothing left to discuss,*

We don't hate you; you're just too different from us.
Go back home, just turn that walleye around,

SHARK:

Adios, shalom, you should be homeward bound.

ALL SHARKS:

Say sayonara, say whatever you like,
It's time for you to leave; it's time for a hike.

ANNIE:

What can I do, how can I hope to get through?
I don't know why you just can't let me go by.

SHARK:

We sharks have sworn to guard each ocean, each sea.

ANNIE:

What would it harm if you would just let me be?

COMPANY A:	COMPANY B:
Let her go	
	Let her go
let her by	
	Let her by

COMPANY:

We must all do our part to let her follow her heart.
We must help her pursue her dream, and help her get through.
You can't give up now that you've traveled so far.

ANNIE:

Come on, my Walleye—show that shark who you are.

(Walleye breaks through as music builds during fight, where Shaman winds up but then taps Shark on the nose. Shark screams and exits, and Annie and Shaman resume swimming.)

SHARK: Oww!!

SHAMAN:

Little mermaid in the sea, you're feeling so out of place

OMANI:

Not yet part of my world

MARY:
Nor part of my race

SHAMAN:
But darling, somehow you must find,
Must leave the world you knew behind,
Yes, you must learn the truth in you,

SHAMAN, OMANI, and MARY:
For truth alone will see you through.

COMPANY:
What will you find at your journey's end?
What will you learn, will you comprehend?
Your history, life's mystery,
What will you see, what will you be?
What will you know when this is through?
Will you know you?

(*The drumming and music get rougher as if a storm comes up,*
and Annie lands alone somewhere.)

ANNIE: Where am I?!

(*Lights go to black.*)

End of Act One.

ACT TWO

Lights come up, and a group of mask dancers enters and performs a mask
dance. But in the middle, a model Hummer enters and drives around the
stage, disrupting the dancers, who exit as crowds of people covered by
umbrellas enter. Annie enters, trying to get someone's attention in vain. By
the end, after the ensemble has exited, Omani and Shaman are sitting at a
bus stop wearing sunglasses and looking cool.

ANNIE: Where am I?
OMANI: You're home.
ANNIE: Where's that?
SHAMAN: Korea, the home you haven't known, Annie.
ANNIE: How do you know my name?
OMANI: Your spirit has always been part of Korea.
ANNIE: But who are you?

OMANI: They call me Omani; it means Mother Korea.
ANNIE: What kind of place is Korea?
OMANI: It's the land of the morning calm.
SHAMAN: The land of your people, the Han.
ANNIE: Is this for real?
OMANI: It's real for us. And we're here to welcome you.

WELCOME TO KOREA

SHAMAN:
Welcome to the land of Korea,
Welcome to the land of morning calm,

OMANI:
Welcome home, my dear, welcome home,
Welcome to the people of the Han.

SHAMAN and OMANI:
It's a modern land,
This place we call our home,

OMANI:
With our cellular phones,

SHAMAN:
And our cars all decked with chrome,

SHAMAN and OMANI:
It's a land of strife,

OMANI:
But a land of life,

SHAMAN and OMANI:
A land that lives inside your blood and bones.

OMANI:	SHAMAN:
Welcome to the land of Korea,	
	Welcome welcome home welcome
Welcome to the land of morning calm,	
	Welcome home now welcome.
Welcome home, my dear, welcome home,	

Welcome to the people of the Han.

Welcome home, now Annie,
welcome home,

We'll be a part of you wherever
you roam.

This is where you'll find your
answers,

Where you find the truth you seek,

Find the key
Now come unlock life's mystery,
Welcome home

Welcome home,
Yes, welcome home,

Yes, welcome home.

Yes welcome home now,
Welcome home.

We're glad you've come back,

We'll get you right on track.

The answer's waiting,

Exhilarating.

That will unlock life's mystery

Welcome home now,
Yes, welcome home now,

Yes, welcome home,
Yes, welcome home.

(*As the song ends, Annie wanders around the stage*
in amazement.)

ANNIE: Can you help me find my birth parents?
OMANI: You have something more important to find.
ANNIE: What's that?
OMANI: Yourself.
ANNIE (*to Shaman*): But you said—
SHAMAN: Trust in Omani, she—
ANNIE: I don't need to find myself. I'm not lost!
OMANI: If you're not lost, then we'd better be going.
SHAMAN: Yes, we're already late. Good luck finding your parents, Annie.
ANNIE: Wait!
SHAMAN: What now?
ANNIE: Can I come with you?
SHAMAN: What do you think?
OMANI: Follow us.

(*Begin* UNDERSCORE *as Omani walks away, followed by Shaman. Annie hes-*
itates, then rushes after them. The following dialogue happens as they walk
around the stage.)

ANNIE: Where we going?

OMANI: To Insa Dong, a neighborhood here in Seoul, the capital of South Korea.

SHAMAN: Insa Dong is where many artists live. It's the soul of Seoul.

(They exit and Ajima, Ajishe, Yoon Mi, Coach Kim, and Sung Say Nim enter to begin setting up the stage for a show.)

AJIMA: Ay Yoh! Yuji neru!

(Annie, Shaman, and Omani enter.)

ANNIE: Are my birth parents here?

OMANI: We don't know.

ANNIE: Then why are we here?

SHAMAN: Today is "Children's Day" in Korea.

OMANI: It's a festival for kids.

ANNIE: I don't have time for kid's stuff.

OMANI: But this is a special festival.

AJIMA: What you doing? That is not the way to set up stage! You are such a bad nephew. I told you: Just go kick your ball and leave us alone!

COACH KIM: Ajima—you are too old to do this alone. Why must you put on shows every year?

SUNG SAY NIM: So our children can learn about our history!

COACH KIM: They'd rather play soccer or videogames.

AJISHE: Anyio *(Koren for "No")*—you cannot argue with your auntie.

YOON MI: She has put on these stories for many years.

(Omani, Shaman, and Annie are noticed by the others.)

ANNIE: Gosh, everyone looks like me!

OMANI: Of course, you are Korean.

(Ajima sees Annie, Omani, and Shaman approaching.)

AJIMA *(in Korean)*: Ah we have been blessed today! Let us welcome our old friends Omani and Shaman.

OMANI: Anyong ha seyo Ajima. *(Bowing deeply.)* It has been too long since our paths have met.

AJIMA *(in Korean)*: Ah—who is this that you bring with you?

OMANI: She is a guest, from America.

COACH KIM *(in Korean)*: She doesn't look American to me.

SHAMAN: She doesn't look American to you because you think all Americans look alike.

OMANI: She was born here and raised there.

AJIMA (*in Korean*): Her family move there?

OMANI: No, she was adopted into an American family in Minneesooota.

CAST: Ahhhh.

(*Ajima, Ajishe, Coach Kim, Yoon Mi,
and Sung Say Nim huddle, murmuring.*)

ANNIE: What are they doing?

SHAMAN: Trying to figure out how to deal with you.

AJISHE (*in Korean*): She speak our language?

SHAMAN: She doesn't speak Korean.

AJISHE: We have to speak English?

OMANI: Let's pretend it's our English lesson.

SUNG SAY NIM: She's one of those babies that got sent away.

COACH KIM: Probably for good reason.

AJISHE: Americans steal many babies from us, after war. I see them take babies from streets.

AJIMA: No, those babies not stolen.

YOON MI: They have no families take care of them.

ANNIE: I have parents at home. I'm here to find my birth parents.

AJIMA: What is your name?

ANNIE: Annie—Annie Gustafson.

AJIMA: Gooffstaff son?

OTHERS: Gustaffffson? Goofstafffson? Gugstafssssson.

AJISHE: You don't know your Korean family name?

ANNIE: No.

COACH KIM: Then how can you find them?

ANNIE: That's why I need your help!

SUNG SAY NIM: I'm sorry, but we have to do a show. No time to look for your parents now. Why don't you have a seat right here? (*Noticing the hang sen.*) Where did you get that?

ANNIE: It was wrapped around me when I was a baby. I don't know what it is.

SUNG SAY NIM: Ajima, look what the child carries.

AJIMA: You have this when you were sent away? This is like sacred hang sen from imperial kingdom of long ago.

AJISHE: Shaman—why didn't you tell us this?

SHAMAN: Nobody asked me.

(*Ajima and others bow and back away.*)

ANNIE: What's she talking about? Why are they doing that?

OMANI: This hang sen. It connects your soul with the heavens. It can heal the place inside you called your Han.

ANNIE: My Han?

OMANI: All Koreans have a Han.

COACH: But she grew up in America and doesn't speak our language. How can she be Korean?

OMANI: She has the ancestral river in her that flows through all of us.

ANNIE: I don't have a river in me.

SUNG SAY NIM: She doesn't understand.

OMANI: It was your Han that brought you back.

ANNIE: Actually, I came on a big walleye. I mean the Shaman.

AJISHE: Why you do that?

SHAMAN: You sound like she's not welcome here.

SUNG SAY NIM: It's only a question.

OMANI: Give me your hand.

(Annie slowly gives her hand to Omani.)

OMANI: Your hands, the skin is so soft, the fingers long and delicate and yet strong. And the lines, of destiny and destruction. I can see the will of your birth mother in them.

ANNIE: Tell me my story . . . please.

OMANI: Then sit down.

SHAMAN: Right here. You have the best seat on the street.

OMANI: Please, begin your story.

AJIMA: Which one would you like?

OMANI: "The Tale of the Two Kingdoms."

AJIMA: Everyone hear that? I need all of you.

COACH KIM: I have to leave in an hour.

SUNG SAY NIM: You have plenty of time, Coach Kim. And remember your lines, in English.

COACH KIM: Why do we have to speak English?

AJISHE *(in Korean)*: Where's my crown?

AJIMA: In your hand, Ajishe, and speak English!

AJISHE: Oh, right. Sorry.

AJIMA: Omani, will you be our narrator?

OMANI: Thank you for the honor.

(Shaman, Ajishe, Ajima, Coach Kim, Yoon Mi, and Sung Say Nim all go offstage. Omani begins moving around the stage as if conjuring up the spirits of the story. Omani and company sing and enact LONG AGO.)

LONG AGO

OMANI:
Long ago in the land of Korea,
There were two mighty kingdoms at war,

For the king of the east
And the king of the west
Could not learn how to share
All that was best

COMPANY and OMANI:
Of the treasures that lay there

OMANI:
On the mountain high and fair

OMANI and COMPANY:
mountain high and fair.

OMANI:
With rice paddies carved in the mountainside,
And forests that grew giant pines.
There were jewels so rare
In the caves hidden there,
Where the hunting was sure
And the rivers ran pure,
There were wonders

COMPANY:
beyond compare

OMANI:
On that mountain high and fair.

(Dialogue break.)

ANNIE: What's all this got to do with me?
OMANI: Do you want to learn your story?
ANNIE: Yes.
OMANI: Then watch and listen.

(Resume song.)

OMANI:
Neither king would decline nor resign from the war,
Neither king would seek peace as before.
So they fought on for years,
Shedding blood, shedding tears,

Turning greed into desperate despair,
But the kings they did not care.

COMPANY:
No they did not care.

OMANI: COMPANY:
Long ago in the land of Korea,
                                                          Long ago in the land of Korea

There were two mighty kingdoms
at war,
                                                          There were two mighty kingdoms
                                                          at war

For the king of the east
                                                          For the king of the east

And the king of the west
                                                          And the king of the west

Could not learn how to share
                                                          Could not learn how to share

All that was best
Of the treasures that lay there
                                                          Of the treasures that lay there
                                                          Of the people in despair
On the mountain high and fair.   *On the mountain high and fair*

(End of song. Suddenly the changgo drums play, and the minister enters
along with Shaman as Daughter.)

ANNIE: Why is the shaman in the show?
OMANI: She loves the theater.
ANNIE: But who is she playing?
OMANI: The daughter of the East King. It's her favorite role. Here comes
the king.

(King enters.)

KING: Now, my precious daughter, will you marry Prince Park of our neigh-
boring clan to the south?
DAUGHTER: Father, I cannot.
KING: What? Why not?
DAUGHTER: How can I marry him if I do not care for him? How can I care
for him if I have not met him?
MINISTER: But his family is our ally against the King of the West!

DAUGHTER: Is that what marriage is for?

KING: Prince Park will be your husband!

DAUGHTER: I have heard from the servants that he is both cold and cruel.

KING: How can you defy me?

DAUGHTER: How can you use me like that?

ANNIE: I don't like this story.

OMANI: Don't you want to see the show?

ANNIE: What does this old tale have to do with me?

OMANI: You'll find out.

KING: Once again, will you take the husband I have chosen for you?

DAUGHTER: What will you do if I refuse?

KING: Send her to the dungeon! I shall never be defied.

(Minister and the soldiers take Shaman/Daughter offstage.)

ANNIE: Shouldn't we help her?

OMANI: I thought you didn't like this story.

ANNIE: I like the daughter.

OMANI: Then let's see what happens.

(Annie and Omani follow Daughter down to the cage of the tigers.)

ANNIE: Isn't that dangerous?

OMANI: She has a special way with those tigers.

(A den keeper enters, sees Daughter and listens to her.)

DAUGHTER: He keeps you here like prizes. We are the same to him, just things he thinks he can control. But he's wrong, and one day we will escape and be free.

(The den keeper drops his bucket of food, and she turns.)

What are you doing here?

PRINCE: I'm the den keeper.

DAUGHTER: Never say a word of this.

PRINCE: Your secret is safe with me.

DAUGHTER: Thank you.

PRINCE: You have a way with the tigers. They trust you. I've seen you down here many times before, feeding them and talking of freedom.

DAUGHTER: And you haven't told anyone?

PRINCE: Never . . .

DAUGHTER: Why not?

PRINCE: Because I am the son of the King of the West. I was captured in the last battle, but he doesn't know it and thinks I am just another soldier.

DAUGHTER: Why should you protect me?

PRINCE: You have a good heart and a strong will. We are the children of enemies, but I feel no hatred for you.

DAUGHTER: Nor I for you.

PRINCE: Good, because I am planning my escape.

DAUGHTER: The guards will stop you.

PRINCE: Not unless someone tells them.

DAUGHTER: Your secret is safe with me.

PRINCE: Good. *(Pause.)* What about you?

DAUGHTER: What?

PRINCE: You were talking to the tigers about getting free.

DAUGHTER: We'll find our own way out.

PRINCE: Why not come with me?

DAUGHTER: I hardly know you.

PRINCE: I am the keeper of your secrets. I've watched over you, protected you from your own guards. If they saw you here talking of freedom, they'd have to report it to your father. Let me help you, that's all I ask. Let me prove to you that I share the love you have for freedom.

DAUGHTER: You speak like a voice from my heart.

PRINCE: Will you join me? Setting free two hearts with one stroke.

DAUGHTER: Yes! And we can take the tigers, too!

PRINCE: Meet me here tomorrow night when the moon is full and we can plan our escape!

(Prince exits.)

ANNIE: I can't wait! They're going to be free!

OMANI: Don't rush or you'll trip.

ANNIE: Look, she's praying.

BEYOND THIS DOOR

DAUGHTER:
What would I find,
What would I see
Beyond my prison door?
A diff'rent life,

A diff'rent world,
There must be so much more,
The life that I've been longing for.
And so I'd search that distant shore,

Seeking what there is in store
For me.
Something more beyond this door.

Ten thousand laws
Can't keep me from
The truth I've never known,
The wondrous myst'ries
Of a life that I am never shown
Surrounded by these walls of stone.
And so I'll search that distant shore
Finding out there is much more,
So much more to life
That I must still explore

Beyond this door.

Beyond that door the world is changing,
Beyond that door so much to see.
Beyond that door a new horizon
Shines on like the sunrise upon me.

(Dialogue break.)

ANNIE: That's how I felt! Is she adopted, too?
OMANI: That was not her fate.
ANNIE: I still like her.
OMANI: Yes, she is a lot like you.

(Resume song.)

ANNIE: OMANI:
I am just like her,
She is just like me,
Deep inside we know
There's so much more
That we must see.
We will find a way,

                                          You must find your way,

Take our chance today.

                                          make your place today,
It's deep within,   *for deep within your heart*
my heart   *you hold the key.*

ANNIE:	DAUGHTER:	OMANI:
So fly with me.		
	Someday I'll send my spirit	
	Soaring 'cross that shining	*Come soar with me*
	sea.	
Across the sea.		
	A part of me will leave these	
	walls,	
	And then I will be free.	*You'll leave these*
		walls behind.
I hope that soon I will		
be free		
	Another world will welcome	*You hold the key.*
	me.	
Will everyone		
welcome me?		
	And so I'll send you on your	
	way,	
You'll stay a part of me	*Knowing how you cannot*	*It's there in you*
	stay,	
	Knowing now a part of me	
	will always be,	
Across the sea	*Across the sea.*	
		Across the sea.

(Daughter exits.)

ANNIE: Is she my birth mother?

OMANI: Why do you think that?

ANNIE: She wants to be with her prince, but her father is against them.

OMANI: This tale is from two hundred years ago.

ANNIE: But she's like my birth mother, right?

OMANI: That's why folk tales tell us so much.

ANNIE: Let's get going.

OMANI: Where now?

ANNIE: We have to help them escape.

OMANI: This is their story, not yours.

ANNIE: OK, but I have to find out what happens.

(Omani leads Annie offstage, and the scene changes from the castle to the mountainside where Prince, Daughter, and the tigers run chased by the soldiers.)

LISTEN TO THE DRUM

SOLDIERS:

Listen to the beat of the drum in the moonlight
Listen to the sound of the wind
Listen to the terrors that hide in the midnight
Listen as your heart pounds within.
Listen, hear the drumming
Listen, hear us coming,
Listen to the hounds of fate
Listen, we will find you
Listen, we will bind you
Listen, we will not a-bate
Listen to the drums.

DAUGHTER:

Lis-ten to the sound of the beat-ing drums,
now the chase is on, and the hunt has come,
yet I do not fear, for our time is near.

Through the dark of night
I can see the light
I can see a flame
burning strong and bright

Love will find a way,
We will see that day we pray.

We'll make our dreams
I've found my home
I'll safely stay right here
in your embrace
'Til the night is gone

PRINCE:

The darkness of night
will hide us
The stars smile on us
And soon love will blossom
in us
That's what we pray

We will make our future
We will find our place
I'll keep you safe
right here in my embrace
Let the drums beat on

KING:

Let her weep, let her cry
let her beg 'til I die
I will not be assuaged
'Til they're both locked and caged
I will not be mocked this way
She has brought me disgrace
Brought this shame to my name
I will search high and low

'Til there's nowhere to go
I will drag them back to pay
Fear the beating drums

(*Dialogue break.*)

ANNIE: The soldiers are getting closer! Can't you do something?
OMANI: The story must be told the way it is.

(*Resume song.*)

SOLDIERS and OMANI:
So we searched far and wide
on that fair moun-tain-side
for the king would not turn from his pride
He would nev-er re-lent
He would nev-er re-pent
He would fight 'til the day he died

KING:
I must never be defied!

SOLDIERS:
Listen, hear the drumming
Listen, hear us coming,
Listen, we will find you
Listen, we will bind you
Listen, hear the beating drum
Listen, fear the beating drum
Listen to the drums
The beating drums

(*Crossfade to Prince and Daughter,*
who are hiding in a cave.)

PRINCE: The soldiers are all around us.
DAUGHTER: How much food do we have?
PRINCE: Enough for another day, or two.
DAUGHTER: Then you must take it and escape.
PRINCE: No.
DAUGHTER: We cannot hide in this cave forever.
PRINCE: I won't leave you like this, with our child to be.
DAUGHTER: You must. You can go to your father and return for me.
PRINCE: No!

DAUGHTER: It is the only way to find freedom for our family.
PRINCE: For our family . . .

*(Prince gives Daughter the sack of food and they
embrace before he leaves.)*

OUR LOVE WILL LAST

DAUGHTER:
Darkness, where is the morning
Where is the sunrise
Is this where love dies

Sunrise, on the horizon

Far from the darkness
Love will live on

(Prince appears on the upstage walkway as if in a distant place.)

PRINCE: DAUGHTER:
Someday . . .
There is hope for tomorrow
there's a world without sorrow
I will bring you that day

                              Someday, when our troubles are over
                              Everything that we strove for

Will be ours at last

DAUGHTER:
Shadows fade far behind us
Your vow will bind us
Filling my heart

PRINCE:
Someday, far from this madness

PRINCE and DAUGHTER:
Out of this sadness
We'll find a way

DAUGHTER:
Someday . . .
Sure as the sunrise,

Pure as our love flies
Our love will last

(*Prince and Daughter exit separately. Korean drumming plays as Prince walks to center of walkway. He is pursued by soldiers and chased down to the main stage, where he is trapped and killed. Lights go to black, then come up again as East King confronts Daughter downstage center.*)

EAST KING: So what have you to say now?
DAUGHTER: We will all be free one day.
EAST KING: Never! Take her to the mountaintop and let her die there!

(*The soldiers are about to take Daughter away.*)

ANNIE: No! Shaman, take me home!
OMANI: But this is your home.
ANNIE: I don't want to watch this!
OMANI: OK, we'll stop the show. (*To rest of cast.*) That's it; the show's over.

(*Cast comes out.*)

COACH KIM: We're not done.
AJISHE: OK with me. I'm tired of playing bad men.
AJIMA: But you're good at it, Ajishe.
SUNG SAY NIM: We haven't got to the best part. The last ten minutes has the meaning.
ANNIE: But they killed the prince and caught the daughter!
AJISHE: She has a point.
AJIMA: Ajishe, don't discourage her!
ANNIE: I know it's not going to turn out OK.
COACH KIM: Why are we doing all this for her?
SHAMAN: Because we care about her.
COACH KIM: Maybe you do.
SHAMAN: Look at her. She is one of us.
SUNG SAY NIM: But she grew up in America.
AJISHE: How can this be her home if she never lived here?
SHAMAN: You are worse than the people in America!
OMANI: Let's all calm down. No use shouting at each other.
ANNIE: Maybe they're right. Maybe this isn't really my home. Maybe it's hopeless anyway. I'll never find my birth parents, I'll never speak the language, I'll always be a stranger here.
AJIMA: No—once Korean, always Korean. She no look like big-eyed American. She is Korean. Yes . . . (*Patting Annie on the body, arms, leg, face.*) I can feel the Han in her blood! You belong here!

ANNIE: But this doesn't feel like home.

AJIMA: Your idea too American. Home for Koreans is hard place, not easy. You have to suffer first, then, if you lucky, something good happen.

ANNIE: When am I going to be lucky?

SUNG SAY NIM: Some people think you already are. Born with no one to give you a name and still you go to America.

YOON MI: Have family to take care of you—

COACH KIM: American family.

YOON MI: They feed you and they take care of you.

SUNG SAY NIM: What you want of us, Annie? To name our shame?

YOON MI: To tell you we have no way to take care of our own?

ANNIE: I'm sorry, but I just want to see my birth parents.

AJIMA: That is one thing we cannot do. We can tell you story like yours but not your story exactly.

ANNIE: Then I came all the way here for nothing?

OMANI: You came for yourself, Annie.

AJIMA: What you say? We finish show?

ANNIE: I don't know.

COACH KIM: If we don't finish the show, I'm going to soccer practice.

SUNG SAY NIM: Wait. What if we do it the modern way. Get rid of all these old costumes.

AJIMA: I made them by hand!

AJISHE: Nobody care these days.

SUNG SAY NIM: What do you think, Annie?

ANNIE: What do you mean?

OMANI: They can do story like it happens today.

ANNIE: But what about the daughter and the king?

SUNG SAY NIM: The daughter is still the daughter, and the king is just another angry father.

COACH: It's the same kind of story. The father is too strict, and daughter falls for some boy.

ANNIE: But the court and the war?

SUN SAY NIM: We don't need the court.

AJISHE: And always some kind of war going on, ha?

ANNIE: Where's the castle dungeon?

SUNG SAY NIM: In the basement.

ANNIE: And the mountainside?

COACH: The streets of Seoul.

SUNG SAY NIM: They can be as cold as any mountainside.

ANNIE: It doesn't sound any better.

SUNG SAY NIM: Well, in modern way, the prince—I mean, boyfriend— disappears. We don't know what happens to him.

ANNIE: So he doesn't have to die?

SUNG SAY NIM: That's right . . .

ANNIE *(pause)*: OK, what happens next?

COACH KIM: Right. Everyone, we're back! But we do it the modern way, right?

ALL: Cho tah! *(Korean for "Good!")*

COACH KIM: Omani, you mind if I tell it?

OMANI: Please do, and I'll back you up!

(Omani takes off coat to reveal nightclub outfit.)

COACH KIM: Lights! Five—six—seven—eight!

(Disco beat begins, and Coach starts disco dancing, with Omani and Mary as backup pair of vocalists.)

OMANI and MARY *(as ensemble member)*:
Accept your fate today.
Give up your willful ways
Accept your fate today.
Give up your willful ways

COACH KIM:
She met him dancing on the floor
His magic hit, she wanted more

CHORUS:
Accept your fate today
Give up your willful ways
Accept your fate today
Give up your willful ways

(Crossfade to platform for twenty-four beats for scene of Daughter dancing with boyfriend. They are interrupted by Father, who drags her away. Crossfade to singers.)

CHORUS:
Accept your fate today
Give up your willful ways
Accept your fate today
Give up your willful ways

COACH KIM:
Her father brought the groom to be
No way she'd be his bride, you see

CHORUS:

> Accept your fate today
> Give up your willful ways
> Accept your fate today
> Give up your willful ways

(Crossfade to platform for twenty-four beats for scene of Father with groom-to-be, who gives Daughter flowers. She tosses them and exits. Crossfade to singers.)

CHORUS:

> Accept your fate today
> Give up your willful ways
> Accept your fate today
> Give up your willful ways

COACH KIM:

> Her father was a man of means
> He knew just how to work the scenes

CHORUS:

> Accept your fate today
> Give up your willful ways
> Accept your fate today
> Give up your willful ways

(Crossfade to platform for twenty-four beats for scene of Father waiting until the boyfriend arrives. Father offers money that the boyfriend takes, and they both exit. Crossfade back to singers.)

CHORUS:

> Accept your fate today
> Give up your willful ways
> Accept your fate today
> Give up your willful ways

COACH KIM:

> She wandered through the streets alone
> Nobody cared when she moaned

CHORUS:

> Accept your fate today
> Give up your willful ways

Accept your fate today
Give up your willful ways

(*Crossfade to platform for twenty-four beats for scene where Daughter
bumps into people on the street until she runs off. Crossfade to singers.*)

CHORUS:
Accept your fate today
Give up your willful ways
Accept your fate today
Give up your willful ways

COACH KIM:
To the clinic, with the blues
The nurses checked, gave her the news

CHORUS:
Accept your fate today
Give up your willful ways
Accept your fate today
Give up your willful ways

(*Crossfade to platform for twenty-four beats for scene of Daughter in chair
facing upstage. Two nurses stand by her. One shows her the charts. Then
they dress her in a hospital gown. Crossfade to singers.*)

CHORUS:
Accept your fate today
Give up your willful ways
Accept your fate today
Give up your willful ways

COACH KIM:
The doctors did the job on the fly
The baby arrived without a sigh

CHORUS:
Accept your fate today
Give up your willful ways
Accept your fate today
Give up your willful ways

(*Crossfade to platform for twenty-four beats for scene of doctors doing
operation and holding up baby. Crossfade back to singers.*)

CHORUS:
>   *Accept your fate today*
>   *Give up your willful ways*
>   *Accept your fate today*
>   *Give up your willful ways*

COACH KIM:
>   *She loved the baby, with heart and soul,*
>   *But poor and alone, that took its toll*

CHORUS:
>   *Accept your fate today*
>   *Give up your willful ways*
>   *Accept your fate today*
>   *Give up your willful ways*

>   *(Crossfade to platform for twenty-four beats for scene of Daughter
>   with baby on streets until she finally kneels down in defeat.)*

DAUGHTER:
>   *Jahng jah jahng u ree ae ki*
>   *Jahl do jahl do jah neun ku nah*
>   *Mung mung kae ya jit jee*
>   *Mah rah kko kko dahl ka u jee*
>   *Mah rah u ree ae ki*
>   *Jahl do jahl dah*

>   *(By the end, Daughter is completely downcast as if she is about to die.)*

ANNIE: Wait! She can't die like that!

>   *(As Omani talks to Annie, Shaman gets up and exits.)*

OMANI: Who said she died?
ANNIE: But she lay down like she was . . . *(Turns to see Shaman gone.)* Where'd
she go?
OMANI: No one knows.
ANNIE: Shaman? Shaman?

>   *(Shaman enters.)*

SHAMAN: Yes?
ANNIE: Where'd the daughter go?
SHAMAN: I don't know. In the story, she just disappears.

ANNIE: But you can't have a story without an ending!

SUNG SAY NIM: Who said it was over?

ANNIE: But who's left to talk about?

OMANI: The baby.

ANNIE: What?

SUNG SAY NIM: They found the baby on the doorstep of the orphanage.

ANNIE: You didn't tell me that!

SHAMAN: We haven't got there yet.

SUNG SAY NIM: No one knew who the baby was or how she got there.

SHAMAN: The daughter disappeared; the boyfriend was gone; and the angry father never knew what happened.

SUNG SAY NIM: There was no one to claim her.

ANNIE: No one in all of Korea wanted her?

SHAMAN: What would you do if you found that baby?

ANNIE: I'd find her a home!

OMANI: Then you should do that.

ANNIE: Me?

OMANI: See if you can find her a home.

SHAMAN: Here, we'll help you.

(Shaman gives the baby to Annie as the others take up positions around the stage facing upstage. As Annie approaches each, they turn to speak to her.)

ANNIE: Will you take this baby into your family?

SUNG SAY NIM: I'm sorry, I have no wife to take care of her, and I have to support my parents who are old and live with me.

ANNIE *(crosses to Coach Kim)*: Will you adopt this baby?

COACH KIM: Our family is packed into a small apartment. We have no room and barely enough food to feed ourselves!

ANNIE *(crosses to Ajima and Ajishe)*: No room in your hearts?

AJISHE: We are too old now to take a baby.

AJIMA: She is not even our child.

ANNIE *(crosses to Yoon Mi)*: You could adopt her, like I was adopted, only she wouldn't have to leave Korea.

YOON MI: Things are different.

AJIMA *(crosses to Annie)*: She not of our blood, our family heritage. It would be impossible to hide that from our neighbors.

ANNIE: How can you talk like that? Doesn't she belong here with you?

AJIMA: It is not so simple for us.

ANNIE: But she needs someone now to take care of her!

YOON MI: Sorry, we are not her family.

AJIMA: And in Korea, family, blood is more important than anything.

SUNG SAY NIM: Only her family can take care of her.

COACH KIM: And her family is gone.

ANNIE: But what will happen to this baby?

OMANI: There is a couple in America who are desperate to adopt her.

SHAMAN: What do you say, Annie? Shall we let them adopt her?

ANNIE: But how could the daughter leave her baby like that?

YOON MI: It's hard to be woman alone with baby, here in Korea.

AJIMA: No one to help you,

AJISHE: Everyone treat you so bad.

YOON MI: No government agency to support you.

COACH KIM: You are like a player with no team.

ANNIE: I know what that's like, when it feels like everyone's against you.

(Annie gives baby to Shaman.)

ANNIE: Can you tell me what happened in the folktale?

OMANI: I thought you didn't like that old story.

ANNIE: I want to know what happened to the baby in that story.

OMANI: She was found by some peasants and was brought up as their own daughter.

SHAMAN: But when she was your age, they told her how they found her on the mountainside.

OMANI: And she climbed the mountain to look for her mother's remains.

ANNIE: Can you take me there?

OMANI: Yes, of course. But you will have to help us tell the story. Will you play the young girl?

ANNIE: Yes.

(Annie walks to the foot of a ladder up to the walkway.)

ANNIE CLIMBS THE MOUNTAIN

ANNIE:

What is it I'll find up there
Up on the highest mountain stair?
What token of the past
Is there to see?

(Dialogue break.)

ANNIE: Why am I doing this? I don't even know what I am looking for!

OMANI: Life is like that most of the time.

ANNIE: Can't you help me? Give me a clue?

OMANI: That would make it too easy for you.

ANNIE: Climbing mountains is not easy.

*(Annie climbs the ladder to the walkway.
Resume song.)*

ANNIE:

> *What memory lingers in this place?*
> *What trace that time could not erase?*
> *What long forgotten sign will there still be?*
> *What will I find that someone left behind?*
> *What is there still for me?*

(Dialogue break.)

ANNIE: Wow, all this searching makes me tired. I need some rest.

*(Annie lies down and goes to sleep. The spirits of Prince and Daughter
enter and look at Annie. A tree branch appears over the sleeping Annie.)*

CHILD OF OUR LOVE

PRINCE:

> *Child of our love,*
> *Child of healing and hope,*
> *Child of our joy and delight.*

DAUGHTER:

> *Blessings we give to you,*
> *Blessings we bring*
> *Blessings we sing here tonight.*

(Spoken break.)

PRINCE: Out of the shadow
DAUGHTER: Your beauty will grow,
PRINCE: In you our love will prevail.
DAUGHTER: Through tears and trials,
PRINCE: Through bitter travail,
DAUGHTER: Hope will not falter, or fail.

(Resume song.)

DAUGHTER:

> *You are the rainbow*
> *That shines through the storm*

PRINCE:

> *You are the flower*
> *That blooms through the thorns*

DAUGHTER:

> *You are the sunrise*
> *That follows the night*

TOGETHER:

> *For you are our joy and delight*
> *you are our joy and delight*

> (*Prince and Daughter exit, and Omani enters*
> *as Annie awakens.*)

OMANI: You have slept the morning away.

ANNIE: Where did you go?

OMANI: I was that tree, my branches hanging over your head, protecting you from the wind and cold.

ANNIE: I had a dream of the prince and the princess.

OMANI: Stories become part of our lives.

DID YOU EVER KNOW?

ANNIE:

> *Did you ever know*
> *Of a princess long ago?*
> *Is there anything at all*
> *You can recall?*
> *Did you ever know*
> *Of her suffering and her shame?*
> *How they caged her yet*
> *Her heart they could not tame?*

> *Did you know her name?*
> *Know how I became?*

> *Could it be no more than just a dream?*
> *No more than just a fantasy?*
> *And when I wake will there be nothing I can hold onto?*
> *Nothing that I'll know of you?*

> (*Dialogue break.*)

OMANI: What are you looking for?

ANNIE: I don't know. Maybe she left something behind.

(Resume song.)

ANNIE:

> *Will it fade away*
> *Like my dream of yesterday?*
> *Just a phantom that I know*
> *Can never stay*
>
> *Drifting in the wind*
> *Without past, and without kin*
> *Never certain of the lives*
> *That once have been*
>
> *Can no one be sure?*
> *Did no trace endure?*
>
> *And could it be no more than just a dream?*
> *No more than just a fantasy?*
> *And when I awake will there be nothing I can hold onto?*
> *Nothing that I'll know of you?*
> *What if you're not true?*

(Annie sees something under the tree branch and pulls out a hang sen. She holds it up, and it is a match to her own hang sen.)

ANNIE: They're the same!

OMANI: They are a match.

ANNIE: But this is for the baby left on the mountain, not me.

OMANI: What does your heart tell you?

ANNIE: It feels strange, holding them together. Like two halves make something whole.

OMANI: Like two hang sen become one heart.

ANNIE *(looking out from the mountain)*: Look, the sky is so clear and blue. It's like I can see all of Korea and over there, across the ocean, America.

(Annie and Omani exit and the rest of the cast comes out downstage. Annie and Omani re-enter downstage. The cast applauds Annie.)

ANNIE: Thank you for doing this show for me.

AJIMA: Did it help you?

ANNIE: Yes . . .

AJIMA: You want to stay? You could join our company. Learn to live in Korea. Let your Han bloom like flower.

OMANI: You want to stay in Korea?

ANNIE: I couldn't leave my folks and everyone back home.

AJISHE: Americans can live without you.

ANNIE: But I want to go home. I found what I was looking for.

AJIMA: What you find?

ANNIE: The land where I came from. The people of the Han. That voice inside me that called me back here . . .

OMANI: You understand.

ANNIE: Yes. When I stood up on that mountaintop and saw all of Korea and America . . . I felt lucky, for the first time in my life. I have my Mom and Dad and Ajima . . . the Han river and baseball, the daughter in the folktale and my birth mother, all inside of me . . . and that's OK . . . because there's a reason for all of that . . . and even though it makes me want to cry . . . it makes me want to stand up and be proud . . .

NOW I CAN STAND

ANNIE:

Now I can stand with my head up high
Now I believe there's a reason why
I have a path that I must take
A destiny that I must make
I know that I was meant to be

(Dialogue break.)

AJIMA: You sing so beautifully.

SUNG SAY NIM: You must be Korean, sing like that.

ANNIE: Thank you, everyone. It was a wonderful show, and it helped me a lot.

COACH KIM: Good. I've got to get to my practice.

ANNIE *(waving good-bye)*: Thanks, Coach Kim!

(Coach Kim exits with his soccer ball.)

AJIMA: You want to join us for our dinner after show? We have lots of kim chee!

ANNIE: I've got to get back.

AJISHE: You leave us behind?

ANNIE: Don't worry, I'm taking you with me, in my heart.

(Music resumes as the other characters exit, leaving Annie alone onstage.)

ANNIE:
> Now I can stand with my head up high
> Now I believe there's a reason why
> I have a home, I have a place
> A future only I can face
> I know that I was meant to be
> Someone loves me.

(*Lights fade to low as Annie moves around the room and settles into the place she started to sleep and the music fades out. Annie sits up.*)

ANNIE: Omani? Shaman? Where did everyone go?

(*Knocking on the door. Lights come up. Annie is asleep and wakes up.*)

MARY (*offstage*): Annie?
ANNIE: What?
MARY (*offstage*): Annie, are you all right?
ANNIE: Mom?
GEORGE (*offstage*): Annie, we have someone here to see you.
ANNIE: Who is it?
GEORGE (*offstage*): Let us in and you'll find out.
ANNIE: Omani? Where are you?
MARY (*offstage*): Annie? Can you let us in, please?
ANNIE: Shaman? Walleye?
GEORGE (*offstage*): Please let us in, Annie!
ANNIE: Just a second!

(*George and Mary enter, and Annie embraces them.*)

Mom, Dad, I'm so glad you're here!
MARY: That's wonderful, Annie, but . . .
GEORGE: Somebody here has something to say to you.

(*Coach Nelson enters.*)

COACH NELSON: Well, Annie, I heard what happened at the ballgame and went lookin' for the other team.
ANNIE: You didn't have to do that . . .
COACH NELSON: Are you kidding? They use that kind of talk against my best player? No way!
ANNIE: But there's nothing you can do.
COACH NELSON: Oh, yeah? Come on in guys.

(Danny, Betty, Billy, and Johnny enter, looking sheepish,
along with Alice and Janet.)

Well, look what we have here. The middle school choir. And who's
singing first?
BETTY: I'm sorry, Annie. For the things we said.
JOHNNY: Yeah, we just got kind of excited, you know?
ALICE: What about you, Danny?

(Pause as Danny looks around.)

DANNY: Well, I just thought you were out.
COACH NELSON: I guess we better look for another pitcher.
DANNY: Wait. I mean, I was just excited, like Johnny said.
COACH NELSON: And?
DANNY: Well, it's too bad that it happened.
COACH NELSON: And?
DANNY: So . . . I'm sorry.
COACH NELSON: Now you got to shake and make amends.
DANNY: Do I have to?
COACH NELSON: Oh yeah, you have to.

(Danny reluctantly extends hand to shake, and Annie takes it.)

KIDS: Yeah, go team!
COACH NELSON: We all missed you at the game, Annie.
ALICE: It wasn't the same without you.
ANNIE: My life wouldn't be the same without all of you.
MARY: I hope this helps you, but if you need more time alone—
ANNIE: No, it's all right now. I've had some time to think about it, my com-
ing here.
COACH NELSON: It was like Homecoming Weekend!

(Enter Uncle Harlan, Aunt Hannah, and Grocer Olsen.)

GROCER OLSEN: Homecoming? I thought this was a serious meeting.
MARY: Don't worry, we're working through it.
AUNT HANNAH: Is Annie all right?
GEORGE: I think she is.
COACH NELSON: Where's the Teach?
AUNT HANNAH: You miss her or something?
COACH NELSON: No, just asking.
AUNT HANNAH: I heard she's getting ready to be your Homecoming Queen!
UNCLE HARLAN: For once you might be right.

(As the others laugh, Shaman enters upstage on platform.)

SHAMAN: Humans are so humorous.

FINALE

COMPANY A:
Gotta throw your line in

COMPANY B:

Just throw it in

Gotta let it go

Just let it go

Gotta take your chances

COMPANY:
See what's down below

KIDS:
Then we will stand with our heads up high
Then we will know there's a reason why.

COMPANY:
We'll make our home
We'll take our place
We'll leave a legacy of grace
We know that we've a destiny

OMANI:
Let us put aside all these masks we wear

SHAMAN:
There is so much more
To us that we must share

COMPANY:
We must embrace the best of who we are
Every part something new will start

COMPANY A:
Gotta put your line in

COMPANY B:

Just throw it in

Gotta let it go

Just let it go

COMPANY:
Gotta take your chances
See what's down below

COMPANY A:
Gotta throw out caution

Throw it to the wind

There's something magical

COMPANY B:

Just throw it out

Blow it away

COMPANY:
about to begin,

COMPANY A:
Just let it in

Just pull it in

COMPANY B:

Gotta take your chances

Gotta let it go

COMPANY:
Just take a chance
Give it a try
Together we'll
JUST PULL IT IN!

END OF MUSICAL

3

Happy Valley

Aurorae Khoo

Introduction, *by Josephine Lee*

Happy Valley was produced by Mu Performing Arts and presented at Intermedia Arts in Minneapolis from September 16, 2005, to October 2, 2005, under the direction of Jennifer Weir.

Happy Valley follows a quartet of memorable characters during Hong Kong's 1997 transition from British to Chinese rule. Each of them—the vulnerable adolescent, Tuppy; her uncle Chester, the Filipino housekeeper, Winnifreda; and Chester's love interest, Victoria—reveals fantasies that sustain their sense of integrity during this tumultuous time. Tuppy clings to her uncle's tales of joining British high society, Chester imagines selling racehorses to the rich and powerful, and Winnifreda dreams about the sons she left in the Philippines. Victoria, a secretary from Mainland China, desires opportunities in her new life in Hong Kong and through her marriage to Chester. In Khoo's memorable staging, pipe dreams and nightmares starring Queen Elizabeth and Deng Xiaoping spring to life, revealing a tangle of colonial, national, ethnic, and familial identities. The action of the play moves inexorably forward, forcing characters toward confrontation with inevitable changes.

Happy Valley ends rather than begins with immigration to North America, connecting what is "Asian American" with the tangible legacies of British Empire, the global importation of Filipinas as domestic labor, and the many faces

Illustration: Sarah Ochs in *Happy Valley.*
(Photograph used by permission of Charissa Uemura Photography.)

of Chinese nationalism. The play reminds us that recent arrivals from Asia bring with them already complicated identities and histories that affect who they become in the United States.

ABOUT THE PLAY

PLACE

Happy Valley, a neighborhood of Hong Kong, and Winnipeg, Manitoba, Canada.

TIME

The eve of the handover of Hong Kong from Britain to China in 1997 and eight years later.

CHARACTERS (ORIGINAL CAST)

TUPPY (Sara Ochs): thirteen, a studious girl, Hong Kong Chinese, precocious

CHESTER (Sherwin Resurreccion): forties, a dapper dandy, Hong Kong Chinese but a severe Anglophile, uncle to Tuppy

WINNIFREDA (Maria Kelly): fifties, short sturdy woman, Filipino, Tuppy and her uncle's longtime nanny and maid

VICTORIA (Jeany Park: early thirties, a horse of a woman but attractive, mainland Chinese, a new immigrant to Hong Kong

TONG TONG (Jeany Park): a chinchilla from Peru (played by a realistic puppet); a chinchilla is like a gerbil but with big mouse ears

The characters Queen Elizabeth II and Deng Xiaoping are performed by the actress playing Victoria.

SYNOPSIS

Set in the year leading up to the handover of Hong Kong from Britain to China in 1997, an adolescent girl searches for happiness in a changing Hong Kong.

As our heroine questions her identity, the nature of family, and origin, the personal, as well as the historic impact of the handover is explored. What does this return to the mainland mean for a people torn between East and West for over a century? How will commerce, politics, culture, and the practicalities of daily life be affected? And are these effects imagined or real?

The play drifts in and out of fantasy as teenage Tuppy longs to leave Hong Kong with her dapper uncle Chester. He is an opportunistic broker of race-horses who is immigrating to London before the People's Republic of China takes over. Standing in Tuppy's way is Chester's gaudy new Mainland Chinese wife, Victoria. The two battle for Chester's affection. Hovering in the background is the family's longtime maid, Winnifreda, who is also torn between mothering Tuppy and escaping the potentially perilous situation.

As for the play's structure, the characters stand in for their political counterparts: Chester represents exiting Britain, the colonial "patron"; Victoria represents the new power and wealth of Mainland China; and Winnifreda is an example of the swelling underclass of imported Third World labor. These forces collide on the vibrant battleground that is Hong Kong—symbolized by the conflicted and lonely young Tuppy.

SCENE 1: AN UNHAPPY BIRTHDAY

In the darkness, the clamor of a late-night city. Lights up on Tuppy, a studious girl, thirteen, wearing a silk jockey shirt and jodphurs. Tuppy stands on a balcony with her pet chinchilla, Tong Tong, in a metal cage next to her. Behind her is the living room of a luxury high-rise apartment. It is dimly lit. Tuppy speaks with an English accent and begins to tell her story to her chinchilla.

TUPPY: Here we are on Floor 21. On a ledge. On the edge. On the end. Of a world. June 30, 1996, Happy Valley, Hong Kong. I know, it's sickening to live here. Everyone is always happy, or at least pretending to be. *(Pointing to different locations in front of her.)* The people in the hospital, where my mother was born, cheer. The ghosts in the Buddhist cemetery clap and cluck their ghost tongues with joy. Even the horses on the racetrack across the way will grin and whinny as the Union Jack goes down.

My uncle works with rich men and those silly horses. But he is smarter than all those other beasts, and good with numbers. In fact, my uncle and I have a lot in common. I'm proud to say, we've both never been happy! We know the truth. Someplace else, better, exists.

(The distant sounds of the city resume. Tuppy continues to watch and listen to the street below.)

(Winnifreda, a short, sensible Filipino woman in her fifties, enters. She wears a nightgown and sleepily rubs her eyes. She calls to Tuppy from the living room.)

WINNIFREDA: *(Filipino accent.)* Miss, why are you still awake? Is this your funny business again?

(Tuppy doesn't move. Doesn't answer back.)

You should be asleep. *(Winnifreda sighs, exasperated, and approaches.)*

TUPPY: Please, I want to stay up.

WINNIFREDA: Come back inside. You'll get sick. (*Winnifreda drapes a crested jacket from a school uniform over Tuppy's shoulders.*) Here's your blazer.

TUPPY: It's too hot.

WINNIFREDA: I kept it in the freezer a while. (*Motions Tuppy to bed.*) Now go.

TUPPY: Even Tong Tong needs air.

WINNIFREDA: I'll get a fan.

TUPPY: But . . . he's not back yet.

WINNIFREDA: He'll be back.

TUPPY: Did you call him?

WINNIFREDA: He doesn't want to be bothered.

TUPPY: He must know I'm waiting.

WINNIFREDA (*stern*): You shouldn't be.

(*Tuppy crosses her arms and bears down. Winnifreda gently lifts the girl's chin, inspects her.*)

Your nose is red.

(*Tuppy turns away, hiding her face in her shoulder. She's been crying.*)

TUPPY: I said it was hot.

WINNIFREDA: When it's cold, you're going to cry, too? (*Takes out a hankie and dabs Tuppy's eyes.*)

TUPPY: Can you just leave me alone?

(*Winnifreda gives up and turns on her heels. She enters the apartment and turns on the lights, then moves off to the dining table, where she begins sorting through a basket of clothes. She holds up a stained shirt, clucks her tongue in disgust.*)

WINNIFREDA: I spent twenty-one dollars of sir's money cleaning these things, and I'll have to do half of it over again.

(*Tuppy remains outside. She and Winnifreda call back and forth to each other.*)

TUPPY (*sarcastic*): I know, back home you used to do it all by hand.

WINNIFREDA: That's right. It turns out better that way.

TUPPY: So why don't you do it that way now?

WINNIFREDA: Because I'm too busy taking care of you.

(*Carrying Tong Tong's cage, Tuppy slowly skulks inside, gravitating to the conversation.*)

Come. If you want to stay up, be of use.

(Tuppy edges toward the dining table, careful not to look too eager. Winnifreda throws the stained shirt aside. Tuppy picks it up and begins folding it.)

Don't fold that.

(Tuppy still folds. Winnifreda tosses aside another soiled garment. Again, Tuppy picks it up.)

Ay naku!

(She bats it out of Tuppy's hands.)

This is helping me? *(Points her away.)* Go do something else.

(The following dialogue is rapid.)

TUPPY *(anxious, impatient)*: For how long?
WINNIFREDA: As long as needed.
TUPPY: He took his toothbrush.
WINNIFREDA *(absorbed with the laundry)*: Doesn't mean it isn't business.
TUPPY: What if he left town?
WINNIFREDA: I'm sure he'll be back.
TUPPY: Everyone else is leaving for good.
WINNIFREDA: Now you're talking nonsense.
TUPPY: What if he was kidnapped by Red Chinese . . .
WINNIFREDA: Ay!
TUPPY: It's the only explanation.
WINNIFREDA *(raising an eyebrow)*: There are other explanations.
TUPPY: You think he's with . . . a woman?
WINNIFREDA: I do not say these things.
TUPPY: Then what are you saying?
WINNIFREDA: There are more important things than your thirteenth birth-day.
TUPPY: He's never missed it.
WINNIFREDA: Miss, you are not small anymore . . .
TUPPY *(interrupts)*: That's right, never missed it in thirteen years . . .
WINNIFREDA *(interrupts)*: It's different now. Ay, the world is ending.
TUPPY: Ohhh, c'mon . . .
WINNIFREDA *(rambling)*: It's true. You see the news today? People's new apart-ments just collapse. Chinese builders don't care about rules in Hong Kong . . .

TUPPY: But we always go to the racetrack.

WINNIFREDA: He should never have started taking you there. Bless the Virgin, he hasn't come home.

TUPPY: Don't say that.

WINNIFREDA: You know what I mean.

TUPPY: Well, if he never comes back, you would have to take care of me.

WINNIFREDA: No I would not.

TUPPY: I'd keep paying you.

WINNIFREDA: Hmmph! I'd go back, to the Pilippines. I have family there.

TUPPY: Aw, they don't remember you.

(Winnifreda is silenced by this. She solemnly gathers the clean clothes in her arms and starts to exit, but she stops.)

WINNIFREDA *(indignant)*: My children would never forget.

(Winnifreda tersely flicks off the apartment lights and marches off-stage. Tuppy is left in the dark.)

TUPPY: Neither would my uncle . . .

SCENE 2: THE RACETRACK: THE LAST BIRTHDAY

In the darkness, the sound of a trumpet, a racing gate snaps. Horses' hooves pound on turf. Upswell of a cheering crowd.

Lights up as Uncle Chester, early forties, dapper with an English accent, jumps out of the living-room closet. He's dressed in a bowtie, straw bowler, and light-colored suit.

CHESTER: Surprise! *(Pumps his arms and begins to sing.)* Happy birthday to you, happy birthday to you . . .

(Uncle Chester leads Tuppy by the arm to another part of the stage. It transforms into the stands at a racetrack. Tuppy is still in her jockey outfit.)

(The scene is snappy, quick, filled with race-day anticipation.)

TUPPY: I knew we'd come here.

CHESTER: Happy twelfth birthday! Would you rather be somewhere else this year?

TUPPY: Of course not. This is perfect.

CHESTER: Good. Because I feel lucky.

TUPPY: So do I.

CHESTER (*shielding his eyes from the sun*): Jesus, it's bloody hot out here. Hurry up now. Where do you want to sit?

TUPPY: Right up front.

CHESTER: All right, right by the rail. You're a real racing fan, not afraid of a little sun.

(*They sit down in the front row of the racing stands. We hear a bad brass band begin to play a watered-down rock song.*)

TUPPY (*shouting over the music*): I like the band.

CHESTER (*shouting back with disdain*): Schoolkids.

(*Over the music.*) In my day, it was real musicians with real uniforms. They played "The King and I" and marches by Sousa.

TUPPY (*over the music*): You know, I'm old enough to be in a band now.

CHESTER (*over the music, teasing*): Ahh, twelve: You're the same age as my watch.

(*They listen. Tuppy swings her legs. The band sputters out, stops playing. Chester takes out his racing program and begins marking it with a pencil.*)

Don't waste your time on bands. You and I've got real talent. We can spot champions; that's why I raised you up around horses.

TUPPY: Isn't that strange?

CHESTER: When did "we" become strange?

(*Tuppy shrugs.*)

TUPPY: It's not normal to live with your uncle.

CHESTER: No, it's extraordinary.

(*Tuppy smiles.*)

(*Chester jumps to his feet. The upswell of a cheering crowd. The sound of horses' hooves pounding on turf.*)

Here they come!

(*Tuppy jumps up also, cranes her neck.*)

Hole In One! Hole In One! Hole In One!

(*The crowd goes wild. Chester leans forward and waves his fist. Tuppy does too.*)

CHESTER and TUPPY: Go, go, go, go!

(He sits down, hat in his hands. Tuppy sits too. The crowd settles down.)

TUPPY: What happened?
CHESTER: *(Lobs an insult at the winning horse.)* Bugger. *(He points with disdain at the results board.)*
TUPPY: We lost?

(Chester grimaces.)

After the handover, will there still be races in Happy Valley?
CHESTER *(stern)*: Don't be silly. Of course.
TUPPY: Winny says, if the Chinese invade, they'll build an airfield right here.
CHESTER: Don't be gloomy.

(Tuppy swings her legs.)

TUPPY: You know what else Winny says?

(Chester groans.)

We shouldn't gamble. We should only work for God.
CHESTER: Tell Winny, God doesn't pay very well.

(Tuppy nods, sits back down. She swings her legs again.)

Here, pick a winner.

(Chester hands her the racing program.)

TUPPY *(reading)*: "Lucky Duck, Super Scallop, Fisherman's Treasure . . ."
CHESTER: Oh bother, it sounds like a menu. *(Rants.)* Only the Chinese would name a horse after a main course. You see, they won't need to invade with tanks. They're sneaky. Already wiggling their way into our minds, our pocketbooks, our sporting events. *(Crinkles his nose.)* Hyping up their horses on hormones and amphetamines. Nothing's a fair bet nowadays. *(With flourish.)* But that's the future, Tup. Genetic engineering.

(Tuppy shrugs.)

Horse cloning. Thoroughbred sperm.
TUPPY *(grimacing)*: Yuchhk.

CHESTER: More valuable than a Rolex. Put Personal Ensign in a test tube mixed with jism from Secretariat. Voila, an instant champion.

TUPPY: What about my genetics?

CHESTER: You're also a champion.

TUPPY *(persistent)*: Why?

CHESTER: You just are.

TUPPY: Didn't my father have bad genes?

CHESTER *(gruffly brushing her off, lying)*: I don't remember him.

TUPPY: Neither do I.

CHESTER: Just as well. But your mother was a thoroughbred.

TUPPY: No she wasn't. She was too plain, had no money, cried all the time . . .

CHESTER *(interrupting)*: But an angel just the same.

TUPPY: . . . a helpless bother . . .

CHESTER *(interrupting)*: We should speak politely of the dead.

TUPPY: . . . and she had me. That's why my father left her.

CHESTER: Don't be melodramatic. He was restless, a cad. C'mon, you said you'd pick me a winner.

TUPPY *(pointing at the race program, glum)*: . . . Seven Year Egg.

CHESTER: Why him?

TUPPY: That's how long I've been living with you. Am *I* a bother to you?

CHESTER: Sometimes.

(Tuppy looks panicked. Chester laughs.)

Oh, c'mon. I've told you a hundred times. My life was ready to be changed.

TUPPY: Did you take me in because no one else would have me?

CHESTER: I did it as an experiment.

(Tuppy gasps in shock.)

Ohhh, I shouldn't have said a word . . .

(Before Tuppy can ask another question, Chester jumps to his feet. The upswell of a cheering crowd. The sound of horses' hooves pounding on turf.)

Here they come!

(Tuppy jumps up also, cranes her neck.)

Seven Year Egg! Seven Year Egg! Seven Year Egg!

(The crowd goes wild. Chester leans forward and waves his fist.
Tuppy does, too.)

CHESTER and TUPPY: Go, go, go, go!

(He sits down, hat in his hands. Tuppy sits, too.
The crowd settles down.)

TUPPY: What happened?

CHESTER: *(Lobs an insult at the winning horse.)* Bugger. *(He points with disdain at the results board.)*

TUPPY: Are you sure I'm not a born loser? *(Beat, glum.)* Like my mother. Winny thinks I should visit her, but I don't want to. I won't anymore.

CHESTER: And now you're twelve, think you can do as you please?

TUPPY: She was horrified by me. I was nothing more than a big hospital bill.

CHESTER: Born two months early, so fragile and small . . .

TUPPY *(overlapping)*: Couldn't even manage to keep me inside of her . . .

CHESTER *(overlapping)*: And now . . .

TUPPY *(overlapping)*: If she hated me, why should I visit?

CHESTER *(overlapping)*: . . . strong and stubborn as a mule.

TUPPY *(insistent)*: You know she thought I ruined her life. Are you listening?

CHESTER: My poor sister, bless her soul. Passed so young. . . . But she wasn't your real mother. *(Then with flourish.)* Your real mum was none other than Queen Elizabeth the Second!

(A fantastic fantasy brass band begins to play a stirring rendition of a Sousa march as Uncle Chester points to another part of the stage—the VIP box. There stands stuffy Queen Elizabeth II, portrayed by the actress playing Victoria. She gives a queenly wave. Tuppy is awed. The Queen is dressed in an ostentatious evening gown, gloves, and tiara.)

QUEEN ELIZABETH *(in an outrageous aristocratic British accent)*: Ohhh, I have such fond memories of Happy Valley. My first visit was in 1983. That old bitch Margaret Thatcher was running things, so believe you me, I needed a holiday. And ohhh, it was the perfect outing. A day at the races in the last imperial colony of the British Empire. It should've been marvelous, watching the Chinky-chonks with their boiled peanuts, horses, and games. But it wasn't. I had this low, sinking feeling . . .

(Her distraught rant builds speed until it's unintelligible.) First, I thought of the Irish. Well, they'd always been bomb toting. Americans quaint, albeit tea dumping; a few irate Islamics; Africa overgrown; India, civil but disobedient . . . *(Hysterical, speeding.)* And what next?! Hong Kong!

My dear, little, malaria-infested island. We British built the place up, you know, until it was glistening with golden pavilions and skyscrapers. And now the damn Chinky-chonks wanted it back?! Well, we won it fair and square. Kicked their little yellow bums in the Opium Wars. Honor called on me to do something. I had to stop the royal fffucking world from falling to pieces!!!

So I met . . . your father.

TUPPY (*excited*): Prince Phillip?

QUEEN ELIZABETH: No, no. Over in the riffraff seats, I spotted the most common, ordinary gambler.

(*Queen Elizabeth makes her way down from the VIP box.
She waves at the crowd as she proceeds.*)

And I was struck by a brilliant plan, my own insidious takeover.

(*She arrives at Tuppy and Chester's bleacher. Motions for them
to scoot over. They do. The queen sits down.*)

I would be like a queen ant and lay my heir among the masses of the colony, her destiny only to be revealed at the appropriate time. So scientists fertilized one of my eggs with the male sprinklings of that Hong Kong gambler—your father.

TUPPY: Was he handsome?

QUEEN ELIZABETH: He had his charms. But you already know he was an irresponsible bastard. Ran off. Didn't stick around to raise you. Fortunately, your uncle Chester stepped in, rescued you, and saved the fate of the empire.

CHESTER: Oh, Your Majesty, you're much too gracious.

QUEEN ELIZABETH: But my hunch was right, Tup. One year after you were born. Margaret "Smarty-Pants" Thatcher signed Hong Kong, lock, stock, and barrel, back to the Chinky-chonks.

TUPPY: But Your Majesty . . .

QUEEN ELIZABETH (*interrupting*): Please, call me Mother.

TUPPY (*blushing*): Mother . . . Uncle Chester's a Chinky-chonk.

QUEEN ELIZABETH: But, you see, there are "good" Chinky-chonks and "bad" ones. Your uncle is "good." Speaks well, has proper manners. Not a Commie bone in his body.

(*Earnest.*) Ohhh, how the "bad" ones will be terribly hard on him.

(*Tuppy gasps. Uncle Chester also fears the warning but brushes it off
and resumes watching the races.*)

(*Blithe.*) Well, I ought to be going. Ta-ta . . .

(The queen gathers herself to leave. Tuppy stands anxiously.)

TUPPY: Wait!

(But Her Majesty doesn't stop. She gives her royal wave and exits with flourish. The terrible brass band strikes up another cacophonous rock medley. It returns us to reality.)

CHESTER: Now, where are you off to?

TUPPY: To join the Queen.

CHESTER *(absorbed in his racing program)*: On your way, be a dear and place a bet for us.

TUPPY *(sits, sullen)*: I don't want to gamble anymore.

CHESTER: Then what do you want?

TUPPY: . . . A mother.

(Chester laughs nervously.)

It isn't funny.

(The band music sputters out. Tuppy is sullen.)

CHESTER: Crikey. *(Throws up his hands.)* I gave you Winny, didn't I? Isn't she like a mother?

TUPPY *(interrupting)*: It's not the same.

CHESTER: Is she asking for a raise?

TUPPY *(interrupting)*: No.

CHESTER *(interrupting, exasperated)*: Then what is it?

TUPPY: Mothers brush your hair. They wait for you to come home from school. They're overprotective.

CHESTER: A good spaniel could do that. Except for brushing the hair.

(He laughs nervously.)

TUPPY: Why do you make a joke out of everything?

CHESTER: Because making jokes is what reasonable adults do.

(He holds up the racing stubs.)

Look, life hands adults these betting stubs, some with big losses, some with small.

TUPPY: What about with wins?

CHESTER: Nowadays, there are rarely wins. It's mainly losses. *(Nervous laugh.)* And what can you do? Nothing. Just look at your silly tickets and laugh.

(He does so—an affected, dapper laugh. He holds up a ticket.)

This one says I'll stub my toe.

(Laughs. Holds up another ticket.)

Ouch, this one says I'll lose gobs of money in a risky investment.

(Shrugs it off. Laughs harder. Looks at the last ticket.)

(Cutting.) Oh, this one says be careful or I'll be useless in the new Hong Kong. Like an old stuffed shirt.

*(Chester laughs and laughs. It's pained, unstoppable.
Tuppy doesn't know what to do.)*

TUPPY: Are you all right?
CHESTER: I'll survive. Laughing. Thinking of the good times.

(He throws the betting stubs up into the air. They float slowly back to the ground. A light snow of other betting stubs begins to fall from the sky— little white squares of paper drifting down.)

TUPPY: Oooh, more tickets . . .

(She catches one, looks at it.)

CHESTER: What does it say? A win or a loss?
TUPPY: *(Frowns.)* A loss.

(But Tuppy shrugs it off, forces out an uncomfortable laugh.)

CHESTER *(pleased)*: There you go. That's growing up.

(Chester opens his umbrella to shield himself from the falling paper. Tuppy stands up on her seat, childishly keeps catching things. Chester thinks for a moment, watches the snowstorm of hundreds of losing tickets.)

(Points to her jodphurs and riding silks.)

Why do you still insist on wearing that?
TUPPY: You bought it for me.
CHESTER: Well, you're getting too old. You look like a runaway jockey. *(He snaps his fingers at her.)* Now sit and stop catching those things.

(Tuppy does so. She sits next to her uncle and leans her head on his shoulder. In turn, Chester tenderly tips his umbrella so it covers and protects her. Chester turns, motions behind them.)

(Annoyed.) I can't believe the gamblers up there in the cheap seats— litterbugs. Throwing their trash down on us. When more Europeans came to the races, this never happened.

TUPPY: I don't mind it.

(The snowfall of tickets gradually stops. Chester holds his palm up to the sky to make sure nothing else is coming down. Then he closes his umbrella.)

CHESTER: You should. We're both getting more refined, mature. Older. *(Ponders.)* What would you think if I got married?

TUPPY: Would you really have to? *(Hesitates.)* We have each other.

CHESTER: What if . . . *(Pauses for dramatic effect.)* She became your new mother.

TUPPY *(curious)*: . . . Would she be pretty?

CHESTER: Of course. Ocean blue eyes.

TUPPY: . . . English?

CHESTER: *(Nods, laughs.)* A princess. Like you!

(Their conversation becomes excited and rapid.)

TUPPY: She'd have to be perfectly graceful. And wear gloves.

CHESTER: And pearls.

TUPPY: And play badminton.

CHESTER: You like badminton?

TUPPY: I'm good at it.

CHESTER: And good with horses?

TUPPY *(rapidly)*: Yes, she'd have to be an excellent horsewoman. Own riding clothes with a red jacket. Help you set up a racetrack in London, Kensington, the center of Picadilly Three Ring Circus! She'd get the Queen to knight you for it.

CHESTER *(pleased)*: Sir Chester. *(Playfully bows to his niece.)* And Lady Tuppy . . .

TUPPY *(Interrupting, curtsies back, still speaking rapidly)*: . . . of the Round Table. We'd go live in her palace. You'd buy her a fountain. She'd throw coins in it and make wishes for me, her little girl.

CHESTER: She sounds wonderful.

TUPPY *(satisfied)*: I'll help you find her.

CHESTER: I warn you, I'll accept nothing less!

TUPPY: Then I promise. Now you promise something.

CHESTER: Yes?

TUPPY: We'll always be together.

(Chester smiles.)

CHESTER: Tup, we'll always be . . .

(One last betting ticket floats down from the sky. Chester picks it up, looks at it curiously, crinkles his nose.)

Why, look at that. . . . A winner.

(He jumps to his feet excited. Tuppy is left alone, sitting on the bench. Chester throws his hands in the air. He dances in celebration; meanwhile, the upswell of a cheering crowd. The sound of horses' hooves pounding on turf. Chester continues to hop about.)

Lights crossfade into . . .

SCENE 3: A BIG DEAL

A spotlight on an overblown portrait of a bushy-eyebrowed, staunch, English patrician posing next to his stunning horse. The rest of the room comes into view. It's evening in the waiting area of an office. Chester sits, waiting anxiously, taps his toes. Victoria, early thirties, is the secretary behind a desk. She is Mainland Chinese, attractive but overly manicured. Victoria eyes Chester from behind her computer.

CHESTER: *(Holds up his shaking hands.)* I've had five blasted cups of coffee already.
VICTORIA: *(Looks up, Chinese accent.)* Would you like another?

(She starts to stand. He shakes his head, motions her to sit down.)

CHESTER: *(Looks at his watch.)* If it wasn't so urgent, I wouldn't still be waiting. . . . Have you called your boss?
VICTORIA: I'm not supposed to call him, sir.

(Chester pulls a few photos out of his briefcase, crisp and quick.)

CHESTER: He'll miss out. Someone's going to snap up one of these horses; you don't want to be responsible for that. What's your name again?
VICTORIA: Call me Victoria.
CHESTER: Vvvvictoria, you chose a nice English name. I like that. I'm Chester.
VICTORIA *(coy)*: I know. I make the appointments.

(Chester approaches her desk.)

CHESTER: You've been working here a while now.
VICTORIA: I recognize you.
CHESTER: So we're fast friends. Can I have a peek at the appointment book?

(Victoria snaps the appointment book shut.)

Do you know anything about horses?

(Victoria shakes her head no.)

You should. Your boss loves them. I'm his blood-stock agent.

(Victoria looks puzzled, plays naïve.)

Sort of a dating service between rich men and horses. *(He shows her a photo of a horse.)* You see this yearling? Look at him, so regal.

*(Victoria flirtatiously leans into Chester,
looks at the picture.)*

VICTORIA: He can make a lot of money?
CHESTER: He's beautiful.
VICTORIA: He can make money?
CHESTER: I suppose. Yearlings are like lottery tickets. They're young, untested, never been raced. So a good-looking fellow like him is still cheap. But if he's trained properly and wins . . . *(Motions.)* His worth goes through the roof.
VICTORIA: And if he doesn't win?
CHESTER: You still get to go to the owners' cocktail party at the Jockey Club. Rub elbows with high society, talk your pony up to a daddy for his little girl.
VICTORIA: So you have to be lucky.
CHESTER: My dear, it's not luck. It's skill. That's where I come in. Your boss, Mr. Hopkinton, works with a savvy middleman, like myself, because I have the sense to find him treasure.
VICTORIA: Do you own a horse?
CHESTER: I, I don't. *(Quickly clarifying.)* But I will. I'm just waiting to find the right one.
VICTORIA: Are you rich?
CHESTER: We don't ask questions like that in proper company. Where are you from?
VICTORIA: China.

CHESTER: *(Mutters to himself.)* Figures.

    (To Victoria.) . . . But I do all right. *(Points at the portrait.)* But your boss, he's more than all right. Comes from old English aristocracy, from the times of knights and castles probably. I'm proud it's more than business between us. I dare say, we're friends.

    (Chester holds his coffee cup up to the portrait and toasts.)

VICTORIA: You must be important.

CHESTER: Can't understand why he wouldn't be here today.

    (Tries to sip the coffee, but his hand shakes.)

    Listen, does he just not want to see me?

    (Victoria looks away, fingers the computer keyboard.)

VICTORIA *(hesitant):* . . . He is preparing to leave, sir.

CHESTER: Back to Surrey?

    (Victoria nods.)

    He didn't tell me.

VICTORIA: Everyone else knows.

CHESTER *(hiding his own humiliation):* And you?

VICTORIA: I'll try to find another job.

CHESTER: And if you don't?

VICTORIA: I have to go home.

CHESTER: I'm sure something will turn up. Your English is "acceptable."

VICTORIA: I practice every night. I listen to the radio.

CHESTER: Pop music?

VICTORIA: Talk programs.

CHESTER: I prefer opera. *(Shakes his head, distraught.)* I can't believe he didn't tell me. He's been avoiding me for weeks.

VICTORIA: He's selling his horses.

CHESTER *(shocked):* To whom?!

VICTORIA: Chinese come into this office.

CHESTER: He'll be robbed blind without me working . . .

VICTORIA: *(Interrupts.)* I translate.

CHESTER: He doesn't want his horses anymore . . . ?

VICTORIA: *(Interrupts.)* Sir, I do not think he cares. He is in a hurry. Just wants to get rid of them.

CHESTER: I . . .

VICTORIA *(interrupting):* Sir, he isn't coming.

CHESTER: I see. (*Looks at his watch.*) It's late. You must want to go home.

VICTORIA (*coy, comforting*): No. I like to hear you talk. Are you married?

CHESTER: No, but I just broke things off with this wonderfully groomed woman.

VICTORIA: Too bad.

CHESTER: No loss. Her legs were too short.

VICTORIA: She have a nice name?

CHESTER: Pamela. But a real nutter. Inconsistent.

VICTORIA: There must be many ladies.

CHESTER: Before her, someone I met on a plane.

VICTORIA: First class?

CHESTER: (*Nods, concocts a grand story.*) The Concord . . . German. A model. And a stewardess. Nice body, nice teeth, healthy. But no real spark.

VICTORIA: Sounds like you're still talking about your horses.

CHESTER: Oh, stop. You make me sound like I've had such an empty, lonely life.

VICTORIA: . . . Have you?

(*Chester is silent. He fidgets.*)

Do I make you uncomfortable?

CHESTER (*defensive*): Why?

VICTORIA: Don't tell me this hasn't happened before.

CHESTER: What?

VICTORIA: A woman, impressed by you.

(*Victoria demurely giggles. Chester smirks, puffs up his chest.*)

Do you think I am a "tidbit?"

CHESTER (*playful*): Tidbit? Where did you learn such a nasty word?

(*Victoria titters. The phone on her desk rings. Victoria doesn't move to answer it. It rings and rings some more.*)

(*Anxious.*) Why is the phone ringing and you're not answering?

VICTORIA: (*Plays earnest, overly romantic.*) I hear nothing but your voice when you are here.

CHESTER: What if it's him?!

(*Chester hurries toward the phone. Before he can pick it up, Victoria answers.*)

VICTORIA (*on phone*): "Wei?" Hopkinton's office. " . . . Qing deng yixia . . ." (*She transfers the call and hangs up.*)

CHESTER: Well . . . ?
VICTORIA: Not him.
CHESTER: So the Reds, interested in his ponies?

(Victoria nods.)

Maybe they'd be interested in some of mine?

(He holds up his sad little photos.)

(Demanding.) Maybe you could slip one of them a note . . .

(Victoria doesn't answer. Chester softens.)

Let's talk it over. Catch an aperitif . . .

(Victoria shrugs, disinterested.)

How 'bout the finest dinner on The Peak?

(She looks more enticed.)

(Desperate.) Look, I really need to sell these horses!

*(Victoria stands, leans over her desk, and kisses Chester.
He swallows his nervousness and . . .)*

*(Lights shift. The sounds of horses' hooves and neighing. Chester heaves
and launches into his sex and sales fantasy, as if at a horse auction. It's a
pitch to the audience—his prospective buyers.)*

(Seductive, confident.) Sixteen to seventeen hands high, a little plump,
muscular, not a wood chewer or a cribber, X-rays clean, no thrush on
the foot, race-tested. But you say to me, "She's bad on turf, could be
faster, blah blah." So you don't buy.

*(The computer screen on the reception desk glows red as Chester's
bravado grows and Victoria flirtatiously prances around.)*

Now, sure, I've got 20 percent commission to lose, but you'll lose
more than that—opportunity. There are some horses who just need a
bit of refinement.

(He pinches Victoria's rump. She whinnies excitedly.)

Still you insist, "The economy might go to hell. No time to fritter away money on a filly."

(Chester prowls around Victoria's desk, swiping it clear of papers, files, and Post-Its.)

I say, in risky times, a filly is the only thing you can count on. You control it. You own this living, breathing thing.

(Victoria neighs submissively.)

VICTORIA *(playing naïve)*: Is this dirty talk?
CHESTER: Ahhh, so you're worried. Maybe after thirty, forty races her legs are shot. What then?

(Chester splays open his briefcase, removes silk sheets, a pillow. He suavely transforms Victoria's desk into a bed.)

Well, how 'bout a stallion with fantastic semen? It's a bit like cheating, his semen works so well. He's brought dozens of mares into foal already.

(Chester takes off his jacket and rips off his tie.)

We all know the bottom line: A horse who studs and mates is the only thing truly worth something. A horse you can respect. A manly man's man of a horse. Grrr.

(He lounges across the makeshift bed and motions for Victoria to trot over. But then . . . the phone rings from under the sheets. Victoria rifles for it and answers, and the fantasy ends.)

VICTORIA: *"Wei?"* . . . *(Passes phone to Chester.)* It's for you.

(Chester nervously takes the call.)

CHESTER *(on phone)*: Hello . . . Hopkinton! Yes, yes . . .
(His heart sinks.) Oh. I see.

The lights fade into . . .

SCENE 4: EARLY THE NEXT MORNING

The family's apartment. Tuppy has her head down on the dining table, snoozing. Tong Tong's cage is in front of her. As she hears the front door rattle, she sits up. Uncle Chester enters. He's disheveled and not his normal dapper self. At last, Chester notices Tuppy.

CHESTER: Tuppy? . . . Why are you up?
TUPPY: I've been waiting for you.
CHESTER: Waiting?

> (*Tuppy is silent, sulks. Chester tries to read what she's thinking.*)

Were you worrying like a granny again? (*Tries to joke.*) . . . You're my niece, not my granny. You know how business goes. I'm on the trail of some big deals.

> (*Winnifreda enters in her robe with a pot of tea.*)

I made a real top-notch connection last night.
WINNIFREDA: (*Clucks her tongue.*) Too long a night.
CHESTER: Tup, aren't you going to ask who your uncle met?

> (*Tuppy doesn't speak, crosses her arms. Chester gives her a puzzled look. Tuppy turns away.*)

Well, if you're going to be sour, run along and get ready for school.
TUPPY: There's no school.

> (*Winnifreda places a cup and saucer on the table and is about to pour Chester tea . . .*)

WINNIFREDA: Tea, sir?
CHESTER: Tea? No time for tea. (*Waves her off with disdain.*) I'll have coffee.

> (*Winnifreda clucks her tongue and exits back to the kitchen. Chester continues to zing from thought to thought like a pinball.*)

(*To Tuppy.*) Lucky you, no school? Well, then you can phone up one of your little friends.
TUPPY: I hate my friends. They're plonkers.
CHESTER (*feigning shock at her nasty mouth*): Tup! (*Then chuckles.*) Yes, plonki-ty-plonk-plonk-plonkers. I hate them, too.

(Winnifreda enters with a decanter of coffee. She pours. Chester quickly downs the beverage, still standing up.)

I really must go.

WINNIFREDA: Sir, it's much too early to run out for business. First we should celebrate . . .

(Winnifreda winks at Chester obviously. He looks puzzled.)

CHESTER: Yes, we should! *(Smug, rapid.)* I'm about to make a fortune! Here I was biting my nails off with pre-handover jitters. Only less than a year left and my British clients want me to sell off all their horses. But to whom? So last night, I go and charm a high-ranking mucker who's going to put me in touch with Shanghai shipping tycoons and Beijing bigwigs, get me jammy with a whole new clientele of Mainland high-rollers. Except we all fear the Mainlanders will eat the beasts, not race them.

(Chester laughs. He prepares to rush off.)

(To Tuppy.) Well, wish me luck . . .

(Tuppy doesn't say anything. Chester stops.)

Do I have to ask what's eating you?

WINNIFREDA: Sir, you missed something important.

(Chester crinkles his nose, puzzled.)

TUPPY: I demand to know where you were last night.

CHESTER: I told you. Out with a real mucker.

TUPPY: I mean, exactly where.

CHESTER *(playfully)*: I see, so you're in charge now?

TUPPY *(murmuring, frustrated)*: Ohhhh . . .

CHESTER: Well, if you're going to act in charge, hurry up and really *be* in charge. *(Demonstrates.)* Winny, get me a fresh shirt.

(Winnifreda shuffles to the closet and returns with a crisp Oxford. Chester quickly changes.)

(To Tuppy.) Your turn. Command me to do something.

TUPPY *(to Chester)*: I command you to get me an ice pop.

CHESTER *(with bravado)*: That's the spirit. Winny, get her an ice pop!

(With a glare, Winnifreda shuffles off to the kitchen.)

TUPPY: I command you to tell Tong Tong you love him.
CHESTER: Oh Tup, there isn't time for this.
TUPPY: But I said!
CHESTER: Oh, Tong Tong, I love you.

(Tuppy motions for more.)

Even if you were scarred in a terrible accident, my undying heart would be yours.

(Winnifreda returns and shoves the ice pop at Tuppy.)

TUPPY: Now I command you to give me the truth.
CHESTER *(reaching)*: I was out . . . gathering proof.

(He holds up his briefcase proudly.)

WINNIFREDA *(skeptical)*: Ay, the briefcase story again.
CHESTER: So I can show paying punters my horses have the best verified pedigree in the industry. Registered ancestors. Markings and spots for the official record. A horse is nothing without it. And now all I've got to do is present these papers and seal the deals.
TUPPY: It's a fib.
CHESTER: All the rich men are waiting for me right now.
TUPPY: C'mon, were you with one of your "pom-pom girls"?
WINNIFREDA *(to Tuppy)*: Shhht! *(To Chester.)* She thinks you forgot.
CHESTER: Forgot?

(He looks to Winnifreda for an answer.)

WINNIFREDA: Shall I bring out the surprise, sir?
CHESTER: *(Still puzzled but plays along.)* Yes, the surprise.

(Winnifreda exits to the kitchen.)

TUPPY *(beginning to brighten)*: For me?
CHESTER: I don't know who else.

(Winnifreda returns with a small, ill-shaped pie with a lone candle on it. She sets it on the table.)

WINNIFREDA: Happy birthday, Miss.

(Tuppy enthusiastically embraces her uncle.)

TUPPY: I knew you didn't forget!

CHESTER (*trying to reassure Tuppy*): There, there. How could it slip my mind?

(*Chester nods to Winnifreda. She nods back.*)

You know your ol' uncle cares for you.

TUPPY: I do, but . . .

(*She lets go of him.*)

CHESTER: But what?

TUPPY (*hesitating*): . . . Why is it a pie, not a cake?

CHESTER (*irritated, cranky*): Well, you know I've been very busy lately. And you're right, the connection I met last night *was* a lady. So perhaps I did for—

(*Tuppy's heart and expression sink. Chester catches himself.*)

WINNIFREDA (*interrupting*): Miss, it's my fault. In the Pilippines, there's no difference between pie and cake.

(*Chester gathers himself.*)

CHESTER: No difference? Ha! Of course, there is. In the Philippines, they're savages.

(*Tuppy breaks a smile.*)

Next year, I'll personally have to buy you two cakes. (*With flourish.*) But for now, my dear, please . . . make a wish!

(*Tuppy closes her eyes and blows.*)

Well, what'd you wish for?

(*Tuppy shies away, hesitates.*)

TUPPY: . . . That you'll always love me best.

CHESTER: Aw, you shouldn't have told me. Now it won't come true.

(*Chester playfully laughs.*)

TUPPY: Oh, Uncle Chester . . .

CHESTER: Tup, of course, I love you best.

(He straightens his coat and picks up the briefcase.)

Now I'm off.

(Chester blows Tuppy a kiss. She reaches into the air and catches it. He rushes out the door.)

Lights crossfade into . . .

SCENE 5: VICTORIA'S ROOM: TWO WEEKS LATER

Really no more than a depressing tenement cubicle. Chester scurries in and finds Victoria clad in gaudy lingerie, reclined on a tattered mattress. She beckons him over and hastily attempts to undress him.

VICTORIA *(demure, coy)*: I am ready for my ride.
CHESTER: Again? I think I'd die.

(She continues to paw at him.)

(Nervous.) Don't you have to work tomorrow? Want some sleep?
VICTORIA: *(Puffs out her bosom.)* First have a look-see.
CHESTER: Please, Vicki.
VICTORIA *(luring Chester)*: Old Hopkinton met with Mr. Lee and Mr. Sun this week.
CHESTER: So they're doing it? Buying out his stitching plant?

(Victoria nods.)

(Shakes his head in disgust.) Awful. Operations being moved entirely across the border. *(Has a glint in his eyes.)* Are those Chinamen coming in again?
VICTORIA: I don't know . . .
CHESTER *(interrupting, anxious)*: You've been promising for the last two weeks I could "happen" to bump into them. *(Points at his briefcase.)* I haven't sold a single animal yet.
VICTORIA: I don't know about appointments. I'm fired. Everyone is fired.
CHESTER: Just like that?

(Victoria nods, forlorn.)

I really ought to go.

(He reaches for his briefcase, which is strewn on the other side of the bed, but Victoria grabs it first. She holds it away from him.)

VICTORIA: You made me awful.

CHESTER: Come on . . .

VICTORIA: *(Plays innocent.)* I am from the old country. Factory worker, not lover. I'd never been with a man.

CHESTER: Hand over my briefcase.

(Victoria pops open the briefcase and fingers through some files. He tries to grab at them.)

Careful there. That's my livelihood!

(Victoria scampers away, off the bed, with the papers. Chester chases after her. They romp over furniture.)

VICTORIA: You should like me better than horses!

CHESTER: C'mon!

(He catches up to her and slaps her on the rump. She squeals, turns, and chases after him.)

I have a feeling this isn't fair.

(Victoria begins whacking him on the back with the folders—hard.)

Owww!

VICTORIA: Now be romantic.

CHESTER: What?! Um, I . . .

(He runs. She chases him more vigorously.)

VICTORIA: Romannnntic . . .

(Chester leaps onto the bed and protects himself with a pillow.)

CHESTER: I'm sorry, but I can't be romantic right now. *(Overly dramatic.)* Free enterprise as we know it is coming to an end!

VICTORIA: And what after the end?

CHESTER: I don't think that far ahead.

VICTORIA: But I can't bear to be away from you.

CHESTER: Really?

(She nods, nuzzles into him.)

(Awkward, honest.) Look, I'm not used to someone making me . . . feel good.

(She kisses him. For an instant, Chester gives over completely
but then resists.)

I can't.

(He removes her.)

I can't make love in a place like this. *(Surveys the cubicle with distaste.)* The walls, everything, so yellow, it's like being stuck in fly paper. I feel cheap. Yellow must be the color of cheap. Melon yellow, bile, dingy dirty cheap.

VICTORIA: So take me away. To your home.
CHESTER: My home is crowded.
VICTORIA: With whom?
CHESTER: I'm responsible for someone.
VICTORIA: There's someone else?
CHESTER: Ohhh, someone else . . .

(Victoria drops the horse papers. Chester quickly takes them, feverishly
tries to straighten out the documents.)

VICTORIA *(with scorn)*: A woman.
CHESTER: No, no. *(Thinks, coy.)* . . . A girl.
VICTORIA: *(Plays hurt.)* She thinks you're handsome?
CHESTER: *(Nods, toys with her.)* She's charming.
VICTORIA: *(Plays forlorn.)* She young?
CHESTER: Thirteen.

(Victoria gasps in shock.)

VICTORIA: Pretty as me?
CHESTER: *(Caresses her face, playful.)* Well, if we fix up your teeth, you'd be quite fine.

(Victoria turns away.)

VICTORIA: She's been to the dentist?
CHESTER: She's been to all the best Western dentists. *(Dances about, laughs.)* Are you jealous? Am I your "man about town"?

(He swaggers.)

VICTORIA: Just leave.

(Chester is sobered. Victoria points to the door.)

To be with *her.*

(Victoria pouts, plays hurt and fragile. Out of the corner of her eye, she watches Chester begin to dress. She switches tactics. Pulls out a large plastic box from under her bed.)

I was going to give you this . . .
CHESTER *(interrupting)*: What?
VICTORIA: . . . but now I can't. It's a Rolodex. Hopkinton's Rolodex.

(Chester leans in, hunger in his eyes.)

CHESTER: You took that?
VICTORIA: All his phone numbers, friends, millionaire contacts. Now I will burn it!
CHESTER: Let me see! It'd take years to put together something like that.
VICTORIA: You could make a lot of business.

(Victoria holds the Rolodex away.)

Say something nice!
CHESTER *(softly)*: I love you?
VICTORIA: You don't.

(She shoves the Rolodex at him anyway. He takes it, flips through the precious address cards, grinning. But Chester's expression soon turns to self-doubt and worry.)

CHESTER: Should I just call them? Won't they wonder who I am?
VICTORIA: There are no more gentlemen. You must push.
CHESTER: *(Nods reluctantly.)* You're right, times have changed. You know a lot. *(Muses.)* Maybe we could be good for each other.
VICTORIA: But all you care about is horses.

(She smiles and turns on all fours, gyrates her round rump, and whinnies seductively. Chester is drawn to her. The lights in the little room dim until Chester and Victoria are merely silhouettes.)

(*Meanwhile, the murmur of a crowd. Suddenly, a trumpet sounds and a racing gate snaps.*)

(*On another part of the stage, spotlight up on the apartment balcony. Tuppy sports binoculars and watches the racetrack across the way.*)

TUPPY (*rapidfire, like a horse-racing announcer*): And they're off!!!

(*Horses' hooves pound on turf. The upswell of a cheering crowd. Chester sits astride Victoria. But perhaps now the horse is in control of the rider. Bucking, bouncing, banging . . . sex, rough stuff. Victoria makes the small man cling on for dear life.*)

Out of the gate, True Hero takes the lead. Fortune Duke up on the right holds the rail. True Hero, Fortune Duke, neck and neck on the backstretch. Making a move on the outside, Fairy King Prawn, from the back of the pack. Coming wide into the turn . . .

(*Chester and Victoria lean to the right.*)

Fortune Duke still holding strong. But Fairy King Prawn closing on Ka Fook, Super Sea Urchin, Made to Figure . . .

(*Chester and Victoria lean to the left.*)

True Hero blocking, Fairy King Prawn breaks through. And it's Fairy King Prawn in the final jump! And here they come! Down the homestretch. Fairy King Prawn and Fortune Duke.

(*Chester rides Victoria vigorously, as if his life depended on it.*)

Fairy King Prawn and Fortune Duke. Fairy King Prawn and Fortune Duke going all out to the finish! And it's Fairy King Prawn by a nose! Fairy King Prawn takes the Hong Kong Mile!

(*Victoria rears up. A spent Chester is limply thrown off with a thud. The sound of a crowd exploding in jubilation.*)

The bedroom lights and crowd sounds crossfade into . . .

SCENE 6: MAKING PLANS

Faint, distant street noise. Night. Tuppy is on the apartment balcony looking out over Happy Valley. She speaks to her chinchilla Tong Tong.

TUPPY: My uncle has taught me everything about horses. He'll own a horse someday, and I'll be the jockey. I'll ride it to victory . . . (*She gives a queenly wave.*) . . . and everyone who's anyone will have to congratulate us—including you. All right, my uncle's never stood in the winner's circle before. But we have a plan—he'll teach me to be a famous rider, and I'll win for him what he's always wanted.

    (*With fear.*) But I can't explain Uncle Chester lately. He says, "Plans aren't predictable. Like between a colony and a country." So I ask, "How 'bout agreements between an uncle and a niece?" He can't take me riding anymore, doesn't have time, says he's met someone and can barely come home.

    (*Brushes it off, jokes.*) C'mon, you know it doesn't bother me. As long as he's found a dame or a duchess, a real *creme de la* creampuff! Uncle Chester wouldn't give up our dream for some ordinary, tasteless biscuit.

(*Meanwhile in the dark of the living room, Winnifreda breezes in from the kitchen and starts a record playing. It's an old, sappy Filipino love ballad.*)

    (*Plays tough, mature.*) Tong Tong, we'll give him our congratulations. Because that's what reasonable adults do.

Lights fade up on the rest of the apartment as . . .

SCENE 7: THE SURPRISE SOUP

Winnifreda hums to the music and begins to set the table. She spots Tuppy on the balcony.

WINNIFREDA (*calling to Tuppy*): Miss, isn't it time to get ready?
TUPPY (*calling back*): I am ready.

(*Winnifreda urges Tuppy inside. It's a familiar tug of war.*)

WINNIFREDA: Then help me prepare for your uncle's surprise.
TUPPY: It's not a sur—
WINNIFREDA (*interrupting*): Act surprised. He's never brought a lady friend home before. Maybe she's special.

*(Tuppy winces at the thought. Winnifreda goes back to humming.
She sets an extra place at the table.)*

TUPPY: Don't hum. You're making me nervous.
WINNIFREDA: Humming is peaceful. You should try.

(Winnifreda hums. Tuppy joins in halfheartedly.)

TUPPY: It doesn't help.

*(Silence. Just Winnifreda's humming and the music
on the record player.)*

WINNIFREDA *(firm)*: It reminds me of home.
TUPPY *(frustrated, mumbling)*: Maybe you should go home. You're always talking about it . . .

(Winnifreda gives Tuppy a stern look.)

(Softly.) I'm sorry.
WINNIFREDA: I have a right to miss my home.
TUPPY: Would you take me back with you?
WINNIFREDA: To the Pilippines??? Ay, Miss, what would you do there? No work. People just stand around all day, humming.
TUPPY *(scared)*: When the Chinese come, will you be sent home to hum?
WINNIFREDA: Eh, to starve. Put all the Filipina maids on one big boat and take our jobs.
TUPPY: Who would want *your* job?
WINNIFREDA: Millions of peasants. Waiting to be your nanny.
TUPPY: But I said I was sorry. I don't want a new nanny.
WINNIFREDA: *(Plays tough.)* Doesn't matter. Sooner or later, I will wipe my hands of you.

*(Winnifreda resumes humming and working.
Tuppy is sobered.)*

TUPPY: If I do get a new nanny, I hope she's young.
WINNIFREDA: Young nannies are trouble.
TUPPY: But the nanny I had before you was young.
WINNIFREDA: Your uncle told me she was a mistake. *(Clucks her tongue with disapproval.)* I heard she dressed like a prostitute.
TUPPY *(earnest)*: Was she *that* pretty?
WINNIFREDA: Ay, wash your mouth. You want to turn your poor mommy over in her grave?

(A moment . . .)

TUPPY: Do you think they'll build skyscrapers on top of her cemetery?

WINNIFREDA: Doesn't matter, you never visit. Besides, your mommy's already in heaven.

TUPPY: I don't think she is.

It wasn't an accident.

WINNIFREDA: We all make mistakes.

TUPPY: What would you do if I took after my mother?

(Winnifreda straightens the dishes on the table nervously.)

(Anxious, rapid.) If I took enough pills to forget the nanny was prettier?

WINNIFREDA: This is morbid talk! Men are just stupid. They like loose women.

TUPPY: . . . Was my father stupid?

WINNIFREDA: *(Shrugs.)* Eh, the whole neighborhood knows, he ran away with the tarty nanny.

(Tuppy is hurt.)

TUPPY: Are your sons stupid?

WINNIFREDA: *(Gives a glare, then proudly.)* My sons are smart. They only like virgins.

(Tuppy crinkles her nose at the strangeness of this.)

TUPPY: I know you think my uncle's stupid.

WINNIFREDA *(trying to hide her true feelings)*: Nooo.

TUPPY: What if he brings home a loose woman?

WINNIFREDA: *Dios ko!*

TUPPY: I hope you didn't cook extra food. If she's not perfect, she won't be staying long.

WINNIFREDA: What makes you think so?

TUPPY: I'll get rid of her.

WINNIFREDA: You can't just get rid of people. Only criminals can do that.

TUPPY: I'll nip the relationship in the bud, simple as that.

(The front door rattles.)

WINNIFREDA *(softly)*: Loose women are never simple.

(Tuppy sits facing the door, anxious. Winnifreda lifts the needle off the record and stands at attention. Uncle Chester enters.)

CHESTER: Oh, hello Tup . . .

TUPPY (*expectantly*): Well, where's the surprise?

WINNIFREDA: Shhht!

CHESTER: Winny, you told her about the surprise?

WINNIFREDA: I did not say a word, sir.

(*Winnifreda helps Chester remove his blazer, hangs it on the coat rack, and returns to preparing for dinner.*)

TUPPY: So where's your lady friend?

CHESTER: "Lady friend" sounds so crass.

TUPPY: Oh, don't be a tosser.

(*Like a football coach, Chester leans on his haunches and clasps his hands. It's a rapid-fire conversation.*)

CHESTER: Now Tup, what's the best surprise I could ever bring you?

TUPPY: A pony.

CHESTER: Better than that.

TUPPY: A big pony.

CHESTER: Come on, you know this family is missing something—incomplete. You said it yourself . . .

TUPPY (*interrupting, nervous*): This family is big enough. Maybe I take back anything I ever said.

(*Uncle Chester keeps going, flamboyantly points to the chinchilla in its cage.*)

CHESTER: Remember when I brought you Tong Tong, smuggled out from the depths of Peru? You were so pleased to have someone to care for, someone who'd care for you right back . . .

TUPPY (*summoning maturity*): Yes, it was nice . . .

CHESTER (*barreling on*): . . . Granted, she's a little rough around the edges. But we make a top-notch team, and this just might make me . . . (*Thinks on it a moment.*) happy. I hope you'll share it with me.

(*Tuppy nods. On this signal, Chester runs out the front door.*)

TUPPY (*calling after him*): Wait! I hope it's just another chinchilla!

(*After a moment, Chester returns carrying Victoria in his arms. He brings her in over the front door's threshold. Victoria is wearing a sexy, shiny red cocktail dress. She is obviously a very "loose woman."*)

CHESTER: Surprise! Meet your new auntie.
WINNIFREDA: Ayyy . . .

(Winnifreda and Tuppy stand shocked and frozen.)

CHESTER: We tied the knot this morning.
VICTORIA: In Macau.

(Victoria holds out the big, ostentatious diamond
ring on her finger.)

TUPPY: Uhhhh. . . .
CHESTER (jumping in): I know, it seems a bit sudden. But we just couldn't
wait.

(The couple giggles, nuzzles noses.)

VICTORIA: Your uncle's a tiger. Has sexy appeal.

(Silence in the room.)

CHESTER: Don't just stand there.
    Tup, come over here and meet your new aunt Victoria.
VICTORIA (to Tuppy): Your uncle says he has a little niece . . .
CHESTER (sincere, to Tuppy): I hope she'll be more like a mother to you.
VICTORIA: . . . but you're not little at all.
TUPPY: "Mother?"

(Tuppy begins a slight groan, which continues through the conversation.)

CHESTER: (Gently.) Yes, wouldn't it be nice to call Vicki "Mother?"

(Victoria uneasily puts on a smile.)

    Stand up, Tup. Stand back to back. Look, Vic, she's almost taller
    than you . . .
TUPPY (interrupting): "Mother?!?!"

(Victoria extends her arms to Tuppy and motions her over. But Tuppy
backs away and dashes to her room. Offstage, her bedroom door slams.)

CHESTER: Winny, make Victoria feel at home.

(Chester leaves Victoria's side and rushes after his niece exits.)

WINNIFREDA: I made soup.

VICTORIA: No soup, just champagne.

*(Winnifreda ladles out bowls of soup anyway.
Victoria motions for her to stop.)*

WINNIFREDA: Soup is sir's favorite.

*(Winnifreda finishes ladling. Victoria, annoyed, sits and slurps loudly
from her spoon. The two women hear Chester's offstage pleas to Tuppy.)*

CHESTER *(offstage, calling)*: Tup, don't be angry at me!

WINNIFREDA: "Victoria"—what kind of name is that?

VICTORIA: It is a name Filipino maids can pronounce.

WINNIFREDA: Yes, "Bictoria." Sir has had many many lady friends, but never one . . . like you.

TUPPY *(offstage)*: Go away!

VICTORIA: Remember, we are more than friends. I am sir's wife.

WINNIFREDA: Pardon, I will call you "Ma'am."

VICTORIA: I am from Fuling, Sichuan, China.

WINNIFREDA: Ahh, there they like spicy food.

*(Vicki slurps down another spoonful of soup.
She doesn't hide her distaste.)*

Sir does not usually like spicy.

(More noise comes from the back hallway.)

CHESTER *(offstage)*: Don't be a rotten apple!

TUPPY *(offstage)*: I won't come out!

(Tuppy's bedroom door slams. Victoria is jarred by the noise.)

VICTORIA *(with trepidation)*: So you take care of her?

WINNIFREDA: Yes, Ma'am.

VICTORIA: Is she always like this?

WINNIFREDA: Miss is just like any other girl.

VICTORIA *(muttering)*: Maybe Hong Kong girls.

(More noise from the back hallway.)

CHESTER *(offstage)*: You're winding your poor uncle up!

TUPPY *(offstage)*: I'll wind if I want!

WINNIFREDA: I'm sure sir hopes *you* will care for her now.

VICTORIA: How?

WINNIFREDA: *(Rapid directions.)* Every morning take her to school. Wake up early, tell her not to stay up late. She yell yell yells at you, and you shouldn't yell back. She will ask many questions about many troubles. And you can pray, ask the Blessed Virgin for help.

VICTORIA: I do not pray.

CHESTER *(offstage)*: You're driving yourself into a mood.

TUPPY *(offstage)*: I'm past moods. I'm sick.

> *(Tuppy slams the bedroom door again. Winnifreda looks to the heavens and crosses herself.)*

VICTORIA: And don't worry, I do not want your job.

WINNIFREDA: Ma'am, it is not just a job. I care about Miss.

> *(Chester returns, trying to cover how frazzled he is.)*

CHESTER: So, Vicki, you feeling at home?

TUPPY *(offstage, calls, groans)*: I'm exploding inside!

CHESTER *(calling back)*: Not tonight, Tup!

> *(Offstage, Tuppy sustains an annoying groan/scream.)*

Winny, go check on her.

> *(Chester authoritatively points. Winnifreda exits, toward Tuppy's room.)*

VICTORIA *(to Chester, pouting)*: I don't think Winny likes me.

CHESTER: She's just the "amah," sturdy as a bread box. Harmless.

> *(During the conversation, Victoria taps and prods at the chinchilla with her soup spoon.)*

(Points to the chinchilla.) But watch out for him. He'll bite your fingers off.

> *(Victoria recoils from the cage.)*

(Crinkles his nose.) Just a tease, dear.

VICTORIA: And your niece?

CHESTER *(lying, trying to reassure himself, as well as Victoria)*: She's just being shy. I'm sure she'll come 'round.

(The crash of a broken object offstage. Chester cringes.)

VICTORIA: Maybe you just leave her be.
CHESTER: Leave her be?
VICTORIA *(demure)*: It is our wedding night.

(Victoria nods, runs her fingers through his hair.)

CHESTER: I can't just leave her . . .
VICTORIA *(interrupting)*: Then tell her our other surprise.
CHESTER *(rolling his eyes)*: Oh no, no more surprises.
VICTORIA: Why not?
CHESTER: What if it makes her more upset? What if she runs away?
VICTORIA *(too eager)*: Run away? . . .
CHESTER *(interrupting, rapid)*: Maybe you'll change your mind, decide not
  to keep it.

(Victoria feigns a sob.)

(Escapes.) Oh, perk up. You haven't seen the rest of your new home.

*(Another crash offstage. Chester ushers Victoria out
to the balcony like a whirlwind.)*

(Blusters on.) The price of this view is what's really burning a hole
  in my pocket.
VICTORIA: Please, just show me the bed.
CHESTER: *(Pats her belly, standoffish.)* Oh, dear, we've done enough damage
  already.

*(Victoria still clings to him, amorous. Tuppy exits from her bedroom
cautiously. She sees Victoria kissing her uncle and moves away distraught.
Winnifreda enters, chasing after her.)*

WINNIFREDA: Wait, Miss!

(Chester jerks away from Victoria.)

CHESTER: Tup!

(Tuppy stumbles to the sofa.)

TUPPY: *(Gags, groans.)* I think I need to go to the hospital!
WINNIFREDA *(skeptical)*: Sir, should I call the ambulance?

VICTORIA: It's just a stomachache.

TUPPY: Why are you with someone like *that?*

CHESTER: Shhh, stop embarrassing me.

TUPPY: And me?!

CHESTER: I'm not acting uncivilized.

TUPPY: You didn't give me any warning about a wife. Didn't even ask me first.

CHESTER: Vicki was about to lose her job, so I thought she should come work for me, 24/7, if you know what I mean. *(Exaggerates.)* She's in a hot spot right now. Got connections to ol' Deng Xiaoping himself.

TUPPY: She's from China? *(To Winnifreda.)* Winny, you were right. They're invading already.

CHESTER: Winny! What nonsense?!

TUPPY: You're not supposed to just get married! . . .

CHESTER *(interrupting)*: You're right. I'm just trying things out!

(Victoria's face falls.)

(Quickly changes the subject.) Winny, the champagne. Let's have a toast.

*(Winnifreda exits. Chester leaves his niece
and goes to the table.)*

VICTORIA: *(Sniffs the air.)* Something smells. I cannot toast. *(Points at the chinchilla.)* It's him.

(Winnifreda returns with the champagne.)

CHESTER: Winny, put Tong Tong in the cupboard.

(Winnifreda hands the champagne to Chester and begins to remove the cage from the table. Tuppy approaches, holding her belly.)

TUPPY: Winny, don't. He makes me feel better.

(Winnifreda puts the cage back down.)

VICTORIA: Dirty animal.

(Winnifreda picks the cage back up.)

TUPPY: You're the dirty animal.

(Winnifreda puts the cage back down once and for all. Tuppy takes Tong Tong out and comforts him. Victoria leans back in fear and disgust.)

CHESTER: Tup! Apologize right now!

(Tuppy springs out of her chair. Still clutching the chinchilla, she lurks about Victoria, interrogates her, rapid fire.)

TUPPY: What do you want from my uncle?
VICTORIA: His . . . his charming company.
TUPPY: What's his proudest moment?
VICTORIA: Ay uh, swimming across Victoria Harbor.
TUPPY: What's his greatest fear?
VICTORIA: I, I don't know.
CHESTER: Vicki, you really don't have to . . .
TUPPY: What are his nervous conditions?
CHESTER: . . . put up with this little test.
VICTORIA *(smug)*: I know something better. I'm pregnant.
WINNIFREDA: But it's before the wedding night. Holy Mother . . .

(Chester glares at her.)

(Sarcastic.) Sir, it's a miracle.

(The room is silent. Tuppy begins to sound her battle cry. It builds.)

TUPPY *(overlapping with Chester)*: Ugggggghhhhh!
CHESTER *(overlapping with Tuppy)*: Now Tup . . .

(Tuppy charges at Victoria, holding Tong Tong out as a weapon. Victoria rears back in fear. Chester jumps between the two of them, intervenes.)

(Overlapping with Tuppy.) . . . we all have to make the best of things!
VICTORIA: Wait! *(Breathless.)* I have another surprise . . .

(Tuppy stops, fearful. Chester turns to his new bride, puzzled.)

(With drama.) A son. *(To Chester.)* You will have a beautiful, perfect son.
WINNIFREDA *(skeptical)*: Ma'am, you're sure?
CHESTER: Isn't it a bit early . . .
VICTORIA: *(Nods to Chester, obsequious.)* He'll be strong. Take after you.
CHESTER: He will? *(Blusters.)* Of course, he will.

TUPPY: You don't need a son. (*Softly.*) You have me.
VICTORIA: Every man needs a boy of his own.

(*Chester gently puts a hand on Victoria's belly. He grins, tickled.*)

CHESTER: Hmmm . . . fancy that.

Lights fade to black.

Intermission.

SCENE 8: FAITH IN THE HOUSE

Lights fade up on the living room of the family's apartment, late night. Tuppy is asleep on the floor, head propped up on her schoolbooks. Victoria, covered by a blanket, yawns and struggles to stay awake. She's pregnant but only slightly round at this stage. Victoria reads from a newspaper spread across her lap. Her reading is somewhat stilted, since English is her second language.

VICTORIA: "Under the leadership of Deng Xiaoping, China has experienced a new brand of capitalism . . . (*She speaks to her stomach with a smile.*) . . . making millionaires in socialist clothing." (*Continues reading.*) "But the aging leader's deteriorating health has fueled speculation hardliners will prevail and prosperity . . . may not last."

(*A moment of concern. She strokes her belly, tries to comfort
the unborn child and herself.*)

WINNIFREDA (*offstage*): Sir, is that you?

(*Winnifreda enters in her nightgown.*)

VICTORIA: He's not back.
WINNIFREDA: Oh, Ma'am, you should get some rest.

(*Tuppy, groggy, awakens.*)

TUPPY: We're waiting up for him.
VICTORIA: I was reading to the baby.
WINNIFREDA: The newspaper? Your baby will be born worrying.
VICTORIA: I'm only reading about lottery winners and stock-market success stories. Tell my baby why his father's not home.
WINNIFREDA: Lately sir is always late.

TUPPY: *(Points at Victoria.)* It's her fault. He's meeting people from her Rolodex.

VICTORIA: He's doing business.

TUPPY: He can't do business all night.

WINNIFREDA: Don't scare your auntie. It isn't good for the baby.

VICTORIA: *(Plays tough.)* I'm not scared.

TUPPY: You should be.

WINNIFREDA: Now, Miss . . .

TUPPY: Your baby could have club feet, like horses' hooves . . .

WINNIFREDA: Shhht!

TUPPY: . . . a broken, twisted body.

WINNIFREDA: Babies are innocent!

TUPPY: . . . a horse of a baby for a horse of a woman. My uncle wouldn't love you then.

(Victoria turns pale, holds her belly.)

WINNIFREDA *(to Tuppy)*: Stop talking nonsense. *(Softens, to Victoria.)* Ma'am, everything will be OK.

VICTORIA: *(Plays tough.)* I know.

TUPPY: You don't. My uncle could leave you at any second. *(Thinks.)* If I were you, I'd go back home.

VICTORIA: I'm not going anywhere. Not even to bed.

(Victoria holds up the newspaper on her lap.)

Here there is opportunity.

WINNIFREDA: Hmmph! Opportunity? It's just money.

VICTORIA: *(Rubs her belly, determined.)* My son will have opportunity.

WINNIFREDA: *(Nods.)* So will mine.

VICTORIA: You have sons?

WINNIFREDA: Two grown boys, Ma'am.

TUPPY: Aw, Winny barely knows them.

WINNIFREDA *(sadly)*: But I pray for them every day.

VICTORIA: Does it help?

WINNIFREDA: God will protect them.

VICTORIA: Teach me to pray, for my son, for my husband.

WINNIFREDA *(surprised, pleased)*: You want to learn?

*(Victoria nods, acts righteous. Winnifreda kneels
by Victoria's side.)*

TUPPY: Winny, don't teach her to pray.

WINNIFREDA: This is a sign from God. She belongs in this house.

TUPPY: Then I want to pray, too.
WINNIFREDA: *Dios ko!*

(*Tuppy rushes to kneel also. Victoria clasps her hands together and closes her eyes. Tuppy does the same in an overblown manner.*)

(*After a moment . . .*)

VICTORIA: (*Yawns.*) This is making me tired.
WINNIFREDA: Good, then you know it's working.

(*Their prayers are interminably long and boring. Tuppy fidgets. . . . Victoria begins to snore.*)

TUPPY (*whispering*): I think she's asleep.
WINNIFREDA: (*Nods.*) Your auntie will talk to God in her dreams.
TUPPY: Isn't it easier to talk to him when you're dead?

(*Winnifreda stands and motions Tuppy to her room.*)

WINNIFREDA (*rolling her eyes*): Enough. Go to bed.

(*But Tuppy lingers, inspects Victoria.*)

TUPPY (*mischievous*): I could kill her . . .
WINNIFREDA: (*Interrupts.*) Ay, terrible girl!
TUPPY: . . . So she can talk with God.

(*Winnifreda drags Tuppy offstage and flicks off the living room lights. The dark apartment is illuminated by blinking streetlights outside. Victoria is left alone, slouched over and snoring. Her sleep is restless. She kicks at her blanket until it flips over to reveal the reverse side—a large Chinese flag. Victoria pulls the flag up under her chin, covers her body from the neck down. She shivers and awakens as her snores become coughs, chokes, and a labored wheeze.*)

(*Victoria transforms into . . . the corpse of Deng Xiaoping. Spotlight on China's paramount leader, ninety-three years old, creaking from rigor mortis. He reclines in the big easy chair, a little cap, with red star, smartly atop his head.*)

DENG XIAOPING: (*Played by Victoria, Chinese accent.*) I, Deng Xiaoping, China's paramount leader, ninety-three years old, welcome you to my final haircut. I die last Wednesday, but still my hair gets cut. I keep all appointments, give radio address, and still make love to wife. The Party says we must all pretend I am still alive. They say last Wednesday not an auspicious day to die, but tomorrow, February 19, 1997, is good official day for death. But I say, why tomorrow? Why not five more months? In warm July, I can see my Hong Kong returned.

Ahh, yes, a man needs a good haircut. But what part of itself can a country afford to get rid of? Hong Kong was no pigtail for British to snip off and take. But soon, China whole and proud again.

I, the great architect, arranged it all. One China, two systems. In one hand, a China very old, farmers smile, told to grow grain. In other hand, China of cellular phone, man free to get rich. I make promise to people of Hong Kong: *"Mah jiu paau, mouh jiu tiuh"*—"The horses will keep running, the dancing will continue."

(Vulnerable, builds speed.) Don't let my promises be stopped by an inconvenience. Death. I'm not ready. So scared. Hong Kong people even more scared. Fear the next leader dislike democracy more than me.

(Clears his throat, spits, and grins.) I ask you, friends, comrades, leaders of the Chinese Communist Party, don't let me die. A country can give its leader a haircut. But cut off his hair, not his whole damn head.

(Meanwhile, Tuppy has crept back into the room. She menacingly looms closer to Deng/Victoria, swinging and twirling a Chinese opera star's sword.)

Lights fade to black . . .

SCENE 9: AFTER THE HAIRCUT:
THE NEXT MORNING

Victoria still asleep in the living room. Tuppy enters in her pajamas. She treads to the front door, opens it, and retrieves a newspaper from the hallway. Tuppy closes the door with a slam. Victoria is jarred awake.

VICTORIA: Chester?!
TUPPY: He's not here.

(Victoria sits up. We see her hair has been jaggedly snipped off. Tuppy begins to laugh.)

VICTORIA *(sleepily)*: What time is it? He never came back?
TUPPY *(through her giggles)*: Maybe he was back . . .
VICTORIA: Stop laughing.
TUPPY: *(Giggles some more.)* But you scared him off.

*(Victoria sees clumps of hair around her. She feels her head
and lets out a horrified cry.)*

VICTORIA: Wh . . . What have you done?!

(Victoria collapses on the sofa and sobs.)

Wicked! So www . . . wicked! Why do this?
TUPPY: You deserve it. You've ruined everything. All my uncle does is work
for you and your stupid baby.

(Victoria pretends to cry even harder. Tuppy edges closer, mischievous.)

Are you afraid of me?

(Victoria looks up.)

(Grins.) Aw, c'mon. You look spiffy.

*(. . . Suddenly, Victoria slaps Tuppy. The girl yelps
and cradles her face.)*

You shouldn't . . . you shouldn't have done that.
(Calling offstage.) Winny!
VICTORIA *(calling offstage)*: Winny!

(Winnifreda enters the living room in her robe.)

TUPPY: She hit me!
WINNIFREDA: Ma'am, your hair!
VICTORIA: Can't even sleep in my own house . . .
TUPPY: She hit me! I was just giving her a makeover.

*(Tuppy holds up the morning's newspaper and points at a large photo on
the front page. She giggles in spite of herself.)*

Now she looks like him.

*(Winnifreda takes the newspaper from Tuppy and inspects it more closely.
She sways uneasily on her feet.)*

WINNIFREDA: Ay, Ma'am, I have a bad feeling. It's much worse than hair . . .

(She hands the paper to Victoria who also reads.)

VICTORIA: . . . Deng Xiaoping is dead?

(A moment.)

    This is not good for my baby. There might be riots. All promises might be broken!

WINNIFREDA: *(Rapid, exaggerated.)* Tanks rolling in, no food, rich people kicked out of their apartments for soldiers to live, your uncle sent to jail—as a spy.

(Victoria gasps.)

TUPPY *(to Victoria)*: Why are you worried? You are one of "them"!

VICTORIA: I'm proud to be one of them. You should be, too.

TUPPY: I, I'm not Chinese. I'm British. My uncle will take me to London, get away from you.

VICTORIA: I am having his son. Maybe *I* will leave with him instead.

WINNIFREDA: Stop, too hard to get a visa. No one can go . . . except Filipino maids shipped home.

(Winnifreda betrays hope for this in spite of herself.)

(The following argument overlaps, a flurry.)

TUPPY: Winny, they wouldn't dare send you away.

VICTORIA *(interruptiung, overlaps)*: They would.

WINNIFREDA: Miss, it might be God's will.

TUPPY: When my uncle comes home, what *he* says is more important than God.

WINNIFREDA *(jumping in, to the heavens)*: Ay, Heavenly Father, she didn't mean that.

VICTORIA *(muttering)*: She meant it.

WINNIFREDA *(looking up)*: We pray you will grant her forgiveness.

(Tuppy and Victoria freeze and fall silent. A heavenly spotlight on Winnifreda as we shift into her fantasy. She prays.)

    . . . And while you are listening . . . please, please bless my sons.

(Tuppy and Victoria assume the roles of her sons.)

    (To the heavens.) I know you hear many prayers from many people, so I will remind you of their names. They are . . .

TUPPY: Horton.

VICTORIA: And Thorton.

WINNIFREDA: Ay, it's better than Cain and Abel. Twin boys, like Gemini. They live in the Pilippines in a muddy village.

TUPPY *(as Horton)*: It's a common story.

WINNIFREDA: But all true. Not some novel.

VICTORIA *(as Thorton)*: Woman leaves home. Goes to the big city—Manila.

WINNIFREDA *(pleased)*: Teaches mathematics. *(Then tired.)* I send home money. Write letters. See the boys on the weekends.

TUPPY and VICTORIA *(as Horton and Thorton)*: Still, not enough money.

WINNIFREDA: So I do what my friends have to do, educated people, nurses, teachers, they go far away.

TUPPY and VICTORIA *(as Horton and Thorton, with resentment)*: Smart people make more money as maids.

WINNIFREDA: It's not that simple, but I came here.

TUPPY and VICTORIA *(as Horton and Thorton)*: And what of Horton and Thorton?

WINNIFREDA: At first, they write and call all the time. Then it becomes every six months. See them once a year. Ay, and before I know it, they are men.

TUPPY *(as Horton)*: . . . I didn't know it was such a sad story.

WINNIFREDA *(forcing a smile)*: But they turn out to be fine young men. Horton, you know, will be a male nurse. He will go to Texas, start a family.

VICTORIA *(as Thorton)*: Horton is gay.

WINNIFREDA: Thorton, more like his father.

TUPPY *(as Horton)*: A layabout.

WINNIFREDA: He will look for his calling in life.

(*Overblown.*) All this because of a mother's greatest power—sacrifice.

> *(As Winnifreda's prayer fantasy ends, the living room
> lights shift back.)*

Heavenly Father, if there's trouble in Hong Kong, I pray, I pray, I will return to my sons.

> *(Winnifreda crosses herself. Tuppy and Victoria's
> rapid-fire argument resumes.)*

TUPPY: Winny, you can't leave. I won't let you go! This is your home.

> *(Winny relents, nods.)*

VICTORIA *(to Tuppy)*: So selfish.

TUPPY *(to Victoria)*: What did *you* pray for?

VICTORIA *(determined, melodramatic)*: . . . That my son will be strong. He will grow up. I, grow old with him. He will take care of me and mourn when I die.

TUPPY: You didn't pray for Uncle Chester?

(Victoria stutters and stumbles.)

. . . And how do you know it's going to be a son?

VICTORIA: I'm a mother.

Lights fade.

SCENE 10: A HISTORY OF SONS

A doctor's waiting room, perhaps signified by two chairs at the front of the stage. Chester and Victoria sit side by side. Chester has a cell phone in his hand and Hopkinton's Rolodex on his lap. He flips through the cards and tries not to be disillusioned. Meanwhile, Victoria looks through a large book of baby names.

CHESTER: Sun Kai-Fong; Sun Kai-Won; Sun Kai-Xing; Tak, Robert Sr.; Tak, Robert Jr.; Tak, Robert O.; Tak, Robert P.; Tak, Robert Q. . . . No bites yet. I'm on to the Ws now.

VICTORIA *(preoccupied with her book)*: Hmmm, "Robert." I like that name.

(Chester insists Victoria look at the Rolodex.)

CHESTER: Look at all these names. Importance is inbred, passed on from grandfather, to father, to son. Power is always related. If one doesn't talk to you, none will. They put up a wall around what they've got, so I've gotta break through.

(On the wall behind them, a projection of a grainy black-and-white image appears. The image is beautiful in its ambiguity and otherworldliness. We begin to recognize anatomical structures—a sonogram.)

(More anxious.) I wonder, is the handover the one thing that can chip through old rock, crack open dynasties? Let a new fella like me have a chance?

VICTORIA *(caressing her belly)*: Here is your best chance.

(The infant in Victoria's grainy sonogram slightly pulses.)

CHESTER: Imagine that, if an ordinary father could have a son who'd become something. Better than himself, well connected, more successful!

VICTORIA *(hesitant)*: And what about a daughter?

CHESTER: I'm a thoroughly modern man, so a daughter's . . . a treasure, clever, accomplished. But no matter, she still can't break her family into the right network without marrying a rich old man and hitching a ride beyond her station.

(The sonogram image projected in the background fades out.)

Daughters upset the very order of the universe. And no phone call or handover's ever going to change that.

(Chester squeezes Victoria's arm.)

Vic, they called your name. The doctor will see you now . . .

(They rise from their seats.)

Lights crossfade into . . .

SCENE 11: WHAT TO BELIEVE

The family's apartment. Chester enters through the front door, head down, demoralized. Victoria comes in after him.

CHESTER *(calling)*: Winny! Tup! . . .

(No answer.)

No one's home.

(An awkward silence.)

VICTORIA: . . . You want to tell them those lies?

CHESTER: I don't think they're lies.

VICTORIA: How can you trust a silly machine, tests, those stupid doctors?

CHESTER *(forcing a smile)*: C'mon, doesn't matter either way. She's healthy. That's what counts.

VICTORIA: They don't know for sure.

CHESTER: Of course, they do. That's why people have these tests.

(The discussion intensifies, more rapid.)

VICTORIA: They're second-rate. Don't know what they're doing.

CHESTER: They said they saw.

VICTORIA: What they see is in their heads.

CHESTER: So you're saying they're liars?

VICTORIA: All the good doctors have left. Moved away.

CHESTER: And everyone left in Hong Kong is half-baked? Shoddy?

(Victoria nods.)

You mean me, too, don't you?

(Victoria takes a moment.)

VICTORIA: You haven't sold your horses.

CHESTER: The contacts you gave me are daft. I've called, even tried to visit.

VICTORIA: Just give up. Let's leave Hong Kong. Before the handover.

CHESTER: On what money? It's only two months 'til July.

VICTORIA: I want better doctors. You will find a way.

CHESTER: Let's wait and see what happens.

VICTORIA: Wait and see? Wait and see? What if people can't get away then?

(Chester moves away to the sofa.)

CHESTER: You think a change of scenery would be good for Tup?

VICTORIA: Why you always think about her?

CHESTER: Still sore about your hair?

VICTORIA: Hair? She'll hate your baby boy! Hurt him.

CHESTER: A little jealousy is . . .

VICTORIA: Cut off his . . .

CHESTER *(interrupting)*: Christ! Once and for all, the doctors said it is *not* a son.

VICTORIA: Who needs these doctors? Chinese predict these things thousands of years. *(Pleads.)* Believe me. I know.

(Chester is silent. Tuppy enters and stands on the other side of her uncle, but not in Victoria's reality. Tuppy is in a separate conversation with Chester. Thus, Victoria's and Tuppy's two divergent scenes play out simultaneously. Chester is too cowardly to look directly at either of them. He keeps his gaze forward.)

Sons are carried low. See, my face stern. My pulse strong in the left wrist. He kicks a lot. I have dreams . . .

(Tuppy's following line begins to overlap here.)

Bright suns, persimmons, three red peppers, carps, dragons flying into the sky right over a mountaintop.

TUPPY (*overlapping with part of Victoria's previous line*): Daughters are carried high. Her face is soft. Pulse on the right wrist. She dreams of clouds and apples, cool damp caves, flowers, butterflies, oysters opening their lips to show one round round pearl.

(*Tuppy covers her mouth, giggles.*)

CHESTER: Stop. (*Hesitates.*) Do you love me?

TUPPY: Do you love her?

VICTORIA: Why do you ask me?

CHESTER: Sometimes I wonder if people get married because they love each other.

TUPPY: So what do you feel about her?

CHESTER (*glum*): For once, I want to be honest. We all do things because we want something else.

VICTORIA: We're having a son. He will carry on your name.

CHESTER: Are we happy?

VICTORIA: Happy?! It's security. Our son will have more possibilities somewhere else.

TUPPY: If she's not what you want, let's send her back. Then you and I will move away . . .

CHESTER: Aw, but what would I do somewhere else?

TUPPY: What's there to do? We're practically royalty, aren't we? (*Fearful.*) Or were you fibbing?

CHESTER (*trying to hide his anxiety, rapid*): I can't just pick up and leave. It's not like they're going to stop horseracing altogether, now will they?

TUPPY (*interrupting*): Will they? I'm boycotting you until you tell me the truth.

(*Chester returns to his bluster and delusions of grandeur. Tuppy exits.*)

VICTORIA: You know, I could go without you. . . . Find some other man.

CHESTER (*frightened*): You'd leave me?

(*Victoria is silent. He thinks a moment.*)

If I leave, who'd take care of Tup?

VICTORIA: Not us. We need a fresh start.

(*Victoria exits to the back bedroom. Chester sits alone, lost in thought.*)

Lights dim . . .

SCENE 12: A FRESH START

The family's apartment. Winnifreda enters through the front door carrying Tuppy's schoolbooks. After a moment, Tuppy plods in behind her. She's wearing her school uniform, drops her jacket to the ground.

WINNIFREDA: Miss, don't treat your school blazer like that.

> *(Tuppy ignores her, treads over to Tong Tong the chinchilla. She halfheartedly plays with him through his cage.)*

TUPPY: Maybe I won't need my blazer. School could be canceled again.

WINNIFREDA: School won't be canceled two days in a row.

TUPPY: What if it happens for ten days? A month? Years?

WINNIFREDA: Ay, it was just your teacher.

TUPPY: It was more than my teacher. We all sat there this morning. Waiting and waiting. And then one of the secretaries came in and wrote on the board: "Your teacher isn't coming. Leaving country A-S-A-P."

WINNIFREDA: Things will calm down. There's always the headmistress and the assistant headmistress.

TUPPY: No, they both left last week. *(Shakes her head, rapid.)* So they ring the recess bell at the wrong time. And all the students just run out into the halls, storm through the library, shouting, hanging off the shelves, pilfering magazines.

WINNIFREDA: You should tell the librarian.

TUPPY: Are you deaf? The librarian's gone, too!

WINNIFREDA: Your aunt Victoria is right. You have no respect!

TUPPY: You're just a Filipino maid. How dare you talk to her about me?!

> *(Winnifreda turns sharply to leave, when . . . Chester hollers from the back bedroom.)*

CHESTER *(offstage, calling)*: Winny?! Tup, is that you?!

WINNIFREDA *(calling back)*: School was canceled, sir.

(Uncle Chester blusters in from the back bedroom. He's wearing Victoria's robe and carrying his briefcase, stacked high with files, and the Rolodex.)

CHESTER: Canceled?

WINNIFREDA *(rolling her eyes)*: It's a long story.

CHESTER: Well, no time for stories. *(He ceremoniously dumps the Rolodex and briefcase into a waste bin.)* I'm proud to say, there'll be no more horses.

TUPPY: What's happened?! But you love horses . . .

CHESTER (*interrupting*): I'm getting out of the business. I have news, time for a family meeting.

(*Winnifreda starts to exit.*)

Oh, you too, Winny.

(*Winnifreda stops, glares at Tuppy.*)

WINNIFREDA: Sir, I am not part of this family.

CHESTER: Nonsense. We're starting a democracy.

(*Chester sits down at the dining table, clasps his hands,
and clears his throat.*)

(*Winnifreda formally stands at attention.*)

TUPPY: What is it Uncle Chester?

(*He gathers himself, ready to ramble on.*)

CHESTER: Now, you see, people are willing to change their entire lives to avoid chaos. If something happens in Hong Kong, it's natural to run for cover. (*The following litany is rapid.*) If you stay and complain, the government sets curfews, turns off your water. Forces you to sit at home thirsty, let alone able to flush your toilet . . .

TUPPY: So why aren't we leaving?

CHESTER: That's what I wanted to run by you. (*Leans into Tuppy, softly.*) . . . What do you think?

(*The following conversation runs on, excited.*)

TUPPY: About leaving?!

WINNIFREDA: For dinner, sir?

CHESTER: No, Hong Kong. Forever. For at least a couple of years. I know you're fond of your school, but . . .

TUPPY: I hate my school.

CHESTER: Perfect! We'll find you a better one. (*Laughs, teases.*) One with boys.

(*Tuppy groans, rolls her eyes. Victoria enters from
the couple's back bedroom.*)

TUPPY (*pointing to Victoria*): Was it *her* idea?!
CHESTER: Vicki's?

(*Victoria grins.*)

TUPPY: Does she have to go too?
CHESTER: (*Stern, he grabs Tuppy's and Victoria's hands.*) Of course. We're going as a family.
TUPPY (*flabbergasted*): Aren't we running out of time?
CHESTER (*pompous*): Don't doubt your uncle. I've got connections in London.
TUPPY: And you're happy about all this?

(*He looks to Victoria for reassurance.*)

CHESTER (*measured*): It's not about happy. It's security.

(*Tuppy thinks on this, not quite sure about the difference between the two.*)

TUPPY: Well . . . I'm sure I'll like it!
CHESTER (*to everyone*): Then it's settled. We're leaving. Winny, get packing.

(*Winnifreda doesn't move.*)

WINNIFREDA: No.

(*The family is stunned.*)

First, Miss needs to say good-bye to someone.
TUPPY: Who?
WINNIFREDA: Your mother.
TUPPY (*sour*): I don't want to.
CHESTER: Aw, what's the hurt in one last time?
TUPPY: Uncle Chester, maybe you could go with . . .
CHESTER (*interrupting, coaxes*): Tup, I can't be gloomy now. Just get it over with.

(*Tuppy nods. Reluctantly, she plods out the front door.*)

(*Calling after her.*) And be back by supper!

(*After a moment . . .*)

There, Winny, satisfied?

(*Winnifreda still doesn't move.*)

WINNIFREDA: Sir, it's so sudden.
VICTORIA: You don't have to go.
CHESTER (*quickly clarifying*): But, of course, we'll arrange for you to come, too. Connections.

(*Winnifreda doesn't respond.*)

You do want to come, don't you?

Lights crossfade with . . .

SCENE 13: THE CEMETERY

It's dusk. Tuppy sits on a bench, surrounded by the shadows of headstones. Winnifreda enters.

WINNIFREDA (*gruff*): Miss, it's time for supper.
TUPPY: You came for me?
WINNIFREDA: Your uncle made me. It's getting dark.
TUPPY: Maybe I'll sit a little longer.

(*Winnifreda also sits.*)

WINNIFREDA: I like this bench. If it wasn't so expensive, your mother should've had one, for visitors.
TUPPY: The dead don't need visitors.

(*A moment.*)

WINNIFREDA: It's good you came anyway.
TUPPY: It's awful.
WINNIFREDA: Cemeteries aren't awful. They're useful. (*Thinks.*) Actually, they're just bus stops. For the dead to catch a bus that is always on time.
TUPPY: A ghost bus?
WINNIFREDA: Ay, a bus that takes you away to a perfect place.
TUPPY (*rolling her eyes*): Heaven?
WINNIFREDA: No clouds or harps, just a subdivision where the apartments are nice and cheap.

(*She points at the headstones farther down the hill. The shadows of the headstones transform. They become silhouettes of a cityscape—shadows of apartment buildings with rooftops, glimmering little windows, and balconies.*)

Down there, a whole valley of townhouses. Inside, dead relatives sleep by candlelight.

(*Tuppy is reluctantly awed.*)

And at night, there's a special bus for mothers. (*Points.*) We catch it by the headstone with the big cross on top. Hundreds of us, with suitcases, picked up and dropped off. We walk the streets in our sensible shoes. Been away for years, working all over the world, lost, and finally we come home, climb the stairs and find our families, waiting, happy to see us. (*With longing.*) This is where I will live someday. In this valley of mothers.

TUPPY: And my mother's here?

WINNIFREDA: Yes, in the nice part of town.

TUPPY (*sheepish*): When I die, what if I don't want to live with her?

WINNIFREDA: Of course, you want.

TUPPY: I've been sitting here trying to remember something beautiful about her, but there's nothing . . .

WINNIFREDA (*interrupting*): Don't say that . . .

TUPPY: She was laying on the kitchen floor, blue as candy. Would rather die than be stuck with me . . .

WINNIFREDA (*interrupting*): I knew your mother. She tried.

TUPPY: A real mother isn't a quitter! I don't want to live with someone who quits like that. (*Rapid, distraught.*) Winny, when we all die, could Uncle Chester and I come live with you instead?

WINNIFREDA (*sharply*): You want to live with the maid?

TUPPY: . . . I'm sorry.

(*Winnifreda doesn't respond.*)

(*Fearful.*) Winny, . . . do you hate me?

WINNIFREDA: You have your moments, Miss.

TUPPY: Aunt Vicki says you must regret raising me.

WINNIFREDA: I don't listen to Aunt Bicki.

TUPPY: You don't?

WINNIFREDA: I listen to my heart.

TUPPY (*hesitant*): . . . And what does your heart say?

WINNIFREDA: Here is a girl who thinks she is big, even though she is small. A girl with angels watching over her. A girl who can be smart and pretty if she is not terrible. . . . A girl like my own.

(Tuppy smiles. The cemetery is dark. Winnifreda stands.)

(Terse.) Come, let's go home. Supper.

Lights fade to black.

SCENE 14: A VAIN ATTEMPT:
TWO MONTHS LATER

Spotlight up on Uncle Chester. The sound of planes landing and taking off denote a crowded airport counter. He speaks to an unseen airline agent, pulls out his billfold, and flashes a wad of cash.

CHESTER: That's right, two adult tickets, one child. *(Listens to the agent.)* She'll be fourteen. *(Listens.)* Of course, she's still a child! *(Listens.)* Fine, then three.

(Reluctantly, he searches his pockets for more money but stops and laughs nervously.)

What do you mean? There must be a mistake. Be a dear and check again. I said check. *(Listens.)* Only two left? *(Sly.)* Perhaps a little more cash? *(Listens.)* No, no, I didn't mean . . . No, don't cancel . . .

(A moment.)

I'll take what I can get.

Lights crossfade with . . .

SCENE 15: THE JUMP:
THE NIGHT OF THE HANDOVER

The apartment. It is now nearly empty. Moving boxes are scattered about. Pictures down from the walls. Winnifreda is covering the furniture with sheets. Tuppy enters from her back bedroom with her suitcase.

WINNIFREDA: Do you have everything, Miss?
TUPPY: Almost.

(Tuppy takes Tong Tong in his cage and rests it on top of her suitcase. She's satisfied.)

There, I'm ready. Are you ready?

WINNIFREDA: *(Changes the subject.)* I've packed all your uncle's things. Such a big trip. *(Winnifreda peers out to the balcony; clucks her tongue.)* Look how it's raining. But people still celebrating. Crazy people.

TUPPY: I hope our plane can take off.

WINNIFREDA: Haven't heard from Sir or Ma'am, so it will take off.

TUPPY: What time is it?

WINNIFREDA: We still have time.

(Tuppy fidgets impatiently.)

(Points.) Ay, look at that! Fireworks.

(The sounds and flashes of fireworks in the distance. Tuppy stands next to Winnifreda at the threshold of the balcony. They crane their necks. On the apartment walls a few splashes of multicolored lights, created by the kaleidoscope of fireworks.)

Careful, don't get wet.

TUPPY: Must be so many if you can see them all the way from the harbor.

(Winnifreda nods.)

You know what I think?

WINNIFREDA *(dry)*: What Miss?

TUPPY: They're not fireworks at all. They're military signals.

WINNIFREDA *(shaking her head)*: Ayyyy. . . .

TUPPY *(mischievous)*: To all of Aunt Victoria's relatives . . .

WINNIFREDA *(interrupting)*: Ay, watch your mouth . . .

TUPPY *(rambling on)*: . . . entire villages, waiting at the border. At midnight, they'll rush across into Hong Kong on crappy bicycles with dirty hair and loud voices. Greedy to take everything over.

WINNIFREDA: Why do you "hate" so much?

TUPPY *(embarrassed)*: It's not hate.

WINNIFREDA: Then what is it?

TUPPY *(earnest)*: . . . I'm sad.

WINNIFREDA *(stern)*: Don't be sad. That is not healthy.

TUPPY: Hong Kong people make me even more sad. Look at them, dancing in the street. Just giving in. Cheery-oh, ho-hum.

WINNIFREDA: What did you expect them to do?

TUPPY: Fight.

WINNIFREDA: You're not fighting.

TUPPY: No. . . . But at least I'm not pretending to be happy.

WINNIFREDA: You know, they're just afraid. People who stay here or run away—all afraid. So they pretend—to be happy, to be rich, to be smart.

And those who move here pretend even harder. Your aunt Victoria had nothing, you know. Not even God. And look what she has to pretend now.

TUPPY: That she loves my uncle?

WINNIFREDA: (Shrugs.) I hope she does love him. I hope you will learn to love her. (Winnifreda takes Tuppy by the shoulders as if saying good-bye and giving advice for the very last time.) She is family.

TUPPY: (Squirms, at last . . .) I'll try.

WINNIFREDA: Good. Family makes you truly happy.

(Victoria enters. She's large, about eight months pregnant, and drenched. Caught out in the rain, she carries a bunch of soggy shopping bags.)

Ma'am, you're back.

VICTORIA (melodramatic, exhausted): I'm barely alive.

(Winnifreda takes the shopping bags from Victoria. Puts her purse on the dining table.)

TUPPY (derisive): You bought a lot.

VICTORIA (to Winnifreda): I had to fight in the shops. People buying everything.

WINNIFREDA: (Inspects the contents of one of the bags.) Batteries, packs of gum, a big bottle of cheap whiskey . . . To drink?

VICTORIA: Pack those things.

TUPPY: Did you remember Tong Tong's niblets?

VICTORIA: Niblets, no, I forgot.

(Tuppy rolls her eyes. She picks up Victoria's purse from the dining table.)

TUPPY: Fine, I'll get them myself.

VICTORIA: Put that down.

TUPPY: I just need a few coins.

WINNIFREDA: Ay, Miss, there isn't time to buy niblets.

(Tuppy begins to open the purse anyway.)

VICTORIA: Stop touching my things!

(Victoria lunges at the handbag. Tuppy holds it away. Victoria grasps her belly in discomfort.)

WINNIFREDA: Remember, Miss, family, respect, love . . .

(Tuppy begins to rummage through the purse.)

VICTORIA: *(Points to the maid.)* Winny . . .

TUPPY: What . . .

VICTORIA: . . . do something!

TUPPY: . . . are you hiding? *(Tuppy digs out two rectangular envelopes from inside the purse.)* What's this? *(She inspects the envelopes more closely. They're airline boarding passes.)* . . . Why are there only two tickets?!

WINNIFREDA *(disturbed)*: Only two?

VICTORIA: Two is all we could get.

TUPPY: What's going on?!

VICTORIA: Your uncle's not "connected" as he says. Ask him.

TUPPY: I will!

VICTORIA: Give those back first!

TUPPY: Call him first!

(Victoria pretends to go into the living room to call but suddenly turns and snatches at the airline tickets instead. Tuppy rushes out to the rainy balcony with them. Victoria follows.)

VICTORIA: *(Panicked, heavy breathing.)* Aiiyah! What are you doing?!

WINNIFREDA *(calling from inside the apartment)*: Miss, are you all right?!

VICTORIA *(to Winnifreda, terse)*: She's fine.

TUPPY: . . . Going once, going twice . . .

(Tuppy winds up as if to throw the airline tickets off into oblivion, but Victoria quickly interrupts.)

VICTORIA: No!!! . . . Fine, I'll call.

(Victoria storms back into the apartment. She sharply points at Winnifreda to dial the phone in the living room.)

TUPPY *(calling to Victoria, taunting)*: You better hurry . . .

(Winnifreda holds the phone receiver as Victoria snatches the handset and speaks.)

VICTORIA *(on the phone)*: Chester, Chester, it's Victoria calling. Where are you?

(Chester appears in a spotlight on a separate part of the stage. He holds an umbrella. He's on his cell phone.)

CHESTER (*to Victoria*): Darling, I was in the queue. Took me forever to get through.

TUPPY: I'm not joking . . .

VICTORIA (*covering the phone, to Tuppy*): Little bitch!

CHESTER (*straining to hear*): What?

VICTORIA: Your sweet niece is being difficult.

CHESTER: Just give her a little nip of brandy. (*Rambling on.*) You should have seen it, Vicki. Lines around the block. The last-minute rush . . . but I got the visas!

VICTORIA (*relieved*): Good. Now come home quick.

(*The dialogue remains very rapid.*)

TUPPY (*calling in from the balcony*): I'm ready to speak with my uncle!

WINNIFREDA (*calling to Tuppy*): Miss, I'm sure he has more tickets!

CHESTER: She found the plane tickets?

VICTORIA: You should've told her. Talk to her now!

CHESTER: Now?

(*Tuppy leans in, crinkles her nose, unable to eavesdrop.*)

VICTORIA: We fly in two hours.

CHESTER: I can't, I can't talk now . . .

(*Chester hangs up his phone. His spotlight goes out. Victoria is left with just a dial tone. Victoria tersely thrusts the phone handset back at Winnifreda and returns to the balcony.*)

TUPPY: So . . . ?

VICTORIA: He hung up.

TUPPY: Then the deal's off.

(*Victoria approaches the girl anyway.*)

Stand back, or I'll jump!

(*Victoria and Winnifreda hover nervously at the balcony's threshold.*)

VICTORIA: You crazy, huh? You'll kill yourself over plane tickets?!

(*Victoria and Tuppy lock eyes, silent for a moment.
The frantic pace resumes.*)

WINNIFREDA: Miss, please be careful!

TUPPY (*to Victoria*): I tell you, I'll jump! My death will be all your fault!

WINNIFREDA: Ay, *dios ko!*

VICTORIA: That's it. Winny, call the police!

(*Victoria sharply points at Winnifreda again.
The maid quickly goes to call.*)

TUPPY (*overlapping with Winny*): She won't be able to get hold of anyone. All the authorities are on the street tonight. Drinking champagne. So stupid.

WINNIFREDA (*overlapping with Tuppy, nervously dialing the phone*): God have mercy!

TUPPY: Look, there's a crowd gathering down there . . .

(*Victoria edges forward a little, cranes her neck
to take a peek down below.*)

There's millions of people on the island tonight just waiting for something to happen. They're looking up here!

VICTORIA (*overlapping with Tuppy*): . . . Please, let us be reasonable.

TUPPY (*calling out to the crowd*): I'll be reasonable with the Chinese army, Tung Chee-Hwa [*the People's Republic of China's provisional governor of Hong Kong*], Governor Chris Patten [*the last British governor of Hong Kong*], the Queen of England!

(*To Victoria.*) But I will not be reasonable with you. Do you really think you could get away with it?

VICTORIA: With what? (*Sweetly.*) The plane tickets are yours. You and your uncle go to London first. Winny and I will follow after.

(*Victoria smiles, reaches out her hand for the tickets.
Tuppy jerks them away.*)

TUPPY: You're going to force my uncle to leave without me!

VICTORIA: I don't have to force anyone. He loves me. More than you.

TUPPY: What do you know about love?

VICTORIA: I know what he tells me when we're in *bed*. Oooh, how happy he is to have a real Chinese wife who knows what it's like to suffer. Girls like you don't even know who they are. You think you're English? You show up at Buckingham Palace tomorrow, you think the Queen Mother will let you in? You are part of a passing hobby, like horses. (*All the while, Victoria has edged over to Tong Tong's cage. She grabs it violently and holds it over the balcony rail.*) Aiiyah!!! Give me the tickets or I'll drop him twenty-one stories. Crack him open like an egg!

(*Chester enters through the front door. He shakes out
his drippy umbrella.*)

CHESTER (*calling*): I'm home!
WINNIFREDA (*still on the phone*): It's terrible, Sir!

(*Victoria runs into the apartment, still clutching Tong Tong's cage.
She embraces Chester.*)

CHESTER: Vicki, is everything under control?
VICTORIA (*swooning*): Ohhh, it's been sooo awful.
CHESTER: You're sweating through your suit!
VICTORIA: Can't breathe. Hold me.
CHESTER: Why are you holding that chinchilla?
TUPPY (*calling*): She was about to murder it!

(*At the sound of Tuppy's agonized voice, Chester breaks away from
Victoria. Tuppy has entered the living room.*)

CHESTER: Tup, don't be upset. I wouldn't let anyone hurt . . .

(*He approaches her, but Tuppy holds up the plane tickets
and threatens to rip them in half.*)

TUPPY: Stay away!

(*Chester stops.*)

VICTORIA: See what a monster she is.
WINNIFREDA (*still on the phone*): We're calling the police.
CHESTER (*tersely, to Winnifreda*): Why call the police? Let's not make a
scene.

(*Winnifreda reluctantly hangs up the phone. Chester cautiously
keeps his distance from the girl.*)

Tuppy dear, why don't you come over here. And we'll have a little
chat.
TUPPY: I don't chat.
CHESTER (*cooing*): Oh, I bet your Tong Tong wants to have a chat. See, he's
nice and safe. Waiting in front of the telly for you.
TUPPY: Stop treating me like a child! Are you leaving without me?!
CHESTER (*sheepish*): It's not that way . . .
TUPPY: Stop lying! Just tell me!

CHESTER (*overlapping*): I tried, really tried, but everyone wants to leave, you know. People can only get out, two by two, like Noah's ark. So I had to make a choice . . .

TUPPY: So you chose her?

CHESTER: Didn't plan it, in desperate times things just happen, figured your aunt Vicki and I could go on ahead. Set up house . . .

TUPPY (*interrupting*): So you're going?!

CHESTER: I, I have to. Spent all my savings on it.

(*Victoria leans in to Chester.*)

VICTORIA (*whispering urgently*): Come on, we're very late.

(*She lumbers away and begins to get her luggage together.*)

CHESTER: If I don't leave now, no one in this family will ever get out. Do you want that?

TUPPY: There's got to be another way . . .

CHESTER: Children can come along after things calm down.

(*Tuppy dashes back out to the rainy balcony.*)

Bloody hell, Tup! Whatcha doing now?!

(*She goes to the precarious edge.*)

TUPPY (*overlapping, launches into a rapid fantasy*): . . . Maybe, maybe, we could run across to the racetrack and escape with the horses. Go on!

CHESTER: What?!

(*Tuppy climbs up on the rail and leans farther out.*)

Tup, stop! Don't move!

TUPPY (*overlapping*): Use them to jump over the hedges, out of the stadium, down the street. Gallop around Bentleys, toward Central, right to the harbor, the pier, the dock, the edge of the landfilled everything, they'd leap, with us on their backs, more like tigers than horses. And we'd land on the boat with Prince Charles sailing away! . . . To London.

CHESTER (*panicked*): Don't be silly!

(*Victoria barges onto the balcony and clings to Chester.*)

VICTORIA (*frightened*): Aiiyah, just grab her! We're going to miss our plane.

TUPPY (*interrupting*): Uncle Chester, you need to take me with you!

*(Tuppy is desperate. Chester shoots Victoria a glare
and slowly moves to his niece.)*

CHESTER: Tup, your uncle Chester will save you. You know, maybe you're right. *(He reaches out to her.)* I haven't tried everything. Come with us to the airport, and I'll pitch a fit with the higher-ups. I'll demand they scavenge up another ticket, and you'll come with us. Directly to London, like a princess. *(He reaches out even farther.)* Come on, Tup. . . . What do you say? . . . Give me your hand.

(Tuppy hesitantly gives her uncle her hand. They connect.)

That's it dear, that's it . . .

(Chester grabs Tuppy, swings her down from the balcony rail. He carries her into the apartment, sets her down on the covered sofa. Tuppy is curled in a little ball, limp with sadness and drenched from the rain. Chester takes the plane tickets from her. Winnifreda runs to the girl and covers her with one of the furniture sheets.)

See, look how happy Tong Tong is that you're all in one piece. He needs you to take care of him.

WINNIFREDA: Ay, Miss, you're soaked through and through.

*(Victoria comes up to Chester and kisses him on the cheek.
He glumly hands her the plane tickets.)*

CHESTER: OK, Tup, let's go! *(Claps his hands.)* Chop, chop. . . . Oh, by the way, you know you'll have to leave Tong Tong behind. They don't let animals like that on international flights.

TUPPY: How do you know? They let dogs on.

VICTORIA: Dogs don't look like rats. He could have diseases. You want all of London to get boils and die because of that thing?

TUPPY: Who asked you?!

WINNIFREDA *(overlapping with Chester)*: Shhht!

CHESTER *(overlapping with Winny)*: Your auntie's right. I'm afraid the customs officers at the airport won't understand a chinchilla. Wouldn't it be best if you stayed here with Tong Tong, for the sake of his feelings? We could send for you later . . .

TUPPY: No! I'm ready to go now!

(Tuppy breaks away from Winnifreda. She violently plucks her chinchilla out of his cage and runs back out to the balcony with it.)

CHESTER: Tuppy, what are you doing?!
WINNIFREDA: Ay, Miss!

(*Tuppy delicately places Tong Tong on the balcony railing.*)

VICTORIA: This will not help! You're not go—
CHESTER: Quiet!

(*He motions for Victoria and Winnifreda to stand back.*)

TUPPY: All right, Tong Tong, go on now. Jump. Jump! Jump, you stupid piss!
CHESTER: Come on Tup, we've got to hurry.
TUPPY (*to her uncle*): He won't do it. (*Through her tears, to Tong Tong.*) Come on. Please, don't be so selfish. Quickly! I have a chance to go to London. To drink tea with milk. To be with my uncle. Don't you want me to be happy!?

(*Tuppy slides to the ground, breathless, overwhelmed with emotion. Victoria rushes out to the balcony.*)

VICTORIA: Grow up! (*She edgily grabs Tong Tong by the scruff of the neck and dumps him in his cage.*) Realize happiness isn't everything.

(*Winnifreda moves to Tuppy, holds and comforts her. Victoria leaves to gather the last of her belongings.*)

(*Calls to Chester, from the front door.*) I'll be waiting for you downstairs.

(*She exits.*)

CHESTER: Winny, dry her eyes. (*Tries to be chipper.*) Now, Tup, chin up. Back inside.

(*Winnifreda leads the girl back in.*)

TUPPY: I'm afraid. For you, Uncle Chester. How will you manage with that awful Victoria?
CHESTER: Look, Tup, she isn't awful.
TUPPY: Please, you will send for me in a month?
CHESTER: A month? You've got a new school to try out.
TUPPY: A new school?
CHESTER (*sheepish*): On scholarship. A place with dormitories, just 'til the end of the term.

(Tuppy is in shock.)

TUPPY *(overlapping, interrupts)*: A boarding school?!
CHESTER: Just 'til Aunt Vicki and I get settled. Winny volunteered to stay with you at a discount salary. It will be just like home . . .
TUPPY *(jerking away from Winnifreda)*: Winny won't make it better!
CHESTER: The truth is, Winny is better at taking care of you than me.

(Chester leaves the balcony, enters the apartment. Tuppy rushes after him. The following dialogue is rapid.)

TUPPY: I don't want Winny!
CHESTER: Tup!
WINNIFREDA: It's all right, Sir.
CHESTER *(flustered, slurred)*: Vicki and I starting a new family and maybe I don't want you to come . . .
TUPPY: Don't say that on my birthday! Or has everyone in the world forgot?!
CHESTER: I haven't forgot; you're fourteen, of course. What do you want me to do?
TUPPY: Promise you'll send for me.
CHESTER: . . . Promise.
TUPPY: Say you love me best.

(Chester is filled with guilt and pity.)

CHESTER: . . . I love you best.

(He gives Tuppy one last look, picks up his suitcase, and exits. Slowly, the front door shuts.)

(Tuppy is motionless. Winnifreda is silent.)

(Finally, the girl finds words . . .)

TUPPY: Winny?
WINNIFREDA: Yes, Miss.
TUPPY: I just want to be happy.
WINNIFREDA: I know, Miss. *(Nods.)* So do I.
TUPPY: Winny?

(Winnifreda looks to Tuppy.)

(Bittersweet.) You're fired. Please, go home.

Lights slowly fade to black.

SCENE 16: EIGHT YEARS LATER:
SOMEWHERE IN CANADA

Lights up on a drab, suburban living room. It's nothing like Hong Kong and all quite unremarkable. Outside the window, it snows. Uncle Chester sits on the sofa watching television. He wears his wife's old robe and slippers.

The doorbell rings. He rushes to answer it. He throws the front door open and Tuppy enters, in puffy jacket and hat, now twenty-two. She carries a suitcase.

CHESTER *(ushering her in)*: Welcome, welcome, Tup. . . . Did you find your way here all right? Long trip. You must be exhausted. *(He brushes the snow off her.)* You must be frrreezing.

TUPPY: I'm fine.

CHESTER: Of course, you are. My big college girl. All grown up. *(He motions at her bag.)* Let me take that for you . . .

TUPPY: I've got it.

CHESTER: *(Chuckles.)* Oh, you better. You're stronger than an ol' man like myself.

(Tuppy puts her suitcase in a corner. Chester turns the TV volume down and scurries to clear off a seat for his niece.)

Here, come sit. Take a load off.

(Tuppy gives a polite half-smile and remains standing. She looks around the living room. Uncle Chester goes ahead and sits back down on the sofa.)

I've tried to keep the place up. But there's only so much you can do with cheap furniture. Remember how things used to be?

(Tuppy nods.)

(Rambles on.) Money was no object. But, you know, had to spend it all paying the fees to move here. Damn Canucks! If we'd moved to London, who knows what could've been. *(Sighs, ignites again.)* Damn Beefeaters! Let us snap some photos, pay a visit, but Hong Kong people not allowed to live there, rotten law. Well, we can't do anything about the law, now can we?

(Tuppy goes to the window.)

TUPPY: Does it snow a lot in Winnipeg?

CHESTER: Feels like every day. Snow kills things.

(A glum, awkward moment between them.)

TUPPY: *(Changes the subject.)* Where's Aunt Vicki?

CHESTER: In her room with the girl. That's right, you haven't met our girl, have you? *(Chuckles.)* I fear you'll be disappointed. She's not as special as you.

(He reaches up to touch Tuppy's face. She bends down to let him touch it but then pulls away again. Tuppy keeps a formal, wary distance.)

(Chipper.) Is it warm back home?

TUPPY: Very.

CHESTER: Ahhh . . .

(Another awkward moment.)

They say Hong Kong hasn't changed much.

TUPPY: It hasn't. Sort of.

CHESTER: *(Nods.)* Sort of.

TUPPY: It looks the same but feels different. Everything's changing under the surface. So you don't quite know what's going to happen. But I don't mind.

CHESTER: Are there lots of Chinese at your uni?

TUPPY: *(Nods.)* I speak Mandarin every day.

CHESTER: *(Exaggerated disbelief.)* *You*, speaking Chinese?!

(Tuppy nods. She and Chester chuckle together.)

You must be making smashing business connections. Be able to travel through the Mainland, make piles of money.

TUPPY: . . . If that's what I wanted. But I'm staying put. In Hong Kong. . . . When you do that, you learn you ought to make things better. Not just run away. Sort of, um, a responsibility for the place, for better or worse.

CHESTER: You want me to say I'm irresponsible?

TUPPY: *(Shakes her head.)* No.

CHESTER: Good.

(Tuppy nods.)

That's good.

(Tuppy nods again.)

I'm afraid I have nothing to say.

(They don't say anything. Tuppy taps her toes
From the back bedroom, a young girl's wail.)

(Motions toward the sound.) Your little cousin doesn't listen. *(Laughs,*
only half-joking.) A disaster.

(He points to a bottle of liquor on a bookshelf.)

(Loud, over the shrill wailing.) Always cries, so we give her brandy.
(The girl's crying suddenly stops. Chester listens for a moment. Shakes his
head, glumly.) I never imagined we'd have a girl. *(Tries to be chipper.)* Never
imagined I'd have a girl of my own.

(Tuppy looks to him.)

TUPPY *(piercing)*: You always did.

(Chester nods, uncomfortable, embarrassed.
At last, he claps his hands.)

CHESTER: The Kentucky Derby's on the telly. *(He reaches over and turns up*
the volume on the television.) That's what they show here.

(From the tinny-sounding television, a trumpet weakly blares and a racing
gate slightly snaps. Horses' hooves patter on turf. The upswell of a cheering
crowd fades in and out with static and a scratchy announcer's voice. Tuppy
and her uncle watch the horse race together.)

It comes in all grainy. I can't afford a satellite.
TUPPY: When I graduate, I'll buy you a satellite.
CHESTER: Oh, that's a sweet girl. Thank you, dear.
TUPPY *(pointing limply at the TV)*: Wow, they're fast.
CHESTER: I watch them all from my old sofa.
TUPPY: I'll get you a new sofa.
CHESTER: I'm not a charity case, you know! I'm still your uncle. You still
   have to love me. You still have to!
TUPPY: I do.

(Chester breaks, hangs his head down. It's something between
a laugh and a cry—pathetic.)

CHESTER (*blubbering rapidly, uncontrolled*): You shouldn't. And don't buy me anything. It's just the Kentucky Derby, damn TV's so boggled, can't see the photo finish, can't see who finished first, just see fuzzy shapes, could be goddamned dogs running, for all I know. Boggled reception!

(*Tuppy bangs the top of the television. The static stops.*
The announcer's voice is clear again.)

(*Meanwhile, the snow outside the living room window slowly stops falling. The sun comes out. It's bright and warm. Something seems to change, becomes alive. A slight hint of green leafy trees.*)

(*Chester calms down. He pulls himself together and turns off the television. Then he digs a rumpled envelope out of his robe pocket.*)

Got a letter from Winny.

(*He passes it to Tuppy. She takes it, inspects it.*)

It's addressed to you.

TUPPY: It's open?

CHESTER: I work for the post office now. (*Forces a smile.*) It's my professional prerogative.

(*Winnifreda appears outside the living room window.*
As Tuppy reads, her former nanny speaks.)

WINNIFREDA (*voicing the letter*): Dear Miss, I am writing you from Texas. It is very warm here, and I am with my sons. Horton has successfully become, a male nurse. I have bought him boots and acid-washed jeans, but he has still not found a wife. (*Grins.*)

My other son, Thorton, has joined community college. He will learn computers. Ay, I pray for them both. And Miss, of course, I pray for you, too. I pray you are as lucky as me, able to find God's blessing. You are a smart girl. Keep working hard.

(*Rapid, evangelical.*) And don't, don't ever use your body for sinful things. Because then you can never respect yourself. God bless you, Miss. Yours Truly, Winnifreda Posedas Busabos.

(*Winnifreda disappears from outside the living room window. Gradually the sunlight fades, and it begins to snow again. Tuppy shakes her head, tickled.*)

CHESTER: She seems happy.
TUPPY (*pleased*): Yes, she does.

(*The sound of the Kentucky Derby on the television fades up, as Tuppy and Chester watch. Then, like their days at the racetrack so many years ago . . . Tuppy, ever so slightly, leans her head on her uncle's shoulder. Not quite a reconciliation, but something.*)

Lights fade to black.

END OF PLAY

4

Asiamnesia

Sun Mee Chomet

INTRODUCTION, *by Josephine Lee*

siamnesia was produced by Mu Performing Arts and presented at the Playwright's Center in Minneapolis from September 13, 2008, to October 5, 2008, under the direction of Randy Reyes.

American popular culture has been rife with the typecasting of Asian women, from the submissive and suicidal Madame Butterfly and the infamous Mata Hari to the prostitute Suzy Wong. *Asiamnesia* begins with a history lesson about famous female performers whose professional careers and personal identities are tied up with these images: Anna May Wong, the famous star of the silent screen; Isabel Rosario Cooper, the Filipina actress famous for the first on-screen kiss in a Filipino movie and the mistress of General Douglas MacArthur; and Oyuki, the celebrated geisha and wife of the millionaire George Morgan. These imagined Asian American "top girls" (with a nod to Caryl Churchill's play) toast the success of Sarah Kim, an Asian American actress who has been cast as another historical figure—the Chinese woman Afong Moy, who in 1834 was displayed as a "Chinese lady" for curious New York onlookers who paid twenty-five or fifty cents for the opportunity to look at her.

Sun Mee Chomet's play happily provides much richer performance opportunities for Asian American women, both individually and as an ensemble. In

Illustration: Rose Le Tran, Katie Ka Vang, Sun Mee Chomet, and Katie Bradley in *Asiamnesia*.
(Photograph used by permission of John Autey Photography.)

the Mu production, the role of Sarah was taken on by each of the actresses in turn, allowing audiences to understand the connections between the many disparate pieces of the play. The play also allows for spirited ensemble playing, inspired by both feminist and pan-ethnic solidarity. Borrowing moments from *Hamlet* to *Madame Butterfly* to *The Wizard of Oz*, *Asiamnesia* tests the versatility and endurance of its performers and celebrates Asian American actresses even while bemoaning the stereotypes that continue to limit them.

––––––––

ABOUT THE PLAY

Asiamnesia was written by Sun Mee Chomet with creative collaboration by the cast. It was directed by Randy Reyes. The artistic designers included Nicholas Golfis (sets), Cana Potter (costumes), Khoo Wu Chen (lighting), Leah Nelson (choreography), Tom Scott (composer), Montana Johnson (sound), Anita Ruth (musical arrangements), and Jesse Golfis (scenic art). The technical crew included Emma Valentine (sound board operation), Stephanie Bertumen (deck crew), and Tim Wilkins and Jennifer Kelley (stage managers). It was presented by Mu Performing Arts, with Rick Shiomi as artistic director, Don Eitel as managing director, and Randy Reyes as artistic associate director. *Asiamnesia* was created through the New Performance Program at Mu Performing Arts, funded by a grant from the Jerome Foundation.

CHARACTERS (ORIGINAL CAST)

KATIE BRADLEY	Sarah Kim, Oyuki, Madame Butterfly, Dragon Lady, Han Yoo
SUN MEE CHOMET	Sarah Kim, Anna May Wong, Barb Lee, Casting Director, Rice Paddy Woman
ROSE LE TRAN	Sarah Kim, Afong Moy, Isabel Rosario Cooper, April, Miss Saigon, Dorothy, Korean Groupie
KATIE KA VANG	Sarah Kim, Korean Groupie, Japanese Tourist

This is an ensemble piece for four Asian American women. Casting for each scene can be distributed as the director wishes, depending on the strengths of each particular cast. My preference is that each actress gets a turn (or two) at playing Sarah throughout the play. This can be indicated with having a costume piece that signifies her journey and can be easily exchanged between the women between scenes—e.g., scarf, skirt, hat.

The costume pieces are elaborate in Scenes 1 and 2; however, they should be built simply to change into and out of as they reappear after the dance sequence and again, at the end of the play.

The set should be minimal, keeping in mind that the entire stage must be cleared for the dance sequence. Using standing screens may be helpful for quick costume changes.

SCENE 1 CHARACTER NOTES

AFONG MOY: First Asian woman arrived in the United States. Came as an exhibit in 1834. She drew huge crowds of curious onlookers.

SCENE 2 CHARACTER NOTES

ANNA MAY WONG (1905–1961): First Chinese American film star; appeared in more than forty films. Most successful Asian American female film star to date.

ISABEL ROSARIO COOPER (nicknamed "Dimples"): Eurasian Filipina actress famous for first onscreen kiss by an Asian woman. Became mistress of General Douglas MacArthur when he was stationed in the Philippines when she was sixteen. She traveled to the United States and lived in Washington, D.C., as his secret mistress. After he refused to make the relationship public, he attempted to send her back to the Philippines, but she insisted on remaining in the United States. She went to Hollywood to try to make it, but to no end. She committed suicide in 1960.

OYUKI: In 1898, she married George D. Morgan (nephew of the millionaire financier J. P. Morgan). He paid $25,000 to her family ($440,000 in modern U.S. currency) for her hand in marriage. They were ostracized on arrival in New York and moved to France, where she had affairs with French men of influence. George Morgan died of a sudden heart attack. Oyuki returned to Kyoto in 1938 as the most celebrated geisha of all time.

SCENE 1

Museum exhibition. New York, 1834.

Lights up on a young woman sitting. It is Afong Moy. She is in full nineteenth-century Chinese dress—a silk gown and four-inch-long slippers on bound feet. She is sitting on an Oriental latticework chair. A bowl of rice and an abacus are placed on a small table next to her. Afong sits for a bit. She stares uncomfortably at the audience. When she gets bored, she eats with chopsticks or counts on the abacus aloud in Chinese (Eee, Arr, San, Suu, Ooh, Lio, Chi, Ba, Djo, Shur); fans herself; or walks, scooting along—it is painful, but she manages to make it look easy. (This scene is done mostly in silence and involves a bit of humorous improvisation and toying with the audience to capture the strangeness of the situation.) She sits again, looking at the audience.

Blackout.

SCENE 2

Upscale sushi restaurant. Los Angeles, today.

Lights up on a dinner party about to begin. Sarah sits, waiting alone at a table for four. She is smiling and happy. Anna enters with a flourish. She wears a smart suit, 1920s trendsetter.

ANNA: Well, darling, it's good to see you. It's been a while; didn't you miss me?

(They kiss on the cheek.)

SARAH: Of course, but you know how it goes. Things get so busy . . .
ANNA: Oh, you don't have to tell me, now do you?
SARAH: No, I suppose not.

(Waitress enters.)

ANNA: I'll have some wine, don't you think? Have you ordered yet?
SARAH: No, I was waiting. . . .
ANNA: Darling, what's the point of waiting. You know we'll all want to drink. *(To the waitress.)* Dear, we'll have a bottle of Pinot Noir to start. Make it tasty, will you? And warm up a bottle of sake, yes?

(Waitress exits.)

It's not smart to mix, but we must consider our company this evening. The other girls are late. *(Sarcastically.)* How unexpected.
SARAH: I know.
ANNA: They're so . . . so . . . what do you say nowadays?
SARAH: High maintenance.
ANNA: Right. Sounds like an automobile repair shop, for Christ's sake. In my day, darling, we *woke up* glamorous. *(Referring to her fabulous self.)* This . . . was second nature. So, what are we dining on this evening? It is, after all, your special night!
SARAH: Yes.
ANNA: Hmmm, the uni looks divine, but I think I'll just have a kaiso salad.
SARAH: Me, too.

(Isabel enters. She wears lingerie with a 1930s bedroom gown over it. She has on matching fluffy slippers, dons red lipstick, and looks like a million bucks.)

ISABEL: So many men, so little time . . .

ANNA: Busy little bee you are.

ISABEL: Sleeping around comes with the job.

ANNA: Oh, a bit of manners, dear.

(Waitress enters with wine.)

Ahh, here we are, a gift from the gods.

(Waitress pours a sip for Anna to taste. Throughout the following, Anna studies and tastes wine.)

ISABEL: Sorry. That's right—Classy, that's your motto, right? . . . It's been a while since I've seen the light of day, forgive me. I don't know what to do with myself now, with all of this freedom.

SARAH *(under her breath)*: A relative term, don't you think?

ANNA *(studying the wine)*: We know, Isabel. Now it's all behind you. So much to look forward, darling. *(Tastes the wine; it's approved. To waitress.)* You are an angel, sweetheart.

(Throughout the following, waitress pours for everyone—Anna, Isabel, and Sarah. She fills fourth glass, as well, even though one person hasn't arrived yet. Waitress knows she's always late.)

(To Isabel, back to business.) So, what's the news from the frontlines, dear?

ISABEL: Four new admirers, two auditions, and one new suit being tailor-made at Saks.

SARAH: That's great!

ANNA: Well, well. You haven't wasted any time.

ISABEL *(to Sarah)*: Thanks, dear. *(Quickly, to Anna.)* Why should I? It's been years. I love this place. I think I'll stay for a while.

ANNA: I'm glad you're being treated like a lady for once.

ISABEL: And why shouldn't I be?

(Oyuki enters. She is in full geisha costume. She is in a state, ready to drink a lot. Sarah sees Oyuki and waves, trying to get her attention.)

ANNA: You should, darling. Every waking moment.

SARAH: Oyuki!

ISABEL: Oh, gorgeous getup!

OYUKI *(bitter and uninterested)*: Oh, this? It's nothing, just something I threw on. Back then I had hundreds of kimono. Back before . . .

ANNA: Now, now, dear. No need to dredge up the past, not on Sarah's special day.

(*Waitress exits.*)

OYUKI: Oh, yes. Forgive me, dear. How thoughtless of me. (*She raises her glass, stands up.*) Please, a toast, shall we?

ISABEL: (*Stands up.*) To Sarah, welcome to Hollywood!

OYUKI: What a thrill!

ANNA: (*Stands up.*) Ahhh, yes. (*Sarcastically.*) Where the silver screen and silicone are idolized.

SARAH: Thank you.

OYUKI: *Kampai!*

ALL: *Kampai!*

(*They all drink, violently savoring the relief that the alcohol gives them.*)

ISABEL: So, is it a meaty part? Do you get to kiss anyone, like I did in the Philippines? Anna, can you imagine? They can kiss onscreen nowadays, in *Hollywood.*

ANNA: I've heard. It kills me, truly, it does. I swear, I was born a decade too early. I would light up the screen now like fireworks, tongue and all . . .

SARAH (*interrupting*): Actually, no. It's a strange role, and there's definitely no kissing.

ANNA (*disappointed*): Some things never change. Well, do you have lines? If you're a principal, you get to speak, yes? I've heard you have those unions *to protect you* nowadays.

SARAH: Yes, I'm SAG, but no, I don't have lines.

ISABEL: You're saggy?

SARAH: No, it's the union. Screen Actors Guild.

ANNA: Sounds like the Kiwanis Club. Couldn't they have made it a bit classier? Go on.

ISABEL: Oh, what a disappointment, you don't have lines. What, Sarah, did silent films come back into fashion?

SARAH (*laughing*): No.

ISABEL: So it is a talkie? Oh, goodie! I hate to read.

SARAH: Yes, it is. But my character is silent.

(*Awkward silence. The other women look to one another, unimpressed.*)

(*Defending her part.*) She's historical, and it's a great part, don't get me wrong. But she doesn't speak.

OYUKI (*changing the subject, drinking a lot*): That's all right, dear. At least you are working. Hmmm, I always thought it'd be wonderful to be on the big screen, seen around the world, ready for my closeup. In my day, you only were able to see us onstage. Very exclusive, especially the Cherry Dances. That's where I met him, the bastard.

ANNA: Oyuki! Now, now, dear . . .

OYUKI: Well, the truth must be told. I was forced into it, more or less. I loved performing; I was at the height of my career. But my parents were enamored of the American and his handsome wallet. They couldn't resist. I had no choice.

ISABEL: I did hear he offered your family a mint.

ANNA: Girls, we're celebrating Sarah's casting, yes?

(No one is listening. Sarah smiles weakly at Anna, acknowledging her effort.)

OYUKI *(ignoring Anna, finishing off the wine)*: $25,000, yes. They thought I would go to the States as a celebrated star. Little did they know it would ruin my life completely. *(Suddenly reflective.)* Although, once he) died . . . I was happy.

(Waitress enters.)

ANNA *(to the waitress)*: I think it's time for the sake.

(Waitress glances at Oyuki and nods to Anna knowingly. She exits.)

OYUKI: Years of training, making my way through the ranks, dance and playing the shamisen . . . wasted. Polite society in New York didn't give a damn or understand what it meant. To them, I was strange bird. George stopped receiving the invitations to balls and tea parties. I had nothing to do. So I had no choice but to seek enjoyment elsewhere, don't you agree?

ISABEL: Oh, of course. A girl has to have her nest tended to.

ANNA: Isabel!

ISABEL: Whoops! Classy, I forgot. *(To Anna.)* Pardon, madam.

OYUKI: Yes, I had lovers all over Paris. A French legionnaire won my heart in the end.

ISABEL *(to Anna, smiling)*: I do love the Frenchmen.

ANNA *(to Isabel, smiling)*: I love the French*women.*

OYUKI: Although the idea of *winning* a heart is a questionable conquest. I know, most definitely, it can be *purchased.*

ISABEL: I agree. D.C. would have been a lonely place had I not snuck out for company. For god's sake, of all the men I could have chosen, I ended up with MacArthur. And I was a star in the Philippines! I come to the States only to realize he only wanted a pet, a secret affair. Where was my head?

OYUKI: In his lap.

ANNA: Ladies, really!

ISABEL: No, not in his lap. How disgusting!

ANNA: (Putting her foot down, she stands.) Please, dear hearts, listen closely. The first rule of stardom is keeping up appearances. Reputation is everything. Let this be a lesson to you, Sarah. As you begin your tumble into the hands of Hollywood casting directors. I live by the motto, "It is important in life to *be* virtuous. But it is more important to . . . "

ANNA, OYUKI, and ISABEL: "*Seem* virtuous.")

ANNA: Are you listening, Sarah?

SARAH: Note taken.

OYUKI: Where's the sake?

(Waitress enters with large bottle of sake and pours for all.
The women love having the waitress to perform for.)

ANNA (to the waitress): Ahhh, divine intervention. Darling, you do know your cue, the perfect entrance. *Merci beaucoup.*

OYUKI: Oh, Anna. You're just showing off. This is a Japanese restaurant, for god's sake. (To waitress.) *Arigatou gozaimasu.*

ISABEL: No dears, I know a sister when I see one. *Maraming Salamat.* (Waitress smiles widely.)

WAITRESS: *Walang anuman.* [Translation: You are quite welcome.]

ISABEL: Ahhh, yes, I do love it here.

(Waitress exits.)

Where was I? Oh, yes, I wanted the glamour! I wanted Clark Gable and Douglas Fairbanks! I wanted Beverly Hills! I thought coming to the U.S. was the next big step.

OYUKI: And you turned into his caged bird.

ISABEL: A prisoner in a penthouse suite in Washington. How miserable. I told him I wanted to go to law school. You know what the general's response was?

OYUKI (tipsy): Bend over?

ANNA: You're hopeless.

ISABEL: He comes home with a black negligee and tells me my duty lay in bed.

OYUKI (in her own world, drinking more): Bastard. The nerve.

ISABEL: So I snuck out and found men in every level of politics in D.C. I'm proud to say that I was most influential in the House and the Senate, whispering policy changes into the ears of many a man over nightcaps. Those were my most politically active years.

SARAH: But you acted, too, right?

ISABEL: Politics is the biggest stage in the world!

ANNA: Sarah, lesson number two is conversational skills. Note: veer with all your might away from overused clichés.

SARAH: Yes, ma'am.

ISABEL: No, I did go to Hollywood, but no one would have me. *(Reflective.)* Looking back, it probably would have been best to return to the Philippines. MacArthur tried to send me back.

OYUKI: Bastard.

ISABEL: But, I was stubborn. *(Suddenly sad.)* The thought of returning home empty-handed, to have to face my family . . . I couldn't do it. No, I was in the States and, damn it, I was determined to make it.

ANNA: Ahh, yet another deluded soul.

OYUKI *(drunk)*: Where's the food? Did we order? I'd like octopus. I'm in the mood. Ohh, I think I'm a bit drunk.

ANNA: None of this at all should sway you from your ambitions, though, Sarah. All of this is so long ago, and the future is full of promise for you, dear.

OYUKI: What happened to your rule against overused clichés?

ANNA: No, all of our chatter is just birds fretting about a different time and place.

ISABEL: As far as I can see, we're still in *la ciudad de los angeles, mi amor.*

ANNA: Indeed, but darling, nothing stands in the way anymore. As you said, Isabel, there are no longer laws forbidding my favorite pastime, kissing.

ISABEL: That didn't stop Marlene from trying with you, Anna!

ANNA: Dear, as I said before, no need to dredge up the past.

ISABEL: Hmmm . . .

ANNA: So you get to legitimately lock lips onscreen nowadays. Am I right, Sarah?

SARAH: That's right.

ANNA: With no contractual terms binding your onscreen death?

SARAH: Correct.

ANNA: Ummm, how delicious.

ISABEL: Well, are you the lead?

SARAH: No. I'm in a supporting role.

ISABEL: Are you listening, Anna? A supporting role and no lines. Anna?

ANNA *(distracted)*: Sorry, I was still thinking about the kissing. What did I miss?

OYUKI *(drunk)*: Supporting role, no lines.

SARAH: Yes.

ANNA: Hmmm, perhaps I'll take back what I said about progress. Reminds me of *Shanghai Express* . . .

ISABEL: What about *The Good Earth?*

ANNA *(suddenly bitter)*: How could I forget? Playing second fiddle to Marlene and losing out to Luise Rainer were not easy pills to swallow.

OYUKI: Who has pills?

SARAH: But, Anna, I actually love the part. I have to start somewhere, right?

ANNA *(touched)*: Yes, dear, you are right. You see, Isabel, this is where being classy pays off in this business.

ISABEL: Humph.

OYUKI *(in her own world)*: Valium.

ANNA: Although I do have to say that you have the option to gracefully bow out. I did, for *The Good Earth*. I was passed over for the lead in a film about Chinese people late in my career. All of the roles went to white actors, for god's sake. And then, dear hearts, I was offered the role of a thief, the only role that portrayed the Chinese in a bad light . . . with my Chinese blood, I couldn't do it.

ISABEL: Good for you.

SARAH: Didn't Mary Wong take your part?

ANNA *(quietly)*: Yes.

ISABEL: That's right. And shortly afterwards, she took her life. Like me.

ANNA: Yes, she hung herself here in the City of Angels in 1940. God rest her soul.

(They all drink.)

ISABEL: But, don't worry, girls. I saw her at an audition yesterday. She's looking fabulous. I think she signed up for a personal trainer.

ANNA: And, to be honest, and I'll just share this with you ladies in confidence. The night that Luise won the Oscar, I wept for hours. I left my flat and found myself aimlessly wandering the night by streetlamp, thinking that if something horrid happened to me, it wouldn't matter a bit. I ended up at the ocean, watching the tide come in and go out until sunrise.

ISABEL: But at least you made it through. You survived it. Mary didn't. I didn't.

OYUKI *(very drunk)*: I did.

ISABEL: No one was intrigued with us. I couldn't bear being shunned. So, you see, dear Anna, you earned your place in history. You live on. But I ended it, and I'm forgotten. On my gravestone, it read only: "Isabel Rosario Cooper, a.k.a, Dimples. 1910–1960. Freelance Actress."

OYUKI: It should have read, "Tortured and Misled by MacArthur: Hypocrite, Misogynist, and Bastard."

ISABEL (*in her own world*): Yes.

ANNA: Yes, I did survive it, but opportunities never presented themselves in my lifetime either. Real opportunities to be someone closer to myself onscreen, that is. I always existed as illusions in other people's minds. (*Smiling, to Sarah.*) You, on the other hand, darling, have tremendous doors open, I imagine. I do envy you a bit, I must admit.

OYUKI: Me, too.

ISABEL: Me, too.

OYUKI (*getting back on track*): So, you're a supporting role, and what is the story about?

ANNA: I hope it's about me. I had quite a fascinating life, darling.

OYUKI: Don't forget me. The Cherry Dances . . .

ISABEL: Or me! Oh, Anna! That would be divine. What a scrumptious idea!

ANNA: What can I say?

SARAH: Unfortunately, no.

ANNA, OYUKI, AND ISABEL (*pausing, then disappointed*): Ohhh.

ANNA (*disappointed*): Ahh, damn, one can only wish. Well, what's the storyline?

SARAH: It's about the rise of P. T. Barnum and his traveling circus.

ANNA: And who, my dear, are you?

SARAH: I'm one of his exhibits.

ISABEL: I don't understand.

SARAH: I play Afong Moy, the first Chinese woman to come to America. She was one of his most successful displays. She drew 20,000 onlookers in six days. And didn't speak a word of English. . . . But the film is mostly about P. T. Barnum.

(*Long, awkward silence.*)

ANNA: Another bottle of wine, darlings, what do you say?

Blackout.

SCENE 3

Chinatown, New York, 2004.

Morning, one year earlier. Lights up on a cluttered office: old coffee cups, Dunkin' Donuts bags, head shots strewn on the desk, etc. This is A+ Talent Agency in Chinatown. Barb sits at a small desk looking at her computer. Framed photographs of her family are buried under paper on her desk. She has on a suit with tennis shoes; she looks sweaty and tired. She has been in the talent business for more than twenty years. Barb speaks fast, with a thick New York accent. April sits at a much tidier desk. She is Barb's newest and only employee; she is ambitious and optimistic. It is a hot, cramped office.

APRIL *(looking at her computer)*: Five new girls, hmmm, one handsome guy. Just arrived from London, looks mixed. Wow, six feet.

BARB *(crossing to April's desk)*: Lemme see. Not bad. He can do some damage. When's he coming in?

APRIL: I'll schedule him for next Thursday. Does that work for you?

BARB *(crossing back to her desk)*: No, honey, bring him in tomorrow, make it work. I need a little eye candy.

APRIL: Got it. And did you hear about the new Meryl Streep film they're casting? Set in Thailand. She's in the Peace Corps, teaching English abroad. Need twenty-five young men and women ages eighteen to twenty-four.

BARB: Is it called *Out of Thailand*? Some originality folks, please. Which office?

APRIL: Jacobson Casting. Starting Wednesday.

BARB: Jesus, they don't give these kids time to prep. How many sides?

APRIL: They just want to put them all on tape, see how pretty they are.

BARB: OK, then call the models, too. But keep them shorter, under five foot six. That's what they'll want. And we gotta send out the smarties, too. 'Cuz if they can't walk and talk, we'll hear about it. Who's producing?

APRIL: Dreamworks.

BARB: Oh, I see. Now, they come to us. . . . Well, I can't complain. If we book half of these, I can get my ass to the Bahamas this year. We gotta get on this pronto. I'll get on the follow-ups from yesterday; you find a hundred to send out to Jacobson.

APRIL: Got it. *(Grabbing her purse and getting up.)* I'm gonna get bagels and coffee before the madness.

BARB: You're a doll, that's why I keep you around.

APRIL: I thought it was 'cuz I am so good at what I do.

BARB: Ai ya!

(April exits. Barb watches her leave, then sneaks a donut or two from her purse and is changing from her walking shoes into heels when Sarah enters.)

SARAH: Excuse me?

(Barb pops up from behind her desk, mouth full of donuts.)

Mrs. Lee? I'm sorry.

*(Barb tries to speak, but her mouth is full. She has on one heel
and is holding her tennis shoe.)*

I'm your ten o'clock. I'm a little early, and I didn't see a waiting
room.

BARB *(mouth full)*: No, come on in, sweetie. Have a seat. Lemme get situated. *(She plops down ungracefully.)* I'm Barb. Barb Lee.

SARAH: Nice to meet you.

BARB *(shuffling through a pile of head shots)*: Now, remind me, how did we
hear about you?

SARAH: April came to my show last week . . . down in the village?

BARB: *(She obviously doesn't have a clue what show it was.)* Right, right. What
was it called?

SARAH: *From the Nile to Yangtze, Tales of Sisterhood.*

BARB: *(Laughs.)* How could I forget? *(Jokingly.)* Wow, it's headed for Broadway, right?

SARAH *(sarcastically)*: Yeah, right.

BARB: You got a résumé? Refresh my memory, what's your name?

SARAH *(giving Barb her résumé)*: Sarah Kim.

BARB: Oh, that's right. OK, OK, it's coming back to me now, the fog is
slowly lifting. I haven't had my coffee yet. *(Looking over résumé.)* Lemme
see, you graduated from <u>Brown</u> in '05, double major in acting and <u>busi</u>-
ness, smart girl.

SARAH: Thanks.

(April enters carrying the coffee and bagels. She doesn't notice Sarah.)

APRIL: Here we go, our ammunition for the day to kill the dreams of many
a young person. . . . *(Seeing Sarah.)* Oh, excuse me . . . good morning.
You must be . . .

SARAH: Sarah Kim.

APRIL: Right, from the show at The Culture Project.

SARAH: Yes.

BARB: This is April, Sarah. She's my eyes and ears and caffeinator in this
city. She's also known as a bright and deluded cheerleader except when
she occasionally comes in and ruins dreams.

APRIL: I think there was a compliment in there somewhere.

BARB: Good luck searching for it.

APRIL *(to Sarah)*: Hey, sorry about that. We have to have a sense of humor
in here.

SARAH: That's OK. I get it.

APRIL: It's good to see you again, Sarah. Wow, you were sooo great. You
totally stole that show.

SARAH: Well, it was more like I was trying to save the show.

BARB: Honey, just take the compliment.

SARAH *(to April)*: Thank you.

APRIL *(to Sarah)*: I told Barb we had to bring you in. You have sooo much potential.

SARAH: Thank you!

BARB: Well, now that we're all nicey-nicey, let's move on before the phones start killing us.

SARAH *(sitting at her desk)*: Sure, I'll start on the hundred for Dreamworks and schedule Mr. Beautiful. Don't mind me.

BARB: So, Sarah Kim, why are you here?

SARAH: I want to break into film.

BARB: You and ten million other girls, honey.

SARAH: April told me that you represent Asian American talent exclusively and that you're in with all of the casting agents for the movie houses.

BARB *(jokingly)*: April, you been talking about me?

APRIL: Sorry, Barb.

BARB: Go on.

SARAH: I just want to cover all my bases.

BARB: Do you have other representation?

SARAH: Yes, I have a manager and an agent.

BARB: Who?

SARAH: I'm with Henderson and Klein.

BARB: Not bad. You're not exclusive?

SARAH: No.

BARB *(looking over résumé)*: Huh, Disneyland commercial. You got a few nationals.

SARAH: Yes.

BARB *(impressed)*: Musicals, Broadway. TV: *Law and Order*—you were Rape Victim Number Four. That's a big accomplishment. And *Boston Public*, Student Number Twelve. *(She looks Sarah over for a bit.)* Hmmm, and, April, she can sing?

APRIL *(from offstage)*: Amazing.

BARB *(suddenly more reflective)*: And what are your goals, long term? I'm asking 'cuz it helps us to know that you're in this for the long haul.

SARAH: Oh, I definitely am. This is all I've ever wanted since I was a kid.

BARB *(loudly)*: Why?

SARAH: I don't know.

(Barb crosses to sit on the desk, speaking a bit too close to Sarah's face.)

BARB: Well, I know it sounds like a silly question, honey. But it actually tells me a lot about who you are, so *(loudly, in Sarah's face)* WHY?

SARAH: I think I just . . . wanted to be . . .

BARB: Rich and famous?

SARAH: No, just for people to see me. I grew up in a small town.

BARB: Where?

SARAH: Avon, Ohio.

BARB: Never heard of it. Go on.

SARAH: I don't know, there weren't a lot of other Asian families, I was pretty shy. . . . Is this what you want to know?

BARB: I know, it feels like group therapy, but *a lot* of actors come through here. Most of them have the chops, but we lose them 'cuz it's a brutal business. We wanna see if you're gonna jump ship when the shit hits the fan.

APRIL: You know, only the strong survive.

SARAH (*determined*): Right. OK, well, I just wanted to be successful, to be seen and heard, I guess. I think when I was in my first school play, I think I was in third grade, around eight years old.

APRIL: Who did you play?

SARAH: It's silly. I played Dorothy. I didn't even know I could really sing. I thought I would get cast as Toto or something, run around the stage barking. But I got the lead, and my parents and everyone . . . well, I loved it. And then it all stopped.

BARB: What stopped?

APRIL (*jokingly*): Time?

BARB (*smiling, to April*): Stop it.

SARAH (*laughing*): No, all of the teasing, all of the feeling invisible, basically . . . Honestly, I wasn't expecting these kinds of questions.

APRIL: What'd you think we'd want to know?

SARAH: I don't know—like, what my singing range was.

APRIL: That stuff is easy. Barb asks the hard questions first. Talent actually isn't the most important thing; it's how much fight you have.

BARB (*sarcastically*): Yeah, like I said, group therapy. We'll pass around the bunny in a bit.

SARAH: And . . . I do want to win an Academy Award.

BARB: (*Pause, then speaks as she crosses to sit down at her desk.*) Well, I'd like to walk around the Village braless, but then reality sets in.

APRIL: You mean gravity.

BARB (*to April*): Watch it, girlie. (*To Sarah.*) Well, one step at a time. I hate to break it to you, but you're not gonna get cast like that in New York or L.A.

SARAH: I know.

APRIL: No *Wizard of Oz*, Miss Dorothy, but maybe *Miss Saigon*.

BARB: Yes, for sure, *Miss Saigon*. It's what sells; it'll pay your bills.

SARAH: Ugh, really?

APRIL: Yeah, this ain't Kansas.

BARB (*looking over her bifocals*): You think you can handle it?

SARAH: Sure.

BARB: I think you have a good look; you'll do well. You could play student or young mother.

APRIL: And everything in between.

SARAH: Really?

BARB: Yeah. . . . (*Looking at watch.*) Well, honey, I like you. We'll try you out.

SARAH: Seriously?

BARB: Yeah, come in tomorrow around. . . . (*Looks to April.*)

APRIL (*looking at computer screen to schedule her*): 1:30.

BARB: 1:30, and we'll get your contracts ready, sign you non-exclusively for six months and see how it goes.

APRIL: Wow, thank you!

BARB: We'll send you out to L.A. for pilot season or if any big films come our way, so stash your piggybank, honey. You'll be flying a lot.

APRIL: Most of our talent is bicoastal.

BARB: Yeah, you gotta play for both teams. The Yankees and the Dodgers.

SARAH: That's fine. I am already bicoastal. I've been bicoastal for a while.

BARB: Well, what you do with your sex life is none of our business.

APRIL (*laughing*): Barb, you kill me!

BARB (*laughing*): I kill me, too! (*Suddenly very serious.*) It's a weird business, you gotta think of yourself as a tennis ball with Velcro. We throw you up against the wall and see where you stick.

APRIL (*laughing*): Sarah, I'm warning you, she's the weird analogy queen. She says this to all of the new talent.

BARB: Or, actually, think of yourself as a . . . hotdog. We throw you into the fire and see what burns. Or try to get you out before you burn.

APRIL: How bout a marshmallow?

BARB: Or a shrinky-dink.

APRIL: See what I mean?

SARAH (*uncertain*): Sounds great.

BARB: You're gonna get weird auditions, and I say just go with it for now.

SARAH: What kind of weird auditions?

(*Barb and April look to each other.*)

BARB AND APRIL: You have no idea.

Blackout.

SCENE 4

Stage transforms to an audition scene, one chair at center stage. Three spotlights up on three women. They are warming up. The casting director stands in the audience. A bit of improv and interaction of casting director with audience is encouraged. The casting director is running three separate auditions simultaneously.

CASTING DIRECTOR (*to Woman 3*): Ready, set, go!

WOMAN 3: My name is Mai Lee. I used to work in the ricefields.

CASTING DIRECTOR: Can you try an accent?

WOMAN 3: But isn't this set in Hawaii?

CASTING DIRECTOR: Yes.

WOMAN 3 (*confused but fully committed with strange accent*): My name is Mai Lee. I used to work in the ricefields. All my parents were killed, my mother and my father. . . .

CASTING DIRECTOR: You sound German.

WOMAN 3: Sorry.

CASTING DIRECTOR (*to Woman 1*): Can you do a haiku?

WOMAN 1: Do a haiku?

CASTING DIRECTOR: Yes.

WOMAN 2: Isn't this an audition for a sitcom?

CASTING DIRECTOR: Yes.

WOMAN 1 (*very uncomfortable*):

Haikus are easy.
But sometimes they don't make sense.
Refrigerator.

CASTING DIRECTOR (*to Woman 2*): I'd like to see you put chopsticks in your hair and hold some rice.

WOMAN 2: But isn't this an audition for *Hamlet*?

CASTING DIRECTOR: It's a concept play.

(*Woman 2 pulls out chopsticks and puts them in her hair as stagehand enters and hands her sushi.*)

WOMAN 2 (*pretending to hand out grains of rice*): Here's fennel for you, and columbines. And there's rue for you, and some for me.

CASTING DIRECTOR: Good. (*To all three women.*) I'd like to see some cleavage please?

(*All three women try to push their boobs up and together, not very successfully.*)

CASTING DIRECTOR: Cleavage! (*To Woman 1.*) Can you hold a belt over your head and growl?

WOMAN 1 (*holding hands up*): Grrrrrrrr!

CASTING DIRECTOR: Great, thank you. *(To Woman 2.)* Next!

WOMAN 2 *(with bad Asian accent)*: What you want? You know, I got double-dildo for you. You like?

CASTING DIRECTOR: This is a frat boy comedy, ladies! You gotta turn on the boys in the suburbs—some humor, please!

WOMAN 1 and WOMAN 3: *(Repeat together.)* What you want? You know, I got double-dildo for you. You like?

CASTING DIRECTOR: That's more like it. *(To all women.)* Can I see some martial arts?

(All women do so badly.)

CASTING DIRECTOR: That wasn't very convincing! Do you want the job or not? Once more, with feeling!

*(All women repeat made-up martial arts badly,
but with much more commitment.)*

CASTING DIRECTOR: That's more like it! *(To all women.)* I'd like to hear you read for Delivery Boy Number Two.

ALL WOMEN: But I'm female.

CASTING DIRECTOR: Doesn't really matter, right?

ALL: Hi dere, I ha yo pork lo mein an fried rice. Seven dolla, please.

CASTING DIRECTOR: Thank you. Next!

WOMAN 3: Umbrella, umbrella, umbrella. Si' dollar for you. OK, fi' dolla, fi' dolla.

CASTING DIRECTOR: Next!

(Woman 3 exits.)

WOMAN 1: Hey, Yankee, fifteen dolla, I give you little sucky-sucky. You like, I love you long time.

CASTING DIRECTOR: Next!

(Woman 1 exits. Single spotlight remains on Woman 2 at center stage.)

I'd like to see you walk.

(Woman 2 does so, awkwardly and self-conscious.)

Use Chinese feet, please.

(Woman 2 tries taking smaller steps, scooting along awkwardly.)

I'd like to see you sit.

(*Woman 2 does so.*)

Can you eat with chopsticks?
WOMAN 2 (*obviously frustrated*): Of course, I can. What do I look like?
CASTING DIRECTOR: Pardon me?
WOMAN 2 (*with forced politeness*): Yes, I can.
CASTING DIRECTOR: (*Crosses onto the stage, approaching Woman 2.*) Can I watch?

(*Woman 2 does so.*)

I'd like to hear you count in Chinese.

(*Woman 2 does so. Her morale is beaten down by this point.*)

WOMAN 2: Eee, Arr, San, Suu, Ooh, Lio, Chi, Ba, Djo, Shur.
CASTING DIRECTOR: Look at me?

(*Woman 2 does so, determined yet suddenly conscious of the audience.*)

(*Mesmerized.*) Great. Freeze.

(*Woman 2 finishes by looking straight out, in the same position as
Afong Moy at the end of Scene 1.*)

Blackout.

SCENE 5

In the ether, suspended in time.

Stage left, spotlight up on Sarah 1 as Kim from Miss Saigon. *This is her
performance; she sings the final song of the show.*

SARAH 1 (*as Kim*):
*Now Tam
my brave boy
our long wait
has ended
Smile Tam
For you have a father
At last*

He has come
To take you home
All I dreamed for you
He'll do
You're still mine
But I can't go along
Don't be sad
Though I'm far away
I'll be watching you
This is the hour
I swore I'd see
I alone can tell now
What the end will be
Look at me one last time
Don't forget what you see
One more kiss
And then say good-bye

(*Second spotlight comes up on Sarah 2 as Madame Butterfly singing.*
The two interweave and overlap. A true duet.)

SARAH 2 (*as Madame Butterfly*):

Tu? tu? tu? tu?	*You? You? You?*
Piccolo ididio!	*Little idol of my heart,*
Amore, amore mio.	*My love, my love,*
Fior di giglio e di rosa.	*flower of the lily and rose,*
Non saperio mai . . . per te,	*Never know that, for you,*
Pei tuoi puri occhi	*For your innocent eyes,*
Muore Butterfly . . .	*Butterfly is about to die...*
Perche tu possa andar	*So that you may go*
Di la dai mare	*Away beyond the sea*
Senza che ti rimorda	*Without being subject to remorse*
Ai di maturi	*In later years*
Il materno abbandono.	*For your mother's desertion.*
O a me, sceso dal trono	*Oh, you who have come down to me*
Dell'alto Paradiso,	*From high heaven,*
Guarda ben fiso, fiso,	*Look well, well*
Di tua madre la faccia!	*On your mother's face,*
Che ten'resti unatraccia,	*That you may keep a faint memory of it,*
Guarda ben!	*Look well!*
Amore, addio, addio!	*Little love, farewell!*
Piccolo amore!	*Farewell, my little love!*
Va, gioca, gioca.	*Go and play.*

(Kim and Madame Butterfly go behind a screen. In silhouette, we see Kim raise a gun to her head and Madame Butterfly reveal a knife. The gunshot and the fatal wound happen simultaneously. Both women fall and are still. Lights out on silhouette.)

(Woman enters; she is Sarah 3. She recites the following from Hamlet. *The following monologue is spoken within the context of the dilemma of being an Asian American actress, of choosing or choosing not to portray stereotypes in order to work—that is, to exist on stage.)*

SARAH 3 *(as Hamlet)*:

To be, or not to be, that is the question:
Whether 'tis nobler in the mind to suffer
The slings and arrows of outrageous fortune,
Or to take arms against a sea of troubles,
And by opposing, end them. To die, to sleep—
No more, and by a sleep to say we end
The heart-ache and the thousand natural shocks
That flesh is heir to; 'tis a consummation
Devoutly to be wish'd. To die, to sleep—
To sleep, perchance to dream—ay, there's the rub,
For in that sleep of death what dreams may come,
When we have shuffled off this mortal coil,
Must give us pause; there's the respect
That makes calamity of so long life:
For who would bear the whips and scorns of time,
Th' oppressor's wrong, the proud man's contumely,
The pangs of despis'd love, the law's delay,
The insolence of office, and the spurns
That patient merit of th' unworthy takes,
When he himself might his quietus make
With a bare bodkin; who would fardels bear,
To grunt and sweat under a weary life,
But that the dread of something after death,
The undiscover'd country, from whose bourn
No traveler returns, puzzles the will,
And makes us rather bear those ills we have,
Than fly to others that we know not of?

(She looks to the screen where we last saw Kim and Butterfly, considering
the security they offer of consistent work.)

Thus conscience does make cowards [of us all],
And thus the native hue of resolution

Is sicklied o'er with the pale cast of thought,
And enterprises of great pitch and moment
With this regard their currents turn awry,
And lose the name of action.

(Sarah 3 surrenders her courage to fight against playing the stereotypes.
She begins to move, a dance with breath audible. As she moves, lights
come up on the other three women who join her in movement. It is a
dance of frustration and what lies beneath the surface, what is not shown.
Sound is a techno-jumble of contemporary songs that refer to Asian
women: David Bowie's "China Girl," "One Night in Bangkok," "Turning
Japanese," "We Are Siamese," as well as classics from Madame Butterfly,
Miss Saigon, *women breathing, women's voices, audio clips from Anna*
May Wong and Isabel Cooper movies, The Good Earth, Apocalypse Now
("Me love you long time"), and other American films about Vietnam, doors
 slamming, etc. It is a mish-mash of sampling; it is, chaotic, funny, with
pockets of silence where we just hear the women onstage breathing as they
dance. The movement sequence is aggressive, revisiting stereotypes, solos,
duets, and all four women moving together. It is percussive. It builds to a
climax.)

Blackout.

SCENE 6

In the ether.

In blackout, we hear sound of jumprope. Spotlight up on woman jumping
rope upstage as a young girl. Second girl enters and bounces ball against the
wall. Third girl enters and plays hopscotch. Percussive harmony. Second
and third girl stop, cross to either side of the stage and sit. Both are sitting
on the floor, tying their shoes. Woman jumping rope speaks. She is Sarah
4. Somewhere in the following, she stops jumping rope.[1]

SARAH 4:
Yellow girl sits on concrete step
Yellow girl sits alone on white concrete step
Pulls the laces of her shoes tight,
tight so they don't come undone,
tight so the blood pumps hard in her feet,
tight so she knows she's alive,
and the day, the morning is hers, and maybe

1. The poem "Yellow Girl," by Katie Hae Leo, is used by permission of the author.

the sunlight, the cool black slick of the playground,
maybe the shadows too, the dark cloud of the convent,
and the children that flow like tributaries from the cafeteria line
and the church that sings its noontime song.
Maybe it all belongs to her today.
Maybe today is different.

> *(The two girls stand and look down center stage*
> *with hope and excitement.)*

She stands, her eight-year-old toes on the kickball diamond,
at a crossroad between two lines,
when outta nowhere
hey, girl!

> *(The girls look at each other as if the taunts are coming from the other.)*

hey, chink, can you see outta those eyes?
hey, flat face, did you get hit by a truck?
and it's like a breath
was stolen
straight out of her lungs,
like a punch

> *(Two girls face out and crumple, as if punched, and slowly*
> *descend into kneeling positions.)*

but slower,
a punch that takes years,
and she wants to tell them

> *(Two girls stay in kneeling position and look out downstage,*
> *focused and fuming.)*

her face isn't flat and she can see just fine,
wants to tell them maybe
she is Anna May Wong,
silent movie star,
Anna May Wong made forty Hollywood films

GIRL 1 *(stands)*:
    did you know that, punks?
    bet not
    bet you can't even read

SARAH 4:

> Her name meant "yellow willows," and she rose
> from the murky waters of Hollywood
> and lit up the sky with her skin

GIRL 2 (*stands*):

> what's your name mean?
> bet you don't even know
> bet it means something like uncombed greasy haired pimplefaced
> momforgottobuyyoupantsthatfitthisyear punkass

SARAH 4:

> She wants to tell those girls she's Isabel Rosario Cooper,
> flower of the Philippines,
> famous at sixteen,
> first Filipina actress to kiss on screen,
> or Oyuki, the fiercest geisha in her time, in anybody's time

GIRL 1 and GIRL 2:

> damn straight before your time punks

> (*The girls jump facing sideways and begin slowly, playfully doing
> tightrope walking in opposite directions. Sarah 4 stands between them.*)

SARAH 4:

> Oyuki, who could make the men melt with one twitch of her pinky
>   finger
> (and some women too), in whose voice the rich Japanese earth still
>   lived,
> or the Trung sisters, warrior women of Vietnam,
> or Lai Choi San, the most dangerous female pirate of the South China
>   seas,
> Yeah, maybe that's who she is.

> (*The girls begin slowly jumping rope throughout the following sentence;
>   it speeds to a frenzy and ends in a yell of delight.*)

> So yellow girl breaks out fourteen or fifteen Kung Fu Karate Tae
>   Kwon Do
> pirate geisha silent film star moves
> and throws down a little white whoop-ass!

> (*Beat.*)

(The girls line up behind Sarah 4, braiding
one another's hair.)

OK, here's the truth:
The year is 1979 and yellow girl wants most of all
to be like Anna May Wong, only she doesn't know it yet.
Isabel Rosario Cooper isn't taught at St. Lawrence School,
the Trung sisters are far away from Avon, Ohio,
and she won't know about Oyuki for many years.
The truth is, to this eight year-old Midwestern yellow girl,
Asians are still somebody else.

But somewhere inside her,
in the deep down marrow of her bones,
yellow girl feels the dim, distant heartbeat
of all the women on whose shoulders she stands,
unsteady on eight year-old toes,
their blood feeding hers, rivers of ancient memory
forming veins in her hands, and she reaches for them
without knowing their names.

If only yellow girl knew about Lai Choi San,
maybe she wouldn't grow up feeling
like herself
in that moment,
toes at the crossroads between two worlds—
America—Asia—
never quite in one, never knowing about the other.
Maybe she wouldn't waste so much time
worrying about how her one bang falls across her forehead.

(All three wipe bangs. All three stay looking out, as if in mirrors,
simply as blank slates.)

Is she funny enough, pretty enough, smart enough?
Maybe she could look in the mirror and see
a fierce Asian woman, not a shy yellow girl.

(During the following, the girls peel away one by one.
Sarah 4 sits alone onstage.)

But this is 1979, and she is the only Asian in the whole second grade
only Asian in her school,

only Asian she knows,
except for the ones on M*A*S*H, and she doesn't think she's like them
  anyway

(Sarah 4 starts to exit. She stops and turns to the audience . . .)

but someday . . .
she'll wake from the gray haze of childhood
and remember

(Pause.)

who they *are and*
who she *is*

one of them

someday . . .

somewhere . . .

Blackout.

SCENE 7

In the ether.

Dorothy enters in full costume, blue dress, blue ribbons in her pigtails, etc.

DOROTHY: Some place where there isn't any trouble. Do you suppose there is such a place, Toto? There must be. It's not a place you can get to by a boat or a train. It's far far away. Behind the moon. Behind the rain . . .

(Throughout the song, stereotypes enter: a dragon lady, a Japanese tourist, and a rice paddy planter. Dorothy notices each one as she sings. She doesn't like them, but they insist on upstaging her. She pulls out a knife as she continues to sing. She kills each one of them in succession. She motions the stagehand offstage to drag each one off. It is funny and demented. She finishes the song with a flourish.)

Somewhere over the rainbow
Way up high

There's a land that I heard of
Once in a lullaby

Somewhere over the rainbow
Skies are blue
And the dreams that you dare to dream
Really do come true

Someday I'll wish upon a star
And wake up where the clouds are far behind me
Where troubles melt like lemondrops
Away above the chimney tops
That's where you'll find me

Somewhere over the rainbow
Bluebirds fly
Birds fly over the rainbow
Why then, oh why can't I?

Some day I'll wish upon a star
And wake up where the clouds are far behind me
Where troubles melt like lemondrops
Away above the chimney tops
That's where you'll find me

Somewhere over the rainbow
Bluebirds fly
Birds fly over the rainbow
Why then, oh why can't I?

If happy little bluebirds fly
Beyond the rainbow
Why, oh why can't I?

(*Spoken.*) **Come on, Toto!** (*Exits.*)

(*Awkward moment with dragon lady lying dead onstage. Finally, stagehand drags her toward stage right. Dragon lady stands up on her own, dusts herself off, and strides off stage right. Stagehand follows.*)

Blackout.

SCENE 8

Seoul, Korea, 2009.

It's the Korean premiere of the P. T. Barnum film. One year after the dinner party. Lights up on a red carpet. A glamorous Asian American woman walks along and stops to pose for pictures. It is Sarah. Cameras are flashing. Screaming Korean girls are trying to get her autograph.

GIRL 1 and GIRL 2 *(in Korean)*: Sarah, can I take a picture with you? Oh my god! Oh my god! Sarah, it's you! Arghhhh!
SARAH: Ne, ne.

> *(Girl 1 poses with Sarah. Girl 2 takes picture.)*

GIRL 1 and GIRL 2: Oh, kamsahamnida, kamsahamnida!
GIRL 2 *(in Korean)*: Sarah, (can we take a picture, all of us)?![2]
SARAH: Ne, ne.

> *(All three pose, Girl 2 holds camera out and takes a picture
> of them scrunched together awkwardly.)*

GIRL 1 *(in Korean)*: (Let me see!)

> *(Grabbing camera, the two girls look together, giggling.)*

GIRL 2 *(in Korean)*: Oh, (so cute. Sarah, do you want to see?)
SARAH: Ne, ne.

> *(Sarah looks at the picture with them. Han Yoo enters and approaches
> Sarah, waiting her turn. She is sixteen. She is pretty, smart, and bookish.)*

GIRL 1 and GIRL 2: Oh, kamsahamnida, kamsahamnida. (You're so cool!
Bye! Arghhhh!)

> *(Girls exit screaming.)*

HAN YOO *(in perfect English)*: Sarah!! Can I get an autograph, please?!
SARAH *(taking Han Yoo's autograph book)*: Ne, ne. Ee rheum ee muh ya?
[Translation: What's your name?]

---

2. Text in parentheses indicates the English translation of dialogue that can be spoken in Korean. It is the director's choice, depending on the audience, whether the lines will be spoken in Korean or a mixture of Korean and English.

HAN YOO: Han Yoo.

SARAH (*signing her book*): "Han Yoo ae gae . . . " (*"Dear Han Yoo . . ."*)

HAN YOO (*in Korean*): (Oh my god, you're writing my name!)

SARAH: Ne . . .

HAN YOO (*in English*): I can't believe it's you!

SARAH: Wow, your English is flawless.

HAN YOO: Well, it should be. I'm American.

SARAH: Oh, really? What brings you here?

HAN YOO: I'm on vacation with my family. Pretty awesome.

SARAH: Yes, Korea is beautiful.

HAN YOO: No, I meant your premiere! I am so your biggest fan. *(Praying.)* Wow, thank you Lord God!

SARAH: Well, I hope you're getting more out of Korea than my premiere. You can see this film in the States.

HAN YOO: I know, but Korea's soooo boring. I mean, seeing you is like the best thing about this trip.

SARAH: I'm not sure that's a good thing.

HAN YOO: I mean, you totally steal the film! Screw P. T. Barnum! I mean, he's amazing and all, but YOU are sooo great! Like the way you sit there. It's like you're talking even though you're not talking at all.

SARAH: Thanks.

HAN YOO: And we are so both Korean! I know you play a Chinese lady, but we all look the same, right?

SARAH: Right.

HAN YOO: Yeah, it's like *Memoirs of a Geisha*. Like, all of the actresses were Chinese playing Japanese-speaking English. That was so messed up.

SARAH: I auditioned for that.

HAN YOO: For real? Awww, you would have been so great.

SARAH: Thank you, but Zhang Ziyi is more famous than any of us in the States.

HAN YOO: That's nuts. Like, you gotta do karate to be famous.

SARAH (*smiling*): Yes, something like that.

HAN YOO: But Zhang Ziyi wasn't nominated for an Oscar. You were.

SARAH (*flattered*): Well . . .

HAN YOO: Like if you win the Oscar, Lord God almighty, you'd be like the first ever!

SARAH: Pardon?

HAN YOO: First ever Asian American woman. Like that is sooo cool.

SARAH: No, I'd be the second.

HAN YOO: No way!

SARAH: Yes.

HAN YOO: Who? When? Dude!

SARAH: Miyoshi Umeki won Best Supporting Actress for the film *Sayonara*.

HAN YOO: Oh, I thought you were going to say Lucy Liu or something back in the eighties.

SARAH: Well, Miyoshi won in *1957.*

HAN YOO (*embarrassed*): Oh, dude. You totally look great for your age. (*Realizes she's put her foot in her mouth.*) No offense.

SARAH (*smiling*): No offense taken.

HAN YOO: I know, sorry. I think . . . I think I talk faster than I think. (*She's confused and talking to herself, trying to calm her hyperactivity.*) . . . I think. . . . Is that right? Yeah. Ugh, chill, Han Yoo. (*Suddenly trying hard to appear very mature to Sarah.*) So you would be like the second?

SARAH: Yes.

HAN YOO: But she wasn't American.

SARAH: Pardon?

HAN YOO: I mean, technically, *was she* American? 'Cuz the name is totally Japanese.

SARAH: (*Pause.*) You're right.

HAN YOO: So, you would be the first Asian *American* woman?

SARAH: Yes!

HAN YOO: Holla!

SARAH: Yes. You're a bright girl. I stand corrected. I can't really think about it. It seems ridiculous.

HAN YOO: No, Sarah. You are amazing! I mean, you don't do a lot, but when you're onscreen, well . . . I love it. 'Cuz I don't get to see that. I mean, when I'm a movie star, I'm going to be just like you. Like, I'm not doing any karate—that's for sure.

SARAH: Is that so?

HAN YOO: Oh yeah.

SARAH: You want to act?

HAN YOO: Yeah! Well, basically I just want men to drool over me, and I'll have to break all their hearts to go shoot a film. 'Cuz that's what I want to do. Break A LOT of hearts. And I mean, like, thousands, like you!

SARAH: You're sweet . . .

HAN YOO: Yeah, dude. That's so what Tila Tequila does. Like, I totally want to be as famous as you or her.

SARAH: Tila Tequila?

HAN YOO: Yeah, like it's a total compliment. I mean, she is hot, so by default that means you're hot, too. I actually want to be *more* famous than you and her, like Hannah Montana.

SARAH: Excuse me? . . .

HAN YOO: Totally. I mean, no offense, but you're just like starting your career, she's like already established.

SARAH: What?

HAN YOO: But, you're like following in her footsteps. I guess she like had her dad to get her going, you know, legacy and stuff. But I have to say,

you are so going in the right direction. Like, if you win the Oscar, it
will so boost your career.

SARAH: Will it?

HAN YOO: Oh, sure, I know the inside stuff. Like, I know all your business,
sorry to say. Perez Hilton says that if you win, and that's a big if, you
will be among the names in Hollywood history like Moon Bloodgood
and Maggie Q. He said, and I quote, "Sarah Kim will be among the
women that are famous today but might not be remembered tomorrow." But I totally disagree with that. I think he meant it as a compliment, right?

*(Pause. Sarah drops the autograph book and pen. She does a movement
sequence echoing the dance. She begins to exit. Han Yoo picks up the
autograph book.)*

Are you OK? . . . Sarah, dude? . . . Did I say something wrong? . . .
What? . . .

(Sarah stops and turns to look at Han Yoo.)

Sarah?

(Pause. Sarah hesitates, then is about to speak . . .)

(Noticing someone offstage left.) Ohmygawd! . . . I'm sorry, is that the
guy that played Barnum? Sarah, can you introduce me? . . . Oh, never
mind, that's OK. No way! Oh my gawd!

*(Han Yoo abruptly exits. Sarah stands alone onstage, devastated. Isabel
enters downstage left, looks at Sarah. Then Oyuki enters downstage left.
Both Isabel and Oyuki look at Sarah encouragingly. Sarah smiles weakly.
The women look at one another. Girl enters jumping rope, remain center
stage, facing the audience. The three watch the girl jumping rope. Women
exit slowly. Lights flash on silhouette of Afong Moy. All lights fade except
for spotlight on girl. She continues to jump rope, wondering about the
future. In blackout, we hear her jumproping.)*

Fade out.

END OF PLAY

5

Sia(b)

MAY LEE-YANG

INTRODUCTION, *by Josephine Lee*

Sia(b) was produced by Mu Performing Arts and performed by May Lee-Yang and Katie Ka Vang at the Playwright's Center in Minneapolis from September 13, 2008, to October 5, 2008, under the direction of Robert Karimi.

In the introduction to *Bamboo among the Oaks: Contemporary Writing by Hmong Americans*, the volume's editor, Mai Neng Moua, describes the relative obscurity of Hmong American writers and the more general invisibility of Hmong individuals and communities even in Asian American representation. Despite local awareness of active political figures such as Minnesota State Senator Mee Moua and a vibrant arts culture that includes a literary journal, *Paj Ntaub Voice*, and arts-based organizations such as the Center for Hmong Arts and Talent, as well as writers, filmmakers, artists, and performers, the larger visibility of Hmong Americans persists in "describing us as simple, pre-literate, illiterate, welfare-dependent, and, most recently, violent"—thus the questions raised in May Lee-Yang's play *Sia(b)* about both invisibility and the

Illustration: May Lee-Yang and Katie Ka Vang in *Sia(b)*.
(Photograph used by permission of John Autey Photography.)

stakes of being represented.[1] As Lee-Yang eloquently states in her program notes for the play:

> I used to believe in the phrase "being a voice for the voiceless" but, one day, the implications of this occurred to me. Being Hmong, female, and a host of other titles that have become part of my identity, I realized I'm supposed to be one of those "voiceless people." But, as one of the characters in this play notes, "We are not voiceless. I am not voiceless. I just became a little more quiet along the way to life." *Sia(b)* is my adult journey to rediscovering the voice and person that was inside me. It is not an attempt to speak on behalf of the whole Hmong community. It is simply my story.

The play, however, is far from simple. *Sia(b)* articulates the stakes of telling the personal story and plays with the fine line between autobiography and fiction, ethnic informant and artist. It confronts the anthropological gaze that tries to reduce Hmong people to primitive objects of fascination or to media clichés of needy refugees. It argues both in Hmong and English about the nature of community and the possibility of translation. And perhaps most movingly, it reframes relationships between parents and children as affected not just by differences in assimilation but also by the legacies of the Cold War. Covert Central Intelligence Agency military operations against communism in Southeast Asia during the 1960s and 1970s involved an entire generation of Hmong men, some of whom, like the father in *Sia(b)*, were later forced to flee Laos with their families. The father's tragedy in the play, his loss of face and name, is thus precipitated well before the action of the play begins.

This history haunts the play and yet does not fully define its meaning. With its own quirky voice, new words for familiar pop tunes, and Hulk Hogan, *Sia(b)* refuses to be yet another predictable story of trauma or empowerment.

ABOUT THE PLAY

Sia(b) was created through the New Performance Program at Mu Performing Arts, funded by a grant from the Jerome Foundation.

CHARACTERS (ORIGINAL CAST)

MAY 1 (May Lee-Yang): The playwright (as herself).

MAY 2 (Katie Ka Vang): The actor playing May. Throughout the play, May 2 morphs into different characters, including the following:

---

1. Mai Neng Moua, ed., *Bamboo among the Oaks: Contemporary Writing by Hmong Americans* (St. Paul: Minnesota Historical Society Press, 2002), 7.

- Mom
- Dad
- Mee (sister)
- Houa (brother)
- ESL Teacher
- Katie, the actress, as herself. (*Note:* The actor may substitute her own name for "Katie.")

SCENE 1: OPENING

May 1 enters stage. As she addresses the audience, she moves in the manner of a Hmong person dancing or telling a folktale.

MAY 1: Hi, everyone! My name is May Lee-Yang, and I want to welcome you to *Siab.*

Siab is the Hmong word for "heart," though it can also mean "liver." According to the Legend of Siab, you can save the world only if you retrieve Siab.

>   *(As May 1 continues to speak, May 2 enters the stage and begins imitating and making fun of her movements.)*

Siab has the power to restore things to their rightful order. Siab can regenerate life. Siab can—

>   *(May 1 notices May 2 making fun of her. May 1 gives May 2 the evil eye but continues to smile and speak to the audience.)*

Siab can clean out all the icky things in our systems to make us whole again and—

>   *(May 1 and May 2 finally meet in the middle of the stage.)*

(To May 2.) What are you doing? Leave me alone. This is my big moment. Everyone came here so they could see an authentic Hmong person.

MAY 2: Authentic? That was authentic?

>   *(May 1 tries to twirl away, but May 2 locks their arms together.)*

MAY 1: Koj tsis txaj muag los? Ws mam tam later.

MAY 2: What do I have to be embarrassed about? You want authentic? Let me show you how it's done.

(There might be some quick improv exchange here, but May 2 gets May 1
to be silent while she addresses the audience.)

How's everyone doing here? How many of you even know what Hmong people are? Anyone? Well, I am a real authentic Hmong person. Here. Take a whiff of me. You want to examine my hands?

(May 2 gets audience to examine her, look at her hands, sniff her. This part is open to improv. Meanwhile, May 1 is uncomfortable but goes along with it and puts on a fake smile. As May 2 talks, she brings May 1 into the audience so they can also examine her more closely.)

You wanna piece of me? People like to study us, after all. You'll find many studies, even headlines like "Hmong Women Oppressed," "Hmong Women Pregnant," "Hmong Man Kills Wife," and "Hmong Man Kills White Man."

Even other Hmong people like to exploit us. On Hmonghotties. com, you'll get see this message:

(May 2 morphs into Hmong Babe Advertiser.)

HMONG BABE ADVERTISER *(speaking like a pimp or salesperson)*: Are you a Hmong Hottie? We are constantly looking for beautiful young Hmong ladies who are openminded and uninhibited. Our goal is to discover new talents and expose them here for the rest of the world to see.

(As May 2.) If you scroll down to the bottom of the site, it says . . .

(Switches to Hmong Babe Advertiser, in a very solemn voice.) **The Hmong in America: A Story of Tragedy and Hope.** We hope that Hmonghotties. com will help you better understand *the Hmong people in the United States, and the tragic events that brought them here.*

(Back to May 2.)

MAY 2: I just love how even an aspiring porn site has to provide some background education on the Hmong culture as though you can't look at my boobs unless you know how my people came to the United States.

But I am tired of getting studied, tired of getting cut up and dissected. I am tired of people saying they are speaking for me, that they are being a voice for the voiceless because *we* are not voiceless. *I* have a voice.

I just became a little more quiet along the way.

SCENE 2: HOW I LOST MY NAME

MAY 2: And because of this, I've lost
- The grayish-green cloth my mom used to wrap around the infant me while we were in the Thai refugee camps
- Walks with my dad to Hamburger Stand, my daily bribe to go to preschool
- The teddy bear my aunt Mai gave me
- And my name . . .

(May 2 grabs the sheets of paper with her name and hands them to May 1. She gestures for May 1 to help her out by going to put the names up.)

When I was born, my father named me Maiv Muam Nkauj Lig Lis.

(Lights change on May 2 as she becomes Dad.)

DAD: Maiv Muam Nkauj Lig Lis.

(May 1 lays out MAIV MUAM NKAUJ LIG LIS
and presents it proudly.)

Your name means "Mongolia," where legends say we originated. I named you, your brothers, and sisters with great names so you will be kings. Great like Rambo, Clint Eastwood, and Hulk Hogan!

(Lights go back to general wash.)

MAY 2: If you read each part of my name separately, this is what each part means: Maiv.
MAY 1: A common name for Hmong girls, similar to Mary.
MAY 2 *(annoyed that May 1 has interrupted her)*: Muam.
MAY 1: Sister.

(May 2 is annoyed she has been interrupted again.)

MAY 2: Nkauj-Lig-Lis.
MAY 1: That was too fast. I didn't get to tell the audience what everything meant . . .

(May 2 walks over to May 1 and ties a piece of Hmong cloth around May 1's mouth, rendering her speechless. Then she returns her attention to the audience.)

MAY 2: When you put all the parts together, they become Maiv Muam Nkauj Lig Lis. Say it with me. *(Gets the audience to say it once.)*

When we came to the United States, the INS [Immigration and Naturalization Service] forgot "Lig," thinking it was the same as my last name. That it was a mistake on our part.

*(May 1 takes LIG off but still smiles to the audience
as she presents her name.)*

When I was in the first grade, my sister taught me how to spell my name.

(Lights change quickly on May 2. She is now Mee.)

MEE: May Moua, you've got it all wrong there. Your name is really spelled "M-A-Y-M-O-U-A-G-H-O-S-T-L-E-E."

(She starts to giggle. Phone rings.)

Hello?

*(May 1 puts up MAY MOUA GHOST LEE uncertainly,
but she still smiles to the audience.)*

(Lights change back to general wash.)

MAY 2: When I was in seventh grade, I became May Moua, but my teacher called me . . .

*(May 1 puts up the signs MAY MOUA and covers MOUA with MOO.
Meanwhile, May 2 transitions into ESL Teacher.)*

ESL TEACHER: May Moo, your English is very good. You're not one of those adopted children from Korea, are you? Where are your parents from, then? You must be Laotian if they're from Laos. No? Not that either? Oh! You're Hmong. Of course, I've heard of your people. I read that the Hmong are nomads.

Class, our new student, May Moo, is Hmong, and the Hmong are nomads. Can you say "nomads"? Noo-mads. *(Gets audience to repeat.)* The family in *Little House on the Prairie* were nomads, too. Can you tell us about *Little House on the Prairie*, May Moo?

*(She turns to May 1, gesturing for her to go on. May 1 takes center stage,
excited to talk. She lowers the cloth that has been tied around her thus far.)*

MAY 1: It's about Mary and Laura and their Ma and Pa. They lived in the woods, but they had to move to the prairie in Kansas 'cause too many people were living on their land. But when they got to the prairie, there were wolves and Indians and fires, but it was the government that kicked them out of Kansas. And my mom says I'm like Laura because I got attitude, and my sister Mee is like Mary because she's nice and pretty. And my dad said that he likes Pa because Pa's like Hmong people. He likes to farm and plant stuff and play with animals. And when we lived in California, we had pet chickens and—

MAY 2: That's bullshit. We were not nomads. We didn't have cattle that needed pastures. We didn't move from Laos to Thailand so we could farm. We moved, packing what we could carry, because someone always wanted us dead.

(May 1 becomes silent, puts the piece of cloth back over her mouth, and returns to the name board.)

By ninth grade, I was just May, and even then, people couldn't get it right. The most common question I get is, "Is your name pronounced 'Mai'?" Worse yet, when they try to spell it, my name comes out as M-A-I, M-E-I, and M-A-E.

(May 1 puts MAI, MEI and MAE on her body, all the while smiling as she presents them.)

But I'm tired of changing, of cutting—of getting dissected, of eliminating pieces of me to make it easier for others to swallow. This is my name: Maiv Muam Nkauj Lig Lis. From here on out, there is no May.

(May 2 goes to the name board and begins taking off the various incorrect names. She solicits May 1 for help in doing this.)

No May Moua, no May Moo, and definitely no Mai. From here on out, my name is Maiv Muam Nkauj Lig Lis. Say it with me. *(Has audience repeat the name until they get it right.)*

SCENE 3: HMONG WOMEN'S NAMES

(May 2 turns to May 1, who still has a cloth around her mouth.)

MAY 2: What about you? You haven't said your name yet.

(May 1 is hesitant, but she takes off the cloth around her mouth.)

MAY 1 (*hesitates, then says to the audience*): You can still call me May. I know the name is really long.

(*May 2 grabs the cloth that was previously on May 1 and puts it on her head, transitioning into Mom.*)

MOM: My Gawh! Tsov tom eh! You want to complain about your name? People don't even remember mine. Before I married your father, I was Nob Yaj. Now I am just Nyab—

MAY 1: Which means daughter-in-law or sister-in-law.

MOM: Nam tij—

MAY 1: Which means—I'm sorry. Were you just speaking in Green Hmong, because White Hmong people don't say that? We say *niam* tij.

MAY 2: You're not Green Hmong?

MAY 1: No. I'm White Hmong. (*To audience.*) White Hmong and Green Hmong are two different dialects of the Hmong language.

MAY 2: Stop that! Am I not doing this right?

MAY 1: No. You're fine. I'm just not Green Hmong. That's OK, though. You're doing a great job. (*Smiles.*)

MAY 2: OK. I guess I can call Mom *Niam*.

MAY 1: Are you sure? Can you speak White Hmong?

MAY 2: I can speak both White Hmong *and* Green Hmong.

(*May 2 transitions back into Mom.*)

MOM: Now I am just nyab, *niam* tij, or Niam Nom Yeej.

Maiv Muam Nkauj Lig Lis, don't you know that when a Hmong woman lives with her parents, they don't think of her as their own daughter. They raise her to take care of her future in-laws. When a Hmong woman marries, she keeps her father's last name. We remain a stranger no matter where we go. Our name is all we have. Say your name for all the women who never got to say their complete names.

(*Mom encourages May 1 to say her name until she feels excited, proud. May 1 savors this small triumph.*)

SCENE 4: THE SIAB, THE PLAWV, AND THE PLACENTA

Mom transitions into May 2.

MAY 2: See. You don't have to be the Quiet Girl.

MAY 1: This is true. I have always been known as the Quiet Girl. I was even voted "Most Quiet" in my graduating high school class. I wasn't really the quiet girl, though. I was always asking questions: "Who's that? What's going on? Why can't we just beat them up?"

MAY 2: I used to raise my hand all the time in school, but the teacher stopped calling on me. I understood. She wanted the quiet kids to talk, so I stopped raising my hand. At home, they said I talked too much. I was annoying. So I learned to keep my mouth shut. It's actually quite easy to be invisible, even with this skin color and this body. (*Beat.*) Well, you don't have to be invisible anymore.

(*The two Mays look at each other in celebration.*)

MAY 1: I get to have the stage?

MAY 2: You got it, girl. You can tell your story now.

(*May 2 leaves the stage, satisfied because she has triumphed.*)

MAY 1 (*to the audience*): So all I have to do now is find out where I'm from. Where is home?

I already know the Hmong believe that, when someone is born, their placenta is buried beneath their house so when they die they can find the way back home. But I don't know where my placenta is.

(*May 1 begins to get back into "dreamy mode" from her first monologue.*)

Maybe my mother dug a grave for my placenta under our shack at the refugee camp in Thailand. If I went back, would I find it?

Or perhaps she didn't even bother. Perhaps she just threw it away in the garbage, in the streets, let it wither and disintegrate into the air. If I don't know where my placenta is, where do I call home? (*Beat.*) So I have to go by what Americans says: Home is where the heart is. I have to find the Hmong heart.

Remember. You can still call me May.

(*May 1 puts the previously discarded name sign MAY over MAIV. Lights change. May 2 enters as Houa.*)

HOUA: You know, for us Hmong, the heart is not here. (*Points to the chest.*) That is the "plawv," the center. The heart is here. (*Points to the liver.*)

But that's the tricky thing about my job interpreting from Hmong into English. You may think it's easy for your big brother, but the words don't always match. If someone says, "Kuv mob siab," it could mean many things: My heart hurts. My liver hurts. My heart is broken.

So I have to make sure I'm interpreting what they really mean. If someone says, "Kuv kho siab," people will say, "That's simple. I'm heart-broken." I've never heard anyone say, "I am fixing my liver." (*Beat.*)

Every time Dad sees me with something new, he starts to complain. "Houa, why did you waste your money?" I can say to him, "Dad, I am buying this because kuv mob siab," but he won't know what I mean. He won't realize that my heart hurts, but in reality I am fixing my liver. I am mending it and setting things to right. Here, check out this Nintendo I just bought. It has a game in it. *The Legend of Zelda.* Maybe it will help your siab.

(*Houa hands May 1 the Nintendo console, then exits the stage.*)

SCENE 5: DESPERATE LOVE, BITTER END

Phone rings. May 2 enters as Mee.

MEE: I'll get it. Hello? Oh, kuv niam tshim nyob lawm os. Nws pais ua teb laws os. Tej zaum zau ntuj. OK. Bye. (*Hangs up phone.*) Dang it! That was just someone calling for Mom.

(*Mee exits stage.*)

(*From offstage.*) Houa, fix the VCR for me. If I have to watch all these lazy brats, I gotta watch *Desperate Love, Bitter End.*

(*Houa enters the stage and teaches May 1 how to set up the videogame system. Sound of hearts. Houa exits.*)

(*Phone rings. Mee enters the stage.*)

I'll get it! (*Starts laughing softly.*) Hi. Yes, this is Mee. No, I'm just babysitting today. (*Physically she should be giving the evil eye to the siblings and kids running around her.*) Yes, just come over later. We just need to be back by 3:30, before all the adults come home. OK. Bye. (*To May 1.*) May Moua, did you fix the VCR for me?
MAY 1: I'm not May Moua, remember? I'm Maiv Muam Nkauj—
MEE: Whatever. I just want to watch *Desperate Love, Bitter End.* The Chi-nese one about Taowha and Shihai. Taowha and Shihai fall in love, and they're planning to get married when they get stopped. This old man wants to marry Taowha, and Shihai's mother doesn't want him to marry Taowha because she's poor. In the end, Taowha is so sad she jumps into a lake, but she doesn't drown. Shihai finds her, and they profess their love for each other before she dies. There's a really sad scene in the end when he carries her dead body to the peach field and

buries her underneath the peach blossoms. God, that was sad. That's Siab. That's Love. Fix the freak'n VCR now!

(The phone rings.)

I'll get it. *(Answers phone.)* Hello? Uh . . . *(Changes her voice so it sounds like a kid.)* She's not home right now. I don't when she'll be home. I'm her younger sister. I'm eleven. My parents don't let me talk to guys yet. OK. Bye. *(Hangs up phone.)*

MAY 1: Why didn't you just say you didn't want to talk to him?

MEE: You think you know everything? What do you know about men or affairs of the plawv? You're just a little girl. Maybe that old guy will come visit you, huh? Then you can have a real boyfriend instead of just being the girl that no one knows exists. Or maybe you'll end up like Mai. It was her own fault that she married an ugly, mean guy. That's what happens when you don't have any standards. But that's not going to happen to me. You'll probably end up playing videogames all your life, alone.

(Mee grabs the videogame control from May 1 and keeps it out of her reach. A car honks.)

Never mind. I gotta go. *(Looks at herself in the mirror one final time.)* If one of the kids poops again, clean them if you want to. Or you can wait until their parents come home. I don't care what you do with the kids.

I'm going to pick up my pictures from Target. God, they better be there. Stupid Hmong people keep stealing my photos at Target.

MAY 1: I'm going to tell Mom and Dad.

MEE: And you better not tattle on me or else you're going to be sorry, niag tsov tom khaus paum!

(May 1 breaks out of character.)

MAY 1: Excuse me? Were you just speaking in Green Hmong? Because White Hmong people don't say that. We say "khaus pim." *(To the audience.)* For those of you who don't speak Hmong, "khaus pim" and "khaus paum" mean "itchy vagina."

(May 2 breaks out of character and become simply herself: Katie.)

KATIE: I can't take this. There is nothing wrong with the way I speak Hmong. Besides, Green Hmong is the right way to speak Hmong.

MAY 1: Excuse me?

KATIE: Green Hmong is the original way Hmong people speak. White Hmong is the lazy person's version.

MAY 1: But most people speak White Hmong. That's the norm.

KATIE: I know you did not just say that . . .

MAY 1: Well, I was just being honest.

KATIE: You have me play you in this play because you are too scared to tell people what you really think, and then you have the nerve to criticize my Hmong pronunciation. I am out, niag tsov tom khaus paum—I mean, niag tsov tom khaus pim!

(Katie starts walking off stage, but May 1 runs after her.)

MAY 1: Wait, Katie—I mean, Maiv Muam Nkauj Lig Lis. I'm sorry. Don't go.

MAY 2: What did you call me?

MAY 1: Maiv Muam Nkauj Lig Lis.

MAY 2: I can't hear you.

MAY 1: Maiv Muam Nkauj Lig Lis!

(May 2 is triumphant and relents, returning to center stage with May 1.)

Why don't we do this next piece together? We can both speak White and Green Hmong.

KATIE: *(Hesitates.)* Yeah. Well, Green Hmong is the original way to speak Hmong.

MAY 1: Sure. Yeah. *(Smiles at the audience.)*

KATIE: What part do you want to play?

MAY 1: I just want to play myself. I never get to play myself. What about you?

KATIE: I want to play your Dad. I really liked the Hulk Hogan thing and—

MAY 1: Oh. OK. I'll play myself.

(Both actors pause for a moment to "get in the zone.")

MAY 2: You ready?

MAY 1: Yeah. Let's do it.

SCENE 6: A REAL AMERICAN HERO

May 1 sets up the TV and sings the Growing Pains *theme song: "Show me that smile again (Ooh show me that smile) / Don't waste another minute on your cryin' / We're nowhere near the end (We're nowhere near . . .) / The best is ready to begin / Ooh . . . / As long as we got each other / We got the world spinnin' right in our hands / Baby, you and me . . . / We got* to be . . . / *The luckiest dreamers who never quit dreamin' / As long as we keep on givin' / We can take anything that comes our way / Baby, rain or shine . . . / All the time . . . / We got each other / Sharin' the laughter and love.")*

Katie transitions from herself into the Dad/Hulk Hogan persona.

MAY 1: If you're Hmong, you know that when people meet you, they automatically ask who your parents are. My dad was born Wang Phia Lee, but when he got older, like most Hmong men, he was given a more distinguished name. He became Nom Yeej, which translates to Important Public Figure Who Will Win and Conquer.

DAD: I named you and your brothers and sisters with great names so you will be kings. Great, like James West. Captain Jim Kirk. James Bond. Rambo. Chuck Norris and Clint Eastwood. Those are real men, but Hulk Hogan is the ultimate hero. He is willing to fall down, but he always gets up.

    (Sings.) "I am a real American. Fighting for the rights of every man."

MAY 1: Dad, can I play videogames on the TV?

DAD: Maiv Muam Nkauj Lig, look at that match. Andre the Giant is so tall, but is Hulk Hogan scared? No. Tsis ntshais li.

MAY 1: Can I watch the TV afterwards?

DAD: *(Can swap some of Dad's English text to Hmong, too.)* Look, Hulk is about to body slam him—oh yo, Andre is too heavy. Hulk, look behind you. Bobby the Brain Heenan is coming. That Bobby the Brain is going to do something bad. I just know it. He's got something in his hand. Hulk, turn around—oh yo! Referee, turn around. Turn around. Tsov tom! How can you not see that? Hulk Hogan got hit by Bobby the Brain Heenan. Now he's so hurt and it's so easy for Andre to hit him.

(Dad starts to rise excitedly from his chair.)

    The match isn't over yet. Look, Maiv Muam Nkauj Lig. Andre can hit Hulk as much as he want, but Hulk is rising. Do you see his eyes? He's mad. He's shaking his head. Oh yo! I knew this would happen. Hulk, hit him. Take him down. One! Two! Three! I told you Hulk Hogan would rise again! He's still the World Federation Heavyweight Cham-pion!

    (Sings.) "I am a real American. Fighting for the rights of every man."

    Maiv Muam Nkauj Lig, when we were still in Laos, I was fighting for my life. We fought just like Hulk Hogan did. Even though the Vietcongs were bigger than us, we weren't afraid, because we knew that, in the end, good can always beat evil. *(Beat.)* Every month, you and your brothers complain that I give away too much money to get back Laos.

(As Dad continues speaking, May 1 returns to her videogame.)

But do you know what? Even though I am an American citizen now, when we get back Laos, we're all going back. I will become a tasseng again.

MAY 1 *(to the audience)*: That's like a governor or something.

DAD: Who are you talking to?

MAY 1: Oh, I'm just educating the non-Hmong in the audience.

DAD: Stop trying to educate others! Educate yourself! *(Looks around and realizes for the first time that Hulk Hogan's theme music has disappeared.)* What happened to my wrestling? What did you do to my TV?

MAY 1: Nothing. I think the cable died.

DAD: We were just watching it.

MAY 1: Dad, they canceled wrestling. It's only on during the daytime now.

DAD: Don't lie to me. You think I'm stupid?

MAY 1: Dad, chill out! You can watch your wrestling next week. I'm almost done playing my videogame. I just need to collect a few more heart pieces; then I'll be ready to face the bad guy. Then you'll get your TV back.

DAD: Connect the TV again!

MAY 1: I don't know why you get so worked up over wrestling. Everything's fake.

DAD: You think that just because we're in America now, we can all act like Americans?

MAY 1: Can't you see that that's why Mr. Fuji always gets away with hitting Macho Man on the side?

DAD: Even though I don't speak English as well as you, I'm still your parent. You can't treat me like a child.

MAY 1: Why do you think the referees pretend they don't see all the cheating going on?

DAD: Don't you know how many times people my age get pushed down, and we have to pretend none of it hurts?

MAY 1: Or why do you think Hulk Hogan always gets hurt in the beginning, then gets up in the end? He's putting on a show just to get the crowd excited. It's all a lie.

DAD: We have to keep going, hiding everything, so that our children will feel proud that we have some dignity even though it's all a lie!

MAY 1: And you know what else? This isn't Laos anymore. You're not a tasseng anymore! You're not in charge! If you want to watch wrestling, then connect the cable cord yourself!

(Dad stares at the TV cord. In the end, he walks to the broom and dances with it like a warrior, a soldier, and a qeej player. May 1 continues playing her videogames until she starts feeling guilty.)

Dad, do you want to watch wrestling? I don't have to play video-games. I'll connect the TV back for you.

(*May 1 reconnects the TV, but Dad ignores her.*)

Dad, the TV's working again.

(*Lights fade low on Dad, up on May 1.*)

In videogames, you use knives to cut down the enemy and protect yourself. I was told that you can tell if there is a man in the house by how sharp the knives are. It is his job to take care of them, to keep them always sharpened.

These are not knives you buy at Target or Walmart. Those knives—the chef's knife, the serrated knife, even steak knives—those are discarded when they become dull.

It is Hmong knives that must be cared for. They have bamboo handles and steel blades. They are so sharp; each has its own sheath.

With a dull knife, you cannot butcher a cow.

You will find it harder to clear bushes and trees at the garden.

You can still cut through chili peppers, but it will take longer.

With a finely honed knife, you can cut through flesh.

Clear away shame with a single slash.

(*Dad cuts himself and falls to the ground. May 1
goes to comfort Dad.*)

This is what happens when you khos siab, when your liver is sad. This is what happens when you poob siab, when you lose your liver, when you lost hope. (*Beat.*) If you're Hmong, you know that when people meet you, they automatically ask who your parents are. When people asked who my dad was and I told them his name, their response was, "Oh, the tasseng?" Nowadays when I tell people who my dad is, their response is, "Oh? That man who tried to kill himself?" So I stopped saying his name.

SCENE 7: FIXING THE LIVER

Lights rise on May 2. May 1 goes to her to see her and to aid her. May 2 hears sound cue to become Houa, but May 1 stops her.

MAY 1: No. I have to do this. Stay. Rest. (*To sound booth operator.*) My Gawh! Tsov tom eh! Wrong cue! It's my mom's turn to talk.

(May 1 transitions into Mom, grabbing the Hmong cloth
May 2 had worn earlier as Mom.)

MOM: Maiv Muam Nkauj Lig-eh, koj txiv neb yuav ruam tag npau li. Sib ceg cuag li cas txoj wrestling cia Nintendo ua cuag lis tsis muaj lawm tus neeg nyob hauv lus neej no na. Kuv niam kes hais tias wrestling yog tiag luas dag na. Koj twb xav hais tias koj yog neeg tshe lawm es koj txawm tab koj txiv ua dabtsis na?

Koj tsis nco qa taum koj ntshawm me, koj txiv twb hlub koj tag npauv li nws tias muaj npe zoo tau koj na. Taum nom koj loj, koj xav hais tias koj tsis tas mlooj lus lawm os?

Koj puas xav kom kuv hais lub tiag tiag rau koj? Koj txiv tsis thog vim hais tias nej sib cej txhoj wrestling tias Nintendo. Koj txiv thog vim hais tias nwspoob npe.

Koj puas nco qab puas ta kuv hais rau koj txhoj poj niam hmoob na? People just call us "nyab, niam tij, niam, phauj, tais."

[Translation: Maiv Muam Nkauj Lig-eh, you and your dad are so stupid fighting over wrestling and Nintendo, acting as if there's no one else in this world. I don't care if wrestling is fake. If you think you're so smart, why do you need to mess around with your dad?

Don't you remember that when you were small, he loved you so much, he gave you a great name? Now that you're older, you don't think you need to listen to him anymore?

Do you want me to speak honestly to you? Your dad didn't fall because you argued over wrestling and Nintendo. Your dad fell because he lost his name.

Do you remember what I said to you earlier about Hmong women? People just call us "daughter-in-law, sister-in-law, mom, aunt, grandma."]

Think about all the Hmong women you know: Phauj Maiv, Tais Mais, Niam Dab Lue, Niam Dab Npawb. There are more people than this, but do you even know what their real names are?

Your father fell because he lost his name. Will you lose your name, too, or will you pick it up?

(May 1 transitions into Houa. Houa enters stage with a microphone.
He signals the stage manager to cue his music.)

HOUA: Dad doesn't understand why I spend my money on electronics. He says it's a waste. I should be saving up for a house. But there are things he doesn't see and can't seem to understand.

I've bought nearly every videogame system since the Atari: Nintendo, Super Nintendo, N64, and Sega Genesis. But the thing that spoke to my siab the most wasn't videogames but the karaoke machine. I didn't even know if I would like singing. No one sang in our family. But one day, a friend said he was selling his karaoke system for cheap, so I bought it.

The discs are as big as those albums from the eighties, only heavier. This album has "Endless Love," "Woman in Love," "Because I Love You." They even have "Love Your More Than I Can Say." I remember that one. Tou Ly Vangkhue sang it in the eighties. (*Sings.*)
Whoa, whoa yea yea
Kuv hlub koj tshaj qhov kuv hais tau
Kuv hlub koj tshaj qhov kuv hais tau
Whoa kuv hlub koj tshaj qhov kuv hais tau

(*Turns to May 1, who is presumably standing next to him.*)

You can also record your voice. You try it.

(*May 1 accepts the microphone and transitions from Houa into herself again.*)

MAY 1: (*Sings.*)
Whoa, whoa yea yea
Kuv hlub koj tshaj qhov kuv hais tau
Kuv hlub koj tshaj qhov kuv hais tau
Whoa kuv hlub koj tshaj qhov kuv hais tau

(*May 1 listens as the recording of her voice is played back to her.*)

Is that really my voice? I guess it's hard to remember what I sound like. It's like what my brother, Houa, says about interpreting.

When you're interpreting, you're not speaking for yourself. But singing is different. Singing come from your siab. When you interpret, people speak through you. They don't want your opinion. They don't even want you to say, "She said so-and-so." I have to speak as if I'm that person. If a Hmong woman says, "Kuv mob siab," I have to say to the doctor, "My heart hurts."

Remember what my brother said before about interpreting for Hmong people? Three words. It could mean many things: "Kuv kho siab. My heart hurts. My liver hurts. My heart is broken." No one ever says, "Kuv kho siab. I am fixing my liver."

(*May 1 sings "Love You More Than I Can Say" as she goes through the ritual of walking around Dad's body and knocking the ground at his head, hands, and feet. May 1 continues the ritual of knocking on the ground, but this time she repeats the names "Wang Phia Lee. Nob Yaj. Maiv Muam Nkauj Lig Lis." She continues to repeat these names as she takes off Dad's shoes and pe Dad's body. [Pe is a gesture that only men and boys do to show respect and honor].*)

(May 1 returns to Dad's head.)

Wang Phia Lee. Sawv los. Sawv los.

(Katie/Dad rises from the ground.)

DAD: Maiv Muam Nkauj Lig Lis—
MAY 1: That's OK. You don't have to do that anymore. We're good.

(Dad breaks out of character and simply becomes Katie.)

KATIE: I could have done the last part.
MAY 1: I know, but I needed to do it on my own. Thank you, though.
KATIE: No problem.

(May 1 helps Katie to her feet, and they walk back toward the audience.)

MAY 1 *(to audience)*: Hi, everyone. My name is Maiv Muam Nkauj Lig Lis, and I'm the daughter of Wang Phia Lee and Nob Yaj. Will you say my name with me one more time? *(Gets audience to repeat her name.)* Actually, now that I'm married, I'm Maiv Muam Nkauj Lig Lis-Yaj. *(Gets audience to repeat this new name.)*

(May 1 turns to Katie with a look indicating, "Your turn.")

Koj nab tib.
KATIE: My name is Maiv Muam Nkauj—
MAY 1: No. Koj lub npe tiag tiag na.
KATIE: Oh! My real name is Katie Vang.
MAY 1: You call that authentic?
KATIE: Well, it's really Ka Vang. Actually, you can call me Katie Ka Vang.
MAY 1: Hais kom lawv roj koj hais na.
KATIE: My name is Katie Ka Vang. Say it with me. *(Gets audience to repeat her name.)*

(May 1 and Katie acknowledge each other with a smile, then begin singing "Love You More Than I Can Say" as they exit the stage.)

END OF PLAY

6

Bahala Na (Let It Go)

CLARENCE COO

INTRODUCTION, *by Josephine Lee*

Bahala Na was produced by Mu Performing Arts and presented at Mixed Blood Theatre in Minneapolis from September 14, 2007, to October 7, 2007, under the direction of Jennifer Weir.

As *Bahala Na* begins, Amah, a one-hundred-year-old Chinese grandmother, lies in a hospital, felled by a stroke; as the play ends, we see her wake to a moment of reconciliation with her gay grandson, Jason, who introduces her to his adopted baby daughter. The story, as we might guess, is a weighty one: one that traces her life from her arranged marriage to a Chinese man in the Philippines through the brutal events of Japanese occupation and her difficult relationship with her only son, who defies her wishes and marries a Filipina. But this is not *Roots*; what at the onset might be a predictable story about the heroism and endurance of our forebears turns out to be something else entirely. Coo depicts Amah's prejudices, idiosyncrasies, and deceptions as openly as he does her will to survive and her longing for love.

Bahala Na depicts an Asian American family history that is told in contradictory ways and shaped by multiple forces of migration, interethnic struggle,

Illustration: Eric Sharp, Katie Bradley, Jeany Park, Mayano Ochi, Alexander Galick, and Rose Le Tran in *Bahala Na*.
(Photograph used by permission of Charissa Uemura Photography.)

class conflict, colonialism, gender, and sexuality. The play deeply questions the integrity and viability of conventional notions of family and makes us think harder about how we are connected by blood, love, and affiliation.

ABOUT THE PLAY

Bahala Na was selected for production through Mu Performing Arts Emerging Writers of Color call for submissions and was further developed and produced with funding from the Ford Foundation.

CHARACTERS (ORIGINAL CAST)

AMAH (Jeany Park): a one-hundred-year-old Chinese woman in a wheelchair
JASON (Eric Sharp): Amah's grandson
WEI WEI (Eric Sharp): Amah's son and Jason's father
YOUNG AMAH (Mayano Ochi): Amah's memory of her younger self
TERESA (Mayano Ochi): Wei Wei's Filipino wife
FIRST DAUGHTER (Katie Bradley): Amah's first daughter, the sour one
ANG CHO AN (Katie Bradley): Amah's husband
SECOND DAUGHTER (Rose Le Tran): Amah's second daughter, the sweet one
AMAH'S FATHER (Rose Le Tran): a memory of a young Japanese man
DAN (Alexander Galick): Jason's partner,

SCENE 1

A room in a hospital in Washington, D.C., 2004. Amah sits motionless in a wheelchair, staring at nothing. Jason and Dan are looking at her.

JASON: Look at her.
DAN: I'll be honest, Jason. I'm kind of sick of looking at your grandmother.
JASON: I come back after all this time and this happens to her.
DAN: I told you. Stop blaming yourself.
JASON: She was always talking. You couldn't shut her up. She had an opinion about everything. Now she's totally silent. It's eerie.
DAN: It is eerie. So let's go.
JASON: Dan, I can't leave her now.
DAN: Yes you can. You're not doing anyone any favors by staying.
JASON: We just got here.
DAN: She doesn't even know we're here.
JASON: Dan, I know she knows we're here.
DAN: And even if she does, what does it matter? I thought she hated me.
JASON: She doesn't hate you.

DAN: She resents me.

JASON: Exactly.

DAN: For not being Chinese. Oh yeah, that I'm not a woman.

JASON: She's old-fashioned.

DAN: Remember how she yelled at me when you introduced me to her.

JASON: Dan, that was five years ago. She won't yell at you now. I promise.

DAN: Come on. Let's go.

JASON: Please, Dan. A little longer?

DAN: You can stay a little longer. I'm going down the street to get some coffee. I haven't had any since we left Chicago. You want any?

JASON: No, thanks.

DAN: And she's OK without coffee, I presume.

(Dan tries to exit, but First Daughter and Second Daughter enter.)

FIRST DAUGHTER *(to Jason)*: Oh, so you're still here.

JASON: Tita Beatriz. Tita Dominga.

FIRST DAUGHTER: You made her this way, you know.

SECOND DAUGHTER: Beatriz, I thought you weren't going to mention that.

FIRST DAUGHTER: I want him to know what he did.

SECOND DAUGHTER: Jason, are you eating enough? You look a little skinny.

FIRST DAUGHTER: Stop asking him if he's eating enough. Look what he did to our mother!

SECOND DAUGHTER: We haven't seen him in five years! I want to express concern about his welfare.

FIRST DAUGHTER: His welfare? Look what he did to our mother!

SECOND DAUGHTER: Beatriz! You promised!

FIRST DAUGHTER: You can't deny it.

SECOND DAUGHTER: Mother was old. These things happen. People get strokes. *(To Jason.)* These things happen, Jason. In fact, we are very glad you decided to come back to Washington.

FIRST DAUGHTER: You just didn't have to bring that man.

SECOND DAUGHTER: Beatriz, stop blaming him.

JASON: Dan, this is why I don't like being around my dad's side of the family.

FIRST DAUGHTER: Then why did you come back!

SECOND DAUGHTER: Beatriz, stop!

FIRST DAUGHTER: First you hurt your grandmother by telling her you're a gay. And then introducing her to this other one. Then you run away from all of us. And you have the nerve to return after five years? To do this to her? You're as irresponsible as your father was!

JASON: Do not talk about my father!

DAN: Hey! This is a hospital! Inside voices. Some respect for the old woman here.

FIRST DAUGHTER: The gay man is correct. I'll cool my nerves by going down to get some cappucino.

SECOND DAUGHTER: Beatriz needs coffee to calm her down.

DAN: I was just going to get some, too. At the café down the street.

FIRST DAUGHTER: Did I say cappucino? I meant pizza. Some nice greasy pizza. You go on to your little café while Dominga and I go somewhere else.

SECOND DAUGHTER: Pizza sounds yummy! Let's go!

(First Daughter and Second Daughter exit.)

DAN: You sure you don't want coffee?

JASON: I'm sure.

(Dan exits. Jason looks at his grandmother and starts to speak to her.)

AMAH: You're here.

JASON: I'm hoping you can hear me. I know you can't talk.

AMAH: I can talk, but no one is listening. No one can hear me.

JASON: But please listen to me.

AMAH: Me? Listen to you? Why should I? You made me this way! Look at me! I can't move! And I'm going to die. I know this. My time is soon.

JASON: I don't even know what to say. This is stupid. My mother warned me not to come.

AMAH: I always know what to say. That's the difference between you and me.

JASON: I make the biggest decision of my life. Then I fly halfway across the country to see you. And this happens.

AMAH: But I know why this happened. Why you're here. So I can change you before it's too late. And make you into a man. Then I will die with no regrets.

(Ang Cho An and Amah's Father enter. Jason does not see them, but Amah does.)

JASON: Why did I come here?

ANG CHO AN: My wife, my wife.

AMAH: Ang Cho An!

AMAH'S FATHER: My daughter, my daughter.

AMAH: Father!

ANG CHO AN: No regrets?

AMAH'S FATHER: We all die with lies.

AMAH: You're both dead! Go away! I'm not dead yet!

ANG CHO AN: We all die with regrets.

AMAH: I won't.

ANG CHO AN: I tell you now that when I died, I did not have my body buried in the Chinese cemetery and laid in place surrounded on all sides with others of my race.

AMAH'S FATHER: I tried so hard to keep the earnings of our name but lost them when the revolution came.

ANG CHO AN: I should have disappeared much earlier. My wife, you should have never seen my face.

AMAH (to Ang Cho An): You coward! You never did your duty! You left your daughters and me behind!

AMAH'S FATHER: My words to you were false when I gave you up to be a wife.

AMAH: That's not true! Your words were right. They made me who I am. (To Jason.) Jason, don't listen to them! They're mad ghosts! Listen to me! I'm still alive!

JASON: Why did I come back to you? My father hated you and died too young.

AMAH: Your father didn't hate me.

JASON: If I'm going to raise a child, I shouldn't be around you at all.

AMAH: Your father loved me!

ANG CHO AN: We all die with regrets.

AMAH'S FATHER: We all die with lies.

AMAH: I was the best mother I could be.

ANG CHO AN: Regrets.

AMAH'S FATHER: Lies.

AMAH: Get out of here! I'm telling him the truth!

(Ang Cho An and Amah's Father exit.)

AMAH (to Jason): You need to understand your father. He was special. You—you can't tell the difference between a man and a woman. If you only knew the story of his life, then you would not be that way. You would know how to be a real man.

JASON: But how can I ever be a father? I never knew my own.

AMAH: You look just like him. It's like he's standing in front of me again. But you're nothing like your father. He was so dependable. One day when he was a young boy, he had this foolish idea to leave school—to work at our store. And I said, "Wei Wei! But why?" And he said, "Mother, I may be a young boy, but I am mature enough to be sensitive to our economic needs." And I said, "But your education! You cannot sacrifice that!" And he said, "But mother, your wisdom is worth far more than a diploma. Please allow me to forego my studies and work here as a shop assistant." I was so moved by his words and his resolve was so strong, I could not refuse.

(Jason becomes his father, Wei Wei, at eight years old.
He hides something in his hands.)

AMAH: Wei Wei was a spirited boy. I remember those wonderful days back
at that grocery store on the island of Negros. The most beautiful island
in the Philippines. My memories are still clear. Unclouded by time. I
can still see the store. The rough wooden walls, the shelves lined with
tin cans, the sacks of rice on the floor. My daughters cooking dinner,
and the smell of food floating in.

SCENE 2

We are now in the past—in a grocery store on the island of Negros, the
Philippines, 1950.

WEI WEI: Mother!
AMAH: Wei Wei! You're back!
WEI WEI: Yes, it's me.
AMAH: I haven't seen you in quite a while.
WEI WEI: I haven't been gone that long.
AMAH: You have. I missed you.
WEI WEI: I took the long way back from school.
AMAH: Must have been very long. You're three hours late.
WEI WEI: Sorry.
AMAH: Your dinner is cold.
WEI WEI: Sorry.
AMAH: First Daughter! Second Daughter! Come here! Now!

(First Daughter and Second Daughter scurry in.)

AMAH: Warm up Wei Wei's dinner! He must be hungry, my baby. Wei Wei,
I made your favorite noodles.

(First Daughter and Second Daughter start to exit, but . . .)

WEI WEI: I'm not hungry. I want to know about my father.

(First Daughter and Second Daughter stop in their tracks.
They want to hear the answer.)

AMAH: What do you mean?
WEI WEI: My father. Who was he?
AMAH: He was a good man. Who died in the war.
WEI WEI: And that's why a bird brought me to you.

AMAH: Yes.

WEI WEI: Did the bird look like this?

*(Wei Wei releases something from his hands into the air.
The sound of wings flapping.)*

FIRST and SECOND DAUGHTER: Aaah!!!

AMAH: What's that?!

WEI WEI: A bird!

AMAH: Why did you bring it here?

WEI WEI: It doesn't know how to get out. It keeps hitting the ceiling.

FIRST DAUGHTER: You will pay!

WEI WEI: It's only a baby.

SECOND DAUGHTER: Oh? I really love babies!

WEI WEI: Does this bird look like the one that brought me to you?

AMAH: Wei Wei. We don't have time to talk about that now.

WEI WEI: I want to know.

AMAH: You have to eat dinner.

WEI WEI: I told you, I'm not hungry.

AMAH: How is that possible? I made your favorite noodles.

WEI WEI: The kids at school were laughing at me.

AMAH: Why?

WEI WEI: Their parents told them to.

AMAH; THE PEOPLE IN THIS TOWN ARE FOOLS.

WEI WEI: Because I said you told me father died during the war, so a bird brought me to you. Which is true, right?

AMAH: Of course, it's true.

WEI WEI: No one believes me.

AMAH: They don't understand.

WEI WEI: I want to know the whole story.

AMAH: That is the whole story.

WEI WEI: Where did the bird come from?

*(Takashi, a Japanese soldier from the Second World War, enters.
He is played by the same actor as Dan.)*

TAKASHI *(reciting)*:
  Bright moon born above the sea.
  This time is shared across the earth.
  Loved ones hate that night is long.
  They miss each other 'til the dawn.

AMAH *(pushing Takashi away from her memory)*: I'll tell you the story. One day.

WEI WEI: Tell me now. Please?

AMAH: Wei Wei.

WEI WEI: I want them to stop teasing.

AMAH: After you eat, I'll tell you the story.

WEI WEI: If you tell me the story now, I'll get my appetite back.

AMAH: You promise to eat afterwards?

WEI WEI: I promise!

AMAH: The true story of where you come from.

WEI WEI (*in awe*): The true story.

FIRST and SECOND DAUGHTER: The true story.

AMAH: Yes. The true story. It begins with the strangers from the East. The Japanese. And how they looked all the way across the world and saw the strangers from the West. Their fancy clothes, their furniture, their factories. But most important, the strangers of the East saw that the strangers of the West owned lands all across the earth. And they wanted that, too.

So a brilliant sun descended on the countries of the Southern Ocean. But this sun was not a sun of light but a sun of darkness.

We in the Philippines were helpless. Our islands were just a few pearls scattered carelessly on the sea. But the strangers of the East snatched us up. The Northern Island. The Southern Island. And all the little islands in between. Including our beautiful island of Negros. And after the Philippines, they wanted more. Like a needle and thread, they strung up all the countries of the Southern Ocean like beads, precious jewelry for their emperor to wear.

I was a beautiful young woman on this island of Negros who lived in a small village far from the town we live in now.

(*Young Amah enters.*)

I worked as a servant for a family of strangers from the West.

(*Young Amah washes clothes.*)

A hard life it was. But with your two sisters and your father, I was content with all I had.

YOUNG AMAH: I am content with all I have!

AMAH: Your father worked in the fields of those strangers from the West. Chopping sugarcane all day.

(*First Daughter becomes Ang Cho An, Amah's husband.
He chops sugarcane.*)

AMAH: He, too, was content with all he had.

ANG CHO AN: I, too, am content with all I have!

AMAH: But sometimes, in the middle of the night, he would pray to Guan Yin, the Buddha who hears the sorrows of the world.

ANG CHO AN: I pray to you to grant me one small wish.

AMAH: He prayed to Guan Yin to grant him one small wish.

ANG CHO AN: Grant me a son so that I may continue the family name.

AMAH: But most of the time—

ANG CHO AN: I am content with all I have!

AMAH: But when the strangers from the East landed on the island of Negros, nothing would ever be the same.

ANG CHO AN and YOUNG AMAH: Nothing will ever be the same!

AMAH: They came down from the sky and all they touched turned to flame. Fields, villages, and even the mansion of the strangers from the West were swallowed in fire and smoke. And when the fields of sugarcane burned in the night, the sky was bright as day and smelled of sweetness and death combined.

And food was nowhere to be found. The island of Negros, which had always been so green, was now filled with cries of starving souls.

YOUNG AMAH (to Ang Cho An): Our two daughters weep with hunger. We have so little rice!

ANG CHO AN: Do not worry. I will sneak over to the next village where I know a man who has a hidden store of rice.

YOUNG AMAH: Oh no, Ang Cho An! That would be dangerous! The Japanese are everywhere. And they are cruel!

AMAH: But your father was brave.

ANG CHO AN: I will run in the cover of the sugarcane. Set your heart at ease.

YOUNG AMAH: They will mistake you for a spy. Or for a rebel soldier. Or for a saboteur. They will kill without a thought.

ANG CHO AN: I do it for you. And for my daughters. Perhaps Guan Yin will reward my bravery by granting us a son.

YOUNG AMAH: You are so brave.

AMAH: And so your father ran as fast as he could between rows of flaming sugarcane to reach the next village. But before he got there—

(Second Daughter becomes a Japanese soldier. The Japanese soldier points a gun at Ang Cho An.)

JAPANESE SOLDIER: Halt! You may be a spy. Or perhaps a rebel soldier. Or even a saboteur.

ANG CHO AN: I am a brave man who wants to feed his family!

JAPANESE SOLDIER: I am Japanese and therefore cruel, so I must shoot you without thought.

ANG CHO AN: Oh Guan Yin, the Buddha who hears the sorrows of the world, be witness to my bravery!

JAPANESE SOLDIER: Bam! Bam!

(Ang Cho An falls to the ground. Japanese Soldier walks away.)

AMAH: When I was told of your father's death, I was so sad, I could not speak for days.

YOUNG AMAH: I cannot speak for days!

AMAH: But Guan Yin did witness your father's bravery. And so came down to the island of Negros in the form of a beautiful bird.

*(First Daughter and Second Daughter link up arms
to become Guan Yin in the form of bird.)*

GUAN YIN *(ethereally)*: I have your wish! But like your husband, you must sacrifice something, too!

(Guan Yin gives Young Amah a baby.)

YOUNG AMAH: Anything for a son!

GUAN YIN: I must take away what a mother does not need.

(Young Amah sinks down to the ground.)

AMAH: And from then on, I could never walk again.

YOUNG AMAH: A son! A son! Finally, I truly am content!

AMAH: And thus, due to your father's bravery during the war and my own small sacrifice, Guan Yin gave you to me, and the lineage of the House of Ang is continued! And that is the true story.

(First Daughter and Second Daughter become themselves again.)

WEI WEI: That's a beautiful story.

AMAH: It is. Now you're old enough to know.
    (To First Daughter and Second Daughter.) What are you waiting for? I told you to warm up his noodles! My baby is hungry.

(First Daughter and Second Daughter scurry off.)

WEI WEI: So that's what I'll tell the other kids at school.

AMAH: The other kids?

WEI WEI: They laughed at me because they didn't understand. Now I'll tell them the truth.

AMAH: I doubt they'll ever understand.

WEI WEI (*pointing to the bird in the ceiling*): And was the bird that brought me to you like that one?

AMAH: Yes, it was.

WEI WEI: Great! Now I know what it looks like.

(*Wei Wei opens the door, and we hear the sound
of a bird escaping the store.*)

AMAH: So just ignore the teasing.

WEI WEI: Bahala na.

AMAH: What's this? Speaking in Filipino?

WEI WEI: Bahala na. Do you know what it means? They say it can't be translated into Chinese.

AMAH: If you can't say it in Chinese, then it's not worth saying.

WEI WEI: But I like the sound of it. Bahala na.

AMAH: Wei Wei, only Chinese is spoken inside this house. No Filipino.

WEI WEI: Why not?

AMAH: No Filipino!

WEI WEI: We have to learn it in school.

AMAH: But I sent you to a Chinese school.

WEI WEI: Even there we have to learn. The teachers say the Philippines is a new nation. So we all should learn the same language.

AMAH: I told you the people in this town are fools. Especially the Chinese! That's why they make it difficult for you. They're jealous because you're special.

WEI WEI: But I'll tell them the story of Guan Yin and the bird. That will make them quiet.

AMAH: You don't have to.

WEI WEI: Why not?

AMAH: I am pulling you out of there. No more school for you.

WEI WEI: You can't do that! I like school!

AMAH: I don't want you around those children and those gossiping parents. And those so-called Chinese teachers who've turned their backs on their own culture. They are not a good influence.

WEI WEI: It's because they don't understand.

AMAH: They never will. You are too special for them. From now on, you'll work at this store.

WEI WEI: I don't want to work at the store.

AMAH: You'll be happy to spend more time with your family. (*Calling.*) First Daughter, Second Daughter! Where are Wei Wei's noodles!

(*First Daughter and Second Daughter return. We are back in the present,
and Wei Wei becomes Jason.*)

SCENE 3

Back at the hospital.

FIRST DAUGHTER: Jason, I brought you back some pizza.

JASON: No thanks, I'm not hungry.

AMAH: Did I not remember that correctly? I thought Wei Wei was the one who wanted to leave school. Was it me who pulled him out?

SECOND DAUGHTER: You've been here three days now. Don't you ever eat?

JASON: I'm OK.

FIRST DAUGHTER: Jason, I might have been hard on you the first day you were here.

AMAH: But the point of the story is that if you loved your family more, you wouldn't be the way you are.

JASON: Amah is sick. It's been difficult for all of us.

SECOND DAUGHTER: I think it's nice that you've been spending so much time with her.

FIRST DAUGHTER: I'm sorry for speaking ill of your father.

JASON: How come you never liked him?

FIRST DAUGHTER: Do you really want to talk about that?

JASON: Did you at least think he was a good father?

FIRST DAUGHTER: He did drink himself to death.

SECOND DAUGHTER: He was a good father and a good brother. He had many positive qualities.

FIRST DAUGHTER: Yes. For example, Wei Wei was very . . . charming.

SECOND DAUGHTER: Charming. A natural salesman.

FIRST DAUGHTER: Which made him very good at business. For a while.

SECOND DAUGHTER: He was very good at business. And supported us with his money.

SCENE 4

AMAH *(to audience)*: Your father was brilliant at business. He loved working at the store, just like he thought he would. And as the years passed, business boomed. Soon, your father caught the eye of important people on the island of Negros. And so he left the store in the hands of his sisters so he could work far away from home. Selling—

FIRST DAUGHTER: Hammers.

SECOND DAUGHTER: Screwdrivers.

FIRST DAUGHTER: Drills.

AMAH: To people in—

SECOND DAUGHTER: Villages.

FIRST DAUGHTER: Towns.

SECOND DAUGHTER: Cities.

AMAH: And not just on the island of Negros! But all over the Philippines!

FIRST DAUGHTER: The Northern Island.

SECOND DAUGHTER: The Southern Island.

FIRST DAUGHTER: And all the little islands in between.

AMAH: And there was money.

SECOND DAUGHTER: Money!

FIRST DAUGHTER: Money!

SECOND DAUGHTER: Money!

AMAH: Money! And soon my youngest child was supporting me and his two sisters. He was rarely home but sent us so much money. Oh how good it was to live a comfortable life.

FIRST DAUGHTER: Custom-made furniture!

SECOND DAUGHTER: Domestic servants!

FIRST DAUGHTER: Imported cars!

AMAH: He gave gifts like smiles. And he acquired even more skills that improved his proficiency in the business world.

SECOND DAUGHTER: Accounting.

FIRST DAUGHTER: Korean.

SECOND DAUGHTER: Marketing.

FIRST DAUGHTER: French.

SECOND DAUGHTER: Golf.

FIRST DAUGHTER: Gambling.

SECOND DAUGHTER: Fine dining.

FIRST DAUGHTER: Drinking.

SECOND DAUGHTER: Dancing.

AMAH: He acquired many things.

FIRST DAUGHTER: Women.

SECOND DAUGHTER: Investing.

FIRST DAUGHTER: Drinking.

SECOND DAUGHTER: Gambling.

FIRST DAUGHTER: Finance.

SECOND DAUGHTER: Women.

FIRST DAUGHTER: Public speaking.

SECOND DAUGHTER: Drinking.

AMAH: So many useful skills.

FIRST DAUGHTER: Gambling.

SECOND DAUGHTER: Women.

FIRST DAUGHTER: Drinking.

SECOND DAUGHTER: Gambling.

FIRST DAUGHTER: Women.

SECOND DAUGHTER: Drinking.

FIRST DAUGHTER: Gambling.

SECOND DAUGHTER: Women.

FIRST DAUGHTER: Waitresses.

SECOND DAUGHTER: Women.
FIRST DAUGHTER: Bar girls.
SECOND DAUGHTER: Women.
FIRST DAUGHTER: Singers.
SECOND DAUGHTER: Women.
FIRST DAUGHTER: Dancers.
SECOND DAUGHTER: Women.
FIRST DAUGHTER: Strippers.
AMAH: He acquired many things.
FIRST and SECOND DAUGHTER: Women!
AMAH: And women adored him. Oh, Jason, your father was such a handsome man. Not like you. You should look at photographs of him and adopt his style. Then women will adore you, too. But Wei Wei was the only one of my children who was beautiful. First Daughter—

(First Daughter pulls down the corners of her mouth with her fingers.)

FIRST DAUGHTER: You will pay!
AMAH: Crooked teeth and sharp fangs that scare most men off. She never found a husband. Second Daughter—

(Second Daughter widens both her eyes with her fingers and smiles.)

SECOND DAUGHTER: I really love babies!
AMAH: Large, dumb eyes that never stayed still. She, too, never found a husband. But Wei Wei, he was special. So strong and healthy and beautiful. Not like your aunts.

(Dan enters.)

SCENE 5

DAN: Oh, the aunties are here! Good day, ladies.
FIRST DAUGHTER: Hello.
SECOND DAUGHTER: Hello.
DAN: How's the vigil?
JASON: The same.
FIRST DAUGHTER: I'm glad you can share in our pain.
DAN: Thank you for sharing it with me. So, Jason, I have some news.
SECOND DAUGHTER: News?
DAN: Um, maybe some privacy?
FIRST DAUGHTER: I know when we're not wanted.

(First Daughter and Second Daughter exit.)

DAN: We got the letter!

JASON: The letter?

DAN: We can fly to China this weekend. To pick her up. A beautiful baby girl from Hunan Province.

JASON: Already?

DAN: What do you mean "already"? We've waited two years for this. And now it's happening!

JASON: We're going to be dads?

DAN: Yes! Isn't that great? So let's start packing.

JASON: Dan, I can't.

DAN: What do you mean you can't?

JASON: I'm not ready.

DAN (*indicating Amah*): You want to wait until she's . . .

JASON: No. I mean, I don't think I'm ready to be a dad.

DAN: Jason, we've waited so long for this.

JASON: I know. I told you we should. But now I don't think we should.

DAN: This is why I stayed at my boring accounting job so I could get that promotion? Why we got a bigger place in a nicer Chicago neighborhood? For the baby? Remember?

JASON: Yes. But.

DAN: But what? The baby's here. It's too late to fight about this now.

AMAH: Fighting? Another way you could learn from your father. Your parents never fought. They were meant for each other.

DAN: Jason, I'm going back to start packing. You can let me know your decision later.

(*Dan exits.*)

AMAH: The instant I met your mother, I knew she was the perfect woman for Wei Wei, the first instant. Tears still well up in my faded eyes when I recall what joy existed between them. And how blessed I was as a mother.

(*Teresa, who is played by the same person as Young Amah, enters. Jason becomes Wei Wei.*)

SCENE 6

The grocery store, 1975. Wei Wei, now an adult, approaches Amah while Teresa keeps her distance.

WEI WEI: Mother?

AMAH: Wei Wei?

WEI WEI: It's me again.

AMAH: Wei Wei! You've returned! First Daughter, Second Daughter, come here! Wei Wei came back!

(First Daughter and Second Daughter enter.)

AMAH: How long has it been?

WEI WEI: Not very long.

AMAH: Three years. Three years since I last saw your face.

WEI WEI: But you've been getting the money?

AMAH: Yes. Every month. The money and a few small words that don't tell me much about your life.

WEI WEI: There wasn't much to tell. Just business.

AMAH: That's not what I heard.

WEI WEI: Is that so?

AMAH: The islands are small. Words move quickly among them.

WEI WEI: Words about what?

FIRST DAUGHTER: Women.

SECOND DAUGHTER: Gambling.

FIRST DAUGHTER: Drinking.

SECOND DAUGHTER: Women.

FIRST DAUGHTER: Gambling.

SECOND DAUGHTER: Drinking.

AMAH: No matter. You're back.

WEI WEI: Yes. Those words—

AMAH: I don't want to hear.

WEI WEI: Mother, I'm here to tell you about someone. Someone unlike anyone else I've met. Mother, this is Teresa.

(Teresa approaches and kisses Amah's hand. She speaks with a Filipino accent, in fragmented sentences.)

TERESA: Honor to meet you, Madam.

AMAH *(to Wei Wei)*: Her Chinese does not sound natural.

WEI WEI: She's not Chinese.

AMAH: I see.

WEI WEI: She's Filipino. I met her on the island just across the water from the island of Negros. She's the purchasing manager of her store. And from my company, she bought—

TERESA: Hammers! Screwdrivers! Drills!

WEI WEI: Yes.

AMAH: Why does this Filipino girl speak Chinese?

WEI WEI: I taught her.

TERESA: He good teacher!

WEI WEI: So she could speak to you.

AMAH: Is that so?

WEI WEI: Yes.

AMAH: But Wei Wei, I don't need any more domestic servants.

WEI WEI: Teresa is my fiancee.

TERESA: Wonderful news, yes?

WEI WEI: I search for the perfect woman all over the Philippines and I find her just one island away.

AMAH: Amusing.

WEI WEI: She's warm and gentle and beautiful.

AMAH: Her feet are enormous.

WEI WEI: And she's a great cook.

AMAH: Filipino food? That takes no skill.

TERESA: And I can dance!

(Teresa begins dancing in circles around Wei Wei and Amah.)

WEI WEI: I never thought I would find someone like her.

AMAH: I never thought you would either.

WEI WEI: What do you think, Mother?

AMAH: Her speech is simple. That has its charms.

WEI WEI: She's just learning Chinese. But when she speaks Filipino, she's well-spoken and deep, and the words she chooses are gentle to the ear.

TERESA: Hammers, screwdrivers, drills!

WEI WEI: She went to university.

AMAH: An educated woman? You know what that means? Endless nagging.

WEI WEI: She's patient and understanding. Unlike any woman I've ever known.

AMAH: You have not known enough Chinese women.

WEI WEI: There is no one like her. *(Pause.)* Mother, we want your blessing.

AMAH: Blessing?

TERESA: Blessing very important, Madam. Please?

WEI WEI: Her parents have cast her out. So she ran away with me.

TERESA: My family do not like Wei Wei.

FIRST DAUGHTER: The Chinese are baffling!

SECOND DAUGHTER: The Chinese are shifty!

FIRST DAUGHTER: The Chinese are bleeding our country to death!

AMAH: And what's wrong with my son?

SECOND DAUGHTER: The Chinese are greedy!

FIRST DAUGHTER: The Chinese are crooked!

SECOND DAUGHTER: They tell you sweet-sounding lies as they rip out your heart!

WEI WEI: Her family hates the Chinese. To them, we are strangers in this country, people without papers.

AMAH: How ignorant! What can you expect from jungle savages?

TERESA: Yes, Madam.

WEI WEI: And according to the law, if she marries a Chinese man, she's no longer a Filipino. Then she'll be without papers, too.

AMAH: Too bad for her.

WEI WEI: We'll have a marriage, but it won't be a legal one.

AMAH: What is your meaning, Wei Wei?

WEI WEI: Our marriage won't be recognized by law. And it won't be recognized by Teresa's family.

(Amah does not respond. Wei Wei wheels her away from Teresa so they can have a private conversation.)

When I left home, I began to drink and gamble and meet all sorts of women. Then I met Teresa. She changed all that. I gave up my old habits. For her. And she told me since she now has no family, she wants to be a part of ours. Please, Mother. Say yes.

(Pause.)

If it wasn't for her, I would have drank myself to death.

AMAH: Is that right?

WEI WEI: Yes.

AMAH: No, I simply cannot give you my blessing. Not to a Filipino woman.

(Takashi enters.)

TAKASHI *(reciting a poem)*:
  Snuff the candle out. A gloomy light.
  Dewdrops felt above the sheet.
  Hands can't touch the other's hands.
  Sleep and dream of good times gone.

WEI WEI: Is being with someone Chinese so important to you?

AMAH: *(Pushes Takashi away from her memory.)* Yes.

(Takashi exits.)

WEI WEI: Then we're getting married anyway.

AMAH: Without my permission?

WEI WEI: We love each other. We don't need your permission.

(Wei Wei and Teresa exit.)

AMAH: Was I so harsh? I must have misremembered some of the details. I am old, forgive me. But the wedding was majestic! Such delicious food. Beautiful decorations. A ceremony filled with laughter and love. Wait. I wasn't at their wedding. That's right. I wasn't. Most likely, the invitation got lost in that unreliable Filipino postal service. But I imagine your parents' wedding to have been quite spectacular, like mine. One day, Jason, you, too, can have a nice wedding. You just haven't met the right woman yet. Just find someone like your mother.

(*Dan enters.*)

SCENE 7

The hospital.

DAN: You're not going with me.

JASON: No.

DAN: I already bought your ticket.

JASON: You just wasted a lot of money.

DAN: Your grandmother was born in China. Don't you want to honor her by going?

JASON: She left China when she was sixteen. And never went back.

AMAH: China was a beautiful land. Every stone had a history about it, every tree had a poem.

DAN: All she talked about was China this and China that. She never returned?

JASON: No. And I don't need to go.

DAN: I'll get you a souvenir. A Chairman Mao alarm clock? A knockoff name-brand handbag?

AMAH: My father taught me so much poetry when I lived in Amoy City.

JASON: You don't need to get me anything.

DAN: Just our child. I think you should get out of here. You're not going to learn to be a father from her.

AMAH: My father had so many wise words.

(*Amah's Father enters.*)

AMAH'S FATHER: My words were lies!

AMAH (*to Amah's Father*): You comforted me when we said good-bye.

DAN: Good-bye.

AMAH'S FATHER: You don't remember? What I said to you?

(*Dan exits.*)

AMAH: Of course, I remember.

SCENE 8

The house in Amoy City, China, 1920. We are even farther back in the past. Young Amah at sixteen enters. Amah watches them.

YOUNG AMAH: I hate good-byes. Father, will my wedding day be the last time I'll see you?

AMAH'S FATHER: Of course not! You'll have opportunities to return!

YOUNG AMAH: Why do I have to get married?

AMAH'S FATHER: You have so many questions!

YOUNG AMAH: I don't want to get married. I don't want to leave China.

AMAH'S FATHER: Lo Chiu Hua, my daughter, my daughter. You've been engaged to Ang Cho An since you were a child. Now you are sixteen years old. It is your time. You should feel joy.

YOUNG AMAH: What if I am unhappy with him? What if there's no joy?

AMAH (*echoing*): What if there's no joy?

AMAH'S FATHER: My daughter, my daughter. Ang Cho An is a clever merchant who has built a fortune in the lush islands of the Philippines. There, riches grow like coconuts on trees. China, though a country of much glory, is governed now by chaos, not by law.

YOUNG AMAH: I am scared to leave.

AMAH'S FATHER: Tomorrow you will board a steamship, depart Amoy City and sail across the Southern Ocean. That night he will take you to bed and you will bleed.

YOUNG AMAH: Bleed?

AMAH'S FATHER: You will enjoy your voyage on the steamship. Three days and nights of sumptuous food, of dancing on the open deck. Then you will arrive in Manila, the jewel of the Philippines. What pride you'll feel as you take your first steps into the mansion of Ang Cho An. You'll be among the strangers of the South, yes, but as a Chinese lady!

YOUNG AMAH: But what if he doesn't like me?

AMAH'S FATHER: My daughter, my daughter. You are beautiful! Like a peach tree in full bloom. And cultured, you who've mastered the poetry of all the dynasties. He cannot help but be impressed.

YOUNG AMAH: Yes, Father.

AMAH'S FATHER: Yes! However . . . you just watch your mouth. You do have a tendency to speak when it is unneeded. Quite unsavory in a woman. Remember, he will take my place as the man to whom you'll listen. Ang Cho An's father is an important business partner.

AMAH: Yes, Father.

YOUNG AMAH: Yes, Father.

AMAH'S FATHER: I hope everything is clear.

YOUNG AMAH: I'm not ready to be a wife!

AMAH'S FATHER: Lo Chiu Hua, my daughter, my daughter. If only your mother was still on earth so that she may alleviate your fears. There are some things only a woman can say to a woman, that I, a man, cannot.

YOUNG AMAH: Father, I have many fears.

AMAH'S FATHER: Listen. When seen from a far distance, or from a far time, each one of us, singly, is insignificant. Small as dust. But in truth, this is not so. You see, we are all part of a scroll of sacred writing that begins high up beyond the sky with the first of our race. With their ancient hands, the ancestors pull up this scroll of descendants, the generations and generations of our people, upward to the heavens. A scroll made up of men, with wives holding tight around their waists. Each embrace becomes a brushstroke on this scroll, the words that all together form the history of our people.

How important that this writing never ends. If any single one of us lets go—of a father, of a husband, of a son—the scroll cannot continue, and our history will end. This is why you must be wed. Do you understand?

YOUNG AMAH and AMAH: Yes, I understand.

AMAH'S FATHER (to Amah): A scroll of sacred writing. You said you understood. But I did not. I needed to keep a business partner happy.

AMAH: But your words remained with me for my whole life. They kept me going when I could not go on.

AMAH'S FATHER: The words were hollow.

AMAH: When I felt hollow, they filled me up.

AMAH'S FATHER: You should have found a husband that you loved.

AMAH: I did.

(Ang Cho An enters.)

ANG CHO AN: Is that true?

AMAH: Yes. Of course, I did. But you betrayed me! And your family. I spent my life protecting your name.

ANG CHO AN: I never cared about my name.

AMAH: Someone had to.

ANG CHO AN: We were never meant to be together.

AMAH: We did not try hard enough.

ANG CHO AN: There was never any chance. You don't remember?

AMAH: Of course, I remember.

SCENE 9

On a ship bound for the Philippines, 1920.

YOUNG AMAH (*reciting*):
  Bright moon born above the sea.
  This time is shared across the earth.
  Loved ones hate that night is long.
  They miss each other 'til the dawn—

ANG CHO AN: No poems, thank you. You'll make me even more seasick.

YOUNG AMAH: Sorry. My father told me that you might enjoy a poem from the Tang Dynasty.

ANG CHO AN: Perhaps later.

YOUNG AMAH: That was a most successful wedding celebration, was it not? And all the most distinguished men of Amoy City were there to wish us all the fortune in the world. All in all, a most joy-filled wedding.

ANG CHO AN: Yes, yes.

YOUNG AMAH: My father wept so many tears when we parted at the pier. Even though he had promised not to shed a single one. Perhaps because he realized I would not see him again. I hope to see him again.

ANG CHO AN: You will.

YOUNG AMAH: I must apologize. Of course, you are my family now, Ang Cho An. Not my father. You are.

ANG CHO AN: Yes, yes.

YOUNG AMAH: You do not talk much, do you?

ANG CHO AN: Talking is not a task that interests me.

YOUNG AMAH: Oh. Do you mean to say you would like to start what newlyweds do this very night?

ANG CHO AN: Lo Chiu Hua, I want to extinguish the light.

AMAH: I had hoped that we could talk some more.

YOUNG AMAH: I had hoped that we could talk some more. To know each other better. Before I bleed for you.

ANG CHO AN: There will be time to bleed another night.

YOUNG AMAH (*relieved*): Thank you, Ang Cho An!

ANG CHO AN: And there will be time for talking another night. Now I am tired and only want to sleep.

YOUNG AMAH: Yes, Ang Cho An. If that is your wish.

ANG CHO AN: It is.

(The light is extinguished.)

YOUNG AMAH: You were very handsome in your photograph, like a Shanghai film star. But in person, you are even more so.

ANG CHO AN: Yes, yes.

YOUNG AMAH: I cannot wait to see the mansion in your compound in Manila.

ANG CHO AN: There is no mansion.

YOUNG AMAH: You have a modest house in your compound, then?

ANG CHO AN: There is no compound.

YOUNG AMAH: So what do you have in Manila?

ANG CHO AN: Manila is a putrid, overcrowded port. I left it long ago.

YOUNG AMAH: I do not understand.

ANG CHO AN: I will tell you all tomorrow. Tonight you can listen to the ocean's words, not mine.

YOUNG AMAH: I do not want to listen to the ocean. You explain!

ANG CHO AN: You talk too much for a woman.

YOUNG AMAH: I will not let you sleep until you explain.

ANG CHO AN: I want to go to bed!

YOUNG AMAH: Explain.

AMAH: Explain!

ANG CHO AN: If it will make you hush.

YOUNG AMAH: Start.

ANG CHO AN: The money that my father gave me three years back—to start a business in the Philippines—has disappeared.

YOUNG AMAH: How?

ANG CHO AN: On cockfights and on dice.

YOUNG AMAH: Gambling?

ANG CHO AN: And then there's the opium.

YOUNG AMAH: Why?

AMAH: Why?

ANG CHO AN: It's lonely over there, among the strangers of the South. We Chinese float about, disconnected from the land. Our spirits hate our flesh. But when I eat the opium, I become without a body. This body of some unhappy man.

YOUNG AMAH: There's no money?

ANG CHO AN: I left Manila for an island full of sugarcane even farther south. An island called Negros. The strangers of the West gave it that name because in their language it means "dark." Because the strangers of the South they found there were dark of skin. And now I live among them. In a hut.

YOUNG AMAH: A hut?

ANG CHO AN: I work in the fields, cutting sugarcane.

YOUNG AMAH: Out in the fields. Like a common Filipino.

AMAH: Like a common Filipino.

ANG CHO AN: But at least I have enough to eat.

YOUNG AMAH: To eat opium.

ANG CHO AN: We eat to live.

YOUNG AMAH: These facts are quite a surprise.

AMAH: Quite.

ANG CHO AN: I promised my father I would come back to China in three years' time to have my bride, which he had selected long ago. If I did not return, he would have lost his name. And, of course, I would not have received your father's generous dowry.

YOUNG AMAH: Quite a surprise.

AMAH: Quite.

ANG CHO AN: The island of Negros is no Manila. But you will learn to like it.

YOUNG AMAH: Quite a surprise.

ANG CHO AN: And appreciate our woven palm-leaf hut.

YOUNG AMAH: I do not think you are a man at all.

ANG CHO AN: Do not talk to me like that.

YOUNG AMAH: You are not a man at all!

AMAH: You are not a man at all!

ANG CHO AN (to Amah): You always spoke of "men" and "women" and what they each must do. But I don't recognize those words. They don't mean much to me.

AMAH (to Ang Cho An): It took me so long to realize.

ANG CHO AN: It took you many years.

AMAH: I had long suspected but could not say in speech. Until the neighbors talked.

ANG CHO AN: Then it's good that neighbors talk.

SCENE 10

The hut on Negros Island, 1935. Young Amah is now thirty-one.

YOUNG AMAH (to Ang Cho An): And the neighbors talk to me, too!

ANG CHO AN: About what?

YOUNG AMAH: About you and your friends. The Filipinos.

AMAH: They are just friends of mine.

ANG CHO AN: They are just friends of mine. That's all.

YOUNG AMAH: And there's that one you spend so much time with—

ANG CHO AN: His name is Miguel.

YOUNG AMAH: Never enough time for your two daughters. But so much time for Miguel.

ANG CHO AN: He is a friend of mine.

YOUNG AMAH: Your friend is so much younger than you.

ANG CHO AN: We are like brothers. I am the elder. He is the younger.

YOUNG AMAH: You can barely speak his language.

ANG CHO AN: Our friendship goes beyond words.

YOUNG AMAH: You spend all our money on him.

ANG CHO AN: Do not forget that it is because of Miguel that I have given up the opium! If it was not for him, I would have drugged myself to death!

AMAH (*as if dictating a letter*): Dear father, I am having a wonderful time in Manila. Ang Cho An's mansion is huge.

AMAH'S FATHER: Our eyes are keen as compass needles.

AMAH: Dear father, the social circuit has kept me busy. I cannot return to Amoy City once again this year.

AMAH'S FATHER: Our minds as sharp as firecrackers.

AMAH: Dear father, Ang Cho An's two sons are growing up so tall.

AMAH'S FATHER: Our feet as quick as printing presses.

AMAH: Dear father, once again entertaining my husband's clients has kept me occupied.

AMAH'S FATHER: And our skin as fine as paper.

AMAH: Maybe next year.

AMAH'S FATHER: Not like the strangers of the South. For we are the Chinese, the descendants of our people.

AMAH: Maybe next year.

ANG CHO AN: The other villagers? Chattering Chinese busybodies.

YOUNG AMAH: But you understand the Filipinos?

ANG CHO AN: They understand me more than you do. Bahala na.

YOUNG AMAH: What does that mean?

ANG CHO AN: There's no translation in Chinese.

YOUNG AMAH: Impossible. Anything worth saying, you can say in Chinese.

ANG CHO AN: It means: Let it go.

YOUNG AMAH: You want me to let this go?

ANG CHO AN: You'll never understand.

YOUNG AMAH: We are part of a great scroll! A scroll of sacred writing that stretches high up into the sky with the—

ANG CHO AN: No more talk of that damn scroll!

YOUNG AMAH: You can't tell the difference between a man and a woman!

AMAH'S FATHER: We are the ones who keep the books, and the books must always balance!

SCENE 11

ANG CHO AN (*to Amah*): I hated that scroll lecture! I hated your Chinese lectures, your Chinese fairytales, and especially your Chinese poems!

AMAH'S FATHER (*to Amah*): He's right. The poems were ancient things. They're dead.

AMAH: No! Our language is the order of our world.

ANG CHO AN: That was not always true for you.

AMAH: Of course, it is. In my head are three hundred poems of the Tang Dynasty. And two hundred from the Song.

ANG CHO AN: You had a moment when your language fell apart. And you smiled.

AMAH: I don't remember.

AMAH'S FATHER: You don't remember?

ANG CHO AN: You don't remember?

(Ang Cho An and Amah's Father exit.)

SCENE 12

The hut on Negros Island, 1941. Young Amah is thirty-seven.

Takashi enters, thinking the hut is empty. He begins rifling through the home, looking for food. Young Amah sees him.

YOUNG AMAH: Who are you? What are you doing here?

(Takashi turns around. Young Amah realizes that he's a soldier.)

Get out of my house!

(Takashi points a gun at her.)

Don't hurt me! Take what you want. Don't hurt me!

(Takashi tries to quiet her down.)

I'll be quiet. I'll be quiet. Please.

SCENE 13

The hospital.

FIRST DAUGHTER: Men are never up to any good. I should have warned you earlier.

SECOND DAUGHTER: He just left you?

JASON: He took a little trip.

FIRST DAUGHTER: The gay man left you. Where'd he go?

JASON: Somewhere far away.

FIRST DAUGHTER: I knew it.

SECOND DAUGHTER: It wasn't us, was it? Sometimes our family can be a bit too much.

JASON: No, it wasn't you, Tita Dominga.

FIRST DAUGHTER: It's because he's a man. That's what men do. They have their fun, then leave.

SECOND DAUGHTER: Maybe you'd be happier with women.

JASON: I'm sure I wouldn't.

FIRST DAUGHTER: Men can never accept responsibility.

SECOND DAUGHTER: They never grow up.

FIRST DAUGHTER: They have their friends. And forget their wives.

SECOND DAUGHTER: That's why we never got married.

AMAH: That's why you never got married?

SECOND DAUGHTER: But then again, Dan is such a good person.

FIRST DAUGHTER: How would you know?

SECOND DAUGHTER: He is so handsome. And has a nice smile.

FIRST DAUGHTER: Those are the worst. They think they can get away with anything. It's a good thing he left you.

JASON: He's coming back.

FIRST DAUGHTER: You can tell yourself that now. But you'll get over it eventually.

JASON: He's bringing back a baby.

AMAH: A baby?

FIRST and SECOND DAUGHTER: A baby?

JASON: We're adopting a girl from China. He's there now to get her.

FIRST DAUGHTER: What are you going to do with a baby?

JASON: Dan and I are going to be fathers.

SECOND DAUGHTER: You?

FIRST DAUGHTER: A father?

AMAH: How can you be a father? You'll disgrace the memory of your own! Wei Wei was a real father. He knew how to raise a child. That's why after he married your mother they moved far from me, far away from the island of Negros, to Manila, the jewel of the Philippines! To earn more money and to start a new life!

SCENE 14

The apartment in Manila.

WEI WEI: To start a new life with my Teresa!

(*Teresa begins to dance with Wei Wei.*)

AMAH: They moved to an expensive high-rise apartment that overlooked Manila Bay. And soon, I grew tired of the island of Negros. How tiny and provincial it seemed! I wanted a share of that cosmopolitan life. So Wei Wei begged me to stay with him in Manila. So generous. I said, "But,

Wei Wei, you are now a husband! I can no longer interfere!" And he said, "Mother, if you live with us, it will be just like the happiest days of my life—when I was a boy." And once again his words moved me so and his resolve was so strong, I could not refuse. *(On the phone.)* Wei Wei!

WEI WEI: Yes, Mother?

AMAH: I've sold the store and will move to Manila next week.

WEI WEI: Where will you stay?

AMAH: I, of course, will stay with you. I am an old woman now. My bones are brittle, and my heart is weak. And I do not want domestic servants watching over me.

WEI WEI: Mother—

AMAH: I do not know how much longer I can walk this mortal world. Oh, I forgot. I cannot walk anyway.

WEI WEI: There's no room for you here.

AMAH: I remember you mentioning a second bedroom.

WEI WEI: Which is where the baby will sleep when it's born.

AMAH: So that is where I can stay and help you be a parent. So you will care for me, and I will care for your child.

WEI WEI: I'll have to ask Teresa.

AMAH: There is, of course, no need to consult with your wife.

WEI WEI: We discuss everything together.

AMAH: You are the man of the family. Do not be infected by that Filipino thinking! I just want to share in your happiness.

WEI WEI: Yes, Mother.

AMAH: How I wish your children will be as kind to you as you are to me.

WEI WEI: Yes, Mother. You may come.

(Teresa begins to argue with Wei Wei. Teresa points at her belly, indicating the child she's carrying.)

AMAH: Was that what really happened? I thought Wei Wei had invited me. Did I invite myself? That sounds so unlike me. But in any case, one night, after listening to Chinese opera on the radio, I came out to the balcony and started back to my room when I heard your parents speaking Filipino. So I crouched by your parents' bedroom window and peered in. Oh what a sight! A pair of lovers in their youth! Speaking in a language I could not share in!

WEI WEI: Bahala na.

(Wei Wei walks away.)

TERESA: Bahala na.

(Teresa becomes Young Amah.)

SCENE 15

The hut on Negros Island, 1941.

Takashi is pointing the gun at Young Amah. Realizing she's harmless, he puts the gun away. He motions that he's hungry.

YOUNG AMAH: I don't understand.
TAKASHI: Food.
YOUNG AMAH: Food?
TAKASHI: Hungry.
YOUNG AMAH: You're hungry?

(*Takashi nods his head. Young Amah backs away slowly and fetches a bowl of rice.*)

YOUNG AMAH: Rice. It's the only food I have.

(*She places the bowl in front of him. He puts the gun on the ground and begins eating ravenously, like a starved animal. When he finishes, he bows.*)

TAKASHI: Thank you.

(*Ang Cho An enters.*)

SCENE 16

ANG CHO AN (*to Amah*): See that?
AMAH: What else could I do?
ANG CHO AN: You could have run.
AMAH: I was not a coward.
ANG CHO AN: You call me a coward? I was only a coward in that I waited so long to do what I had to do.
AMAH: What you had to do? You deserted me! And our daughters!
ANG CHO AN: You left them, too!
AMAH: I did not. Don't speak of such a thing.
ANG CHO AN: You don't remember?
AMAH: I don't remember.
YOUNG AMAH (*to Ang Cho An*): The daughters!
ANG CHO AN (*to Young Amah*): And what about the daughters?
YOUNG AMAH: You cannot leave our daughters!
ANG CHO AN: The war has already come to the Philippines. The Japanese arrive this week. They'll turn our island upside down to plunder all its wealth. Nothing will be the same.

YOUNG AMAH: So you're leaving us behind?

ANG CHO AN: I'm free of you. But this means that you are also free.

YOUNG AMAH: Free?

ANG CHO AN: Don't play dumb. For more than twenty years we've been a burden to each other.

YOUNG AMAH: Without a husband what am I? And our daughters?

ANG CHO AN: They were never mine to want.

YOUNG AMAH: Deserting us in a time of war. You are not a man at all!

ANG CHO AN: Say what you want.

AMAH: It's that Filipino boy.

YOUNG AMAH: It's that Filipino boy.

ANG CHO AN: I'm leaving this hut forever. And for your sake and for the daughters, do the same.

AMAH: I'm not leaving.

YOUNG AMAH: I'm not leaving. I'll stay until you return. You will change your mind.

ANG CHO AN: Are you listening? I'm not coming back! Do not be here when the Japanese arrive! At least get the daughters far away. Don't leave them in the village.

(Pause.)

I'll find a neighbor to take them to the mountains. They will live without a father. They will live without a mother. But they will live. To hate us both.

YOUNG AMAH: Let the Japanese come.

SCENE 17

The hut on Negros Island. Takashi has finished his bowl of rice. He displays the empty bowl to her.

YOUNG AMAH: You're still hungry? You want more?

(Takashi nods his head. Young Amah approaches him, motioning toward the bowl. But she grabs the gun instead. She stands and points the gun at him. Takashi puts his hands in front of him, pleading with her to put the gun down.)

TAKASHI: No! Please! Don't! I justed wanted food. I didn't want to hurt you. Please!

YOUNG AMAH: I don't understand you. I don't understand what you're saying.

TAKASHI: Don't! I was only hungry.

YOUNG AMAH: I only speak Chinese. Chinese.

TAKASHI: Chinese? I took Chinese at school. But all I remember are the poems. I don't remember any grammar. "Hello." "Good-bye." "Nice to meet you." Really, all I remember are the poems. (*Takashi stops to recall a memory. He recites.*)
Bright moon born above the sea.
This time is shared across the earth.
Loved ones hate that night is long.
They miss each other 'til the dawn.
Snuff the candle out. A gloomy light.
Dewdrops felt above the sheet.
Hands can't touch the other's hands.
Sleep and dream of good times gone.

(*Young Amah is stunned. She lowers the gun.*)

SCENE 18

The hospital.

FIRST DAUGHTER: So Dan went to China, and you're still here?

JASON: You only need one person to pick up a child.

FIRST DAUGHTER: Yes, but you're going to be a father.

SECOND DAUGHTER: I think it's great that he decided to stay here. With his grandmother. He's thinking of his family.

JASON: That's right. I'm thinking of my family.

FIRST DAUGHTER: Dan and the baby are your family now.

JASON: Yes, that's right.

FIRST DAUGHTER: So how is that a family if you're still here and he's over there?

SECOND DAUGHTER: Don't be so hard on him. He's never been a dad before.

FIRST DAUGHTER: Jason, I don't think you're ready to be a dad.

AMAH: When you were born, your father was so excited. He had no doubts about wanting to raise a child. Now look at you. So indecisive. Perhaps it's because you grew up without your father, so you don't know how to be one. This must be all your mother's fault. She must have spoiled you growing up.

SCENE 19

The apartment in Manila. Teresa enters, carrying a baby.

AMAH (*to Teresa*): Will you stop spoiling him?

TERESA: What you mean, Mother-in-law?

AMAH: The way you dote on Jason, it makes me sick.

TERESA: How should I speak to him then?

AMAH: Sternly.

TERESA: But he is not even one year old!

AMAH: Starting early is the best. This is how to be a parent.

(*Teresa begins to sob.*)

AMAH: What's wrong?

TERESA: You have to ask?

AMAH: I cannot read your mind.

TERESA: Your son! I knew he liked to drink.

FIRST DAUGHTER: Drinking!

TERESA: I thought he stop when we marry, but after Jason born, he start again.

SECOND DAUGHTER: Drinking!

AMAH: Sure, a few glasses now and then.

TERESA: First with his friends. He goes out all night, coming home only when it's late.

FIRST DAUGHTER: Drinking!

TERESA: And now he start gambling again. Play mahjongg.

SECOND DAUGHTER: Gambling!

AMAH: He plays for fun.

TERESA: First he gamble away his wages. And then when he has no money, he go to my store and demand from me.

FIRST DAUGHTER: Gambling!

TERESA: He owe people money.

SECOND DAUGHTER: Gambling!

AMAH: That doesn't sound like my son. You exaggerate.

TERESA: And then—

FIRST DAUGHTER: Women!

TERESA: Once I follow him. He go to hotel.

SECOND DAUGHTER: Women!

TERESA: And who is waiting there? To go with him inside?

FIRST DAUGHTER: Women!

TERESA: My worst fears! Another woman.

AMAH: Stop telling me these lies!

SECOND DAUGHTER: Drinking.

FIRST DAUGHTER: Gambling.

SECOND DAUGHTER: Women.

TERESA: The others who work with him. They tell me. He see many women. But I never believe them. Until now.

FIRST DAUGHTER: Drinking.

SECOND DAUGHTER: Gambling.

FIRST DAUGHTER: Women.

AMAH: I don't believe you! He's the perfect son!

TERESA: He no longer man I married! He is now son you raised!

(Teresa, First Daughter, and Second Daughter exit. Wei Wei enters.)

WEI WEI: You're awake.

AMAH *(to Wei Wei)*: You're home. Jason can walk now, do you know that?

WEI WEI: No.

AMAH: He took his first steps today.

WEI WEI: I'm going to bed.

AMAH: We talk so little now.

WEI WEI: It's late. I'm tired.

AMAH: Wei Wei, look at you, you have grown so thin.

(Wei Wei sits down and holds his stomach.)

AMAH: Wei Wei . . .

WEI WEI: I need to go to the hospital.

AMAH: What's wrong?

WEI WEI: Teresa!

(Teresa enters. She sees Wei Wei in pain, then embraces him.)

TERESA: Wei Wei!

AMAH: And one night, he began to cough up blood. The doctors said he would need an operation. They said he had drank so much his liver had begun to rot. But the doctors were just being overdramatic. Really, it was all the stress he felt. Work was very hard. Also, Filipino food was not good for him. So I encouraged Wei Wei to take a short vacation. Away from the Philippines. And that's why he decided to leave the country with your mother and yourself.

WEI WEI: Dear Mother—

AMAH: Wei Wei! Where are you?

WEI WEI:—I haven't spoken to you in seven years. After my operation, Teresa decided we would leave the Philippines. So we are in America now, in Washington, D.C. One day I'll repay all my debts. I worry about you. I know all you want is to hear that I am well. So I write you. I am well.

AMAH:

Dearest Wei Wei,

Expect to see me by the end of the month.

Since you've been gone, my eyes have been cloudy and my hands shake. I worry that with every day I am closer to leaving this world. One thought only makes me happy. Let me live with you in America.

Please do not deny me this pleasure. Seven years have passed without me seeing your face. Let me see you again before I die.

I have already bought my ticket to America. I am so excited.

Love, your mother.

SCENE 20

The house in Washington, 1984. Wei Wei enters, with Teresa supporting him as he walks.

WEI WEI *(to Amah)*: I don't feel well.

AMAH *(to Wei Wei)*: I've finished rearranging the kitchen. Wei Wei, you must tell your wife that she must be more organized. I know this is America, but there still must be limits to her freedom.

WEI WEI: Can we talk about that later?

AMAH: You looked so healthy when I arrived. Now a month later, you can barely walk? Teresa's disorganization must be no help.

WEI WEI: She's busy with work.

AMAH: Too busy to take care of you. Good thing I'm here. And your son, Jason! Every night, banging, clanging, running all around the house. How can you get a good amount of sleep? He's already eight years old. He should understand some things.

WEI WEI: I will speak with him.

(First Daughter enters.)

AMAH: There's something else I wanted to tell you. First Daughter wants to move in with us.

WEI WEI: No.

AMAH: You owe her a lot of money, right? For your medical bills?

FIRST DAUGHTER: You will pay!

AMAH: So don't complain. She wants to watch you to make sure you don't go back to bad habits. And she wants her money back. Also Second Daughter.

(Second Daughter enters.)

WEI WEI: What about her?

AMAH: She's moving in, too.

WEI WEI: Why?

AMAH: Second Daughter has mentioned that she should adopt Jason. You know she wants children.

SECOND DAUGHTER: Because I really love babies!

AMAH: How generous she is, Wei Wei. I agree that this plan is perfect for all involved.

WEI WEI: I'm not giving up my son.

AMAH: Well, see how she is with Jason. You just might change your mind.

WEI WEI: There is not enough room in this house.

AMAH: Of course, there is.

FIRST DAUGHTER: You will pay!

AMAH: You have one extra room here and also the basement.

SECOND DAUGHTER: Because I really love babies!

FIRST DAUGHTER: You will pay!

SECOND DAUGHTER: Because I really love babies!

WEI WEI: The house will be too crowded.

AMAH: Crowded, but we can all take care of each other.

FIRST DAUGHTER: You will pay!

SECOND DAUGHTER: Because I really love babies!

AMAH: It will be just like when you were a boy!

FIRST DAUGHTER: You will pay!

SECOND DAUGHTER: Because I really love babies!

(Wei Wei collapses to the ground.)

TERESA: Wei Wei! *(She rushes toward Wei Wei.)* His heart stop.

AMAH: His heart stopped?

TERESA: He's not breathing!

(Wei Wei rises, looks back at Amah and Teresa, then exits.)

WEI WEI IS DEAD!

AMAH: My son is dead!

TERESA: He's dead!

AMAH *(to herself)*: I loved my son too much. So he could never be the son or husband or father that he wished that he could be. I couldn't let him go, and he died too young! Was it because he was the only happiness in my life? How was that possible? What about him made me love him more than he deserved?

SCENE 21

The hospital.

SECOND DAUGHTER: Did you talk to him?

FIRST DAUGHTER: Why aren't you at the airport?

JASON: I told you, I have to be with Amah.

FIRST DAUGHTER: When are they supposed to get here?
JASON: Any moment now. Why do you keep asking me these questions?
SECOND DAUGHTER: What are you going to say to him?
JASON: I'll know when he gets here, OK?

(*Dan enters, holding a baby.*)

DAN: We missed you.

(*First Daughter and Second Daughter melt when they see the baby.*)

Aren't you going to say something?
FIRST DAUGHTER: She's so cute!
SECOND DAUGHTER: Look at you!
DAN: Her name is Lili.

(*First Daughter and Second Daughter scramble
to take turns holding the baby.*)

SECOND DAUGHTER: Jason, don't you want to hold the baby?

(*Jason doesn't move.*)

FIRST DAUGHTER: Jason, she's your daughter.
SECOND DAUGHTER: Jason?
FIRST DAUGHTER: Your daughter?
DAN: I'll take her. (*Dan takes the baby and starts to leave the room.*)
SECOND DAUGHTER: You're not going to ignore your daughter, are you?

SCENE 22

A cave on Negros Island, 1941.

AMAH: Where am I?
FIRST DAUGHTER: Mother! You're awake.
AMAH: Who are you?
SECOND DAUGHTER: Your daughters. We're here.
AMAH: My daughters?
FIRST DAUGHTER: You've been asleep for so long. We're safe now. We're in
    the caves. The villagers found you in the ruins of our hut.
SECOND DAUGHTER: We're so glad you're still alive!
AMAH: Alive?

FIRST DAUGHTER: The Japanese hit our village. We saw it from up here in the mountains.

SECOND DAUGHTER: Explosions and fire swallowed up the earth. The village destroyed. They found you half-alive.

AMAH: My legs!

FIRST DAUGHTER: Your legs were crushed. They had to pull you out.

AMAH: What about—anyone else? In the village? Did they find anyone else alive?

SECOND DAUGHTER: They couldn't find our father.

FIRST DAUGHTER: Yes, where is he? Where did father go?

AMAH: Your father?

FIRST DAUGHTER: The neighbors brought us here to hide. They said father went back for you.

SECOND DAUGHTER: Did you see him?

AMAH: Your father?

FIRST DAUGHTER: Yes, what happened to him?

AMAH: He told me he would go get rice. For you and me. He said he would sneak over to the next village—where he knew a man with a hidden store of rice.

SECOND DAUGHTER: He did not come back?

AMAH: No. He must have been—your father was brave. A brave man who thought only of his family. The Japanese are cruel.

FIRST DAUGHTER: And you, mother? Why did you not come to the cave with us?

SECOND DAUGHTER: We were so scared. We felt alone.

FIRST DAUGHTER: We wept for days. We thought you had forgotten us.

AMAH: I got lost. I couldn't find the cave. The trails were overgrown.

FIRST DAUGHTER: Is that true?

AMAH: Yes. I got lost. I couldn't find the cave.

SECOND DAUGHTER: That's the true story?

AMAH: Yes, that is the true story.

FIRST and SECOND DAUGHTER: That is the true story.

(First and Second Daughter exit.)

SCENE 23

The hut on Negros Island. Takashi and Young Amah are reciting poems.

TAKASHI: Before the bed.

YOUNG AMAH: Bright moonlight.

TAKASHI: The ground perhaps?

YOUNG AMAH: Frosty, white.
TAKASHI: The head lifts up.
YOUNG AMAH: A moonlit dome.
TAKASHI: The head bows down.
YOUNG AMAH: Thoughts of home.

(Young Amah thinks of another poem.)

YOUNG AMAH: In early youth he left home.
TAKASHI: Older, he returns one day.
YOUNG AMAH: His local accent hasn't changed.
TAKASHI: But his temple hairs have faded gray.
YOUNG AMAH: Children come to take a look.
TAKASHI: They do not know his face.
YOUNG AMAH: They laugh and ask the visitor:
TAKASHI: You've come here from what place?

(They're both quiet for a moment.)

YOUNG AMAH: You speak Chinese?
TAKASHI: I don't really speak Chinese.
YOUNG AMAH: Sorry, I don't understand you.
TAKASHI: I don't understand. I learned those poems in school. In Chinese class.
YOUNG AMAH: I don't speak your language.
TAKASHI: I only learned the poems. Not the language. But I love the poems.
YOUNG AMAH: I haven't heard those poems in twenty years. My father taught them to me. I miss him. I haven't seen him since I left China. My husband doesn't care for poems. He doesn't think that words are beautiful. But they're the only things I have in my life. The poems are always there. They can't abandon you.
TAKASHI: I hate this war. I wanted to become a writer, not a soldier. But I had to join the army. Otherwise I would have been disgraced. But I couldn't kill. That made me an awful soldier. So I ran away. Now I have nowhere to turn. If the Japanese find me, they'll kill me. If the Filipinos find me, they'll kill me.
YOUNG AMAH: Did you understand what I just said?
TAKASHI: Did you understand what I just said?
YOUNG AMAH *(speaking to him slowly)*: What's your name?
TAKASHI: "Name?"
YOUNG AMAH: Yes. What's your name?

(She gestures toward him.)

TAKASHI: Takashi. You?
YOUNG AMAH: Lo Chiu Hua.

(They approach each other. The sound of flapping wings.)

YOUNG AMAH: What's that?
TAKASHI: A bird. It must have flown inside.
YOUNG AMAH: A bird. It can't get out.

(Young Amah opens the door. The sound of wings flapping away.
Stillness. Then the sound of airplanes in the distance.)

YOUNG AMAH: What's that sound?
TAKASHI: Airplanes.
YOUNG AMAH: "Airplanes"? I don't understand.
TAKASHI: Airplanes.
YOUNG AMAH: Airplanes.
TAKASHI: Yes. We need to go.
YOUNG AMAH: Ignore them.

(Young Amah closes the door.)

TAKASHI: We need to go.
YOUNG AMAH: Ignore them.
TAKASHI: But—

(Young Amah pulls Takashi toward her.
The airplanes get louder.)

YOUNG AMAH: I want to stay here.
TAKASHI: I don't understand.
YOUNG AMAH: With you.

(Takashi puts his arms around Young Amah.)

YOUNG AMAH: I don't even know how to describe how I'm feeling. I have
no words for this.
TAKASHI: "No words."
YOUNG AMAH: No words.
AMAH: No words.
YOUNG AMAH: There's this silly Filipino phrase. The people here say it all
the time. Bahala na.
TAKASHI: "Bahala na." What does it mean?
YOUNG AMAH: Let it go.

TAKASHI: I don't understand.

YOUNG AMAH: Don't worry. I do. I understand it now.

(Amah's Father and Ang Cho An enter.)

SCENE 24

AMAH: I understand it now. Though no words were said and language fell apart. I knew joy. A single moment. I understood. Not in words. But still I understood.

ANG CHO AN: When I died, I did not have my body buried in the Chinese cemetery and laid in place surrounded on all sides with others of my race. With my name carved in stone to stand eternal keep guard above my bones, to guard against disgrace.

AMAH: So now I know why you hated words and disappeared.

(Ang Cho An exits.)

AMAH'S FATHER: My daughter, my daughter! I gave you up to grow accounts. I tried so hard to keep the earnings of our name but lost them when the revolution came to Amoy City. The people carried torches and burned our house down to the ground and all the records, deeds, agreements, and accounts. The scroll of sacred writing was just a ledger book. That was finally set to flame.

AMAH: That's not true. The scroll continues, but not the scroll we thought it was. With every generation, the scroll's redone and retranslated with different words. Only then can it have meaning to our children. With new language that we can't imagine yet. The scroll continues but never looks the same.

AMAH'S FATHER: The people cursed and kicked me 'til I could breathe no more. But when I closed my eyes for one last time, I thought of my daughter in the Philippines whom I gave up long ago.

AMAH: Your greatest gift was taking back your name from me when I became a wife. You let me go but spared my life.

AMAH'S FATHER: I let you go but spared your life.

AMAH: So I am still alive.

SCENE 25

The hospital. Amah awakens. She recognizes the people around her. They are stunned when she speaks.

AMAH: Jason. Beatriz. Dominga. Dan. *(Noticing the baby Dan is holding.)* And who's that?

JASON: Her name is Lili. She's my daughter.

AMAH: Your daughter?

JASON: And Dan's.

AMAH: Both of yours? Is that possible?

(Jason and Dan nod their heads.)

AMAH: Give her to me!

(Dan hands the baby to Amah.)

AMAH *(to the baby)*: My great-granddaughter, you are blessed. Your family is here.

(Amah hands the baby to Jason. At first, Jason is too stunned to move. He looks at Dan. He looks at Amah. He looks at his aunts. He looks at the baby and finally accepts it from his grandmother.)

AMAH *(to Jason)*: Your daughter. Bahala na.

END OF PLAY

7

Ching Chong Chinaman

LAUREN YEE

INTRODUCTION, *by Josephine Lee*

*C*hing Chong Chinaman* was produced by Mu Performing Arts and presented at Mixed Blood Theatre from February 14, 2009, to March 1,
2009, under the direction of Jennifer Weir.

In Frank Chin's play *The Chickencoop Chinaman* (1972), the aptly named
character Tom lectures the rebellious Tam Lum on the value of being the
"model minority": "We used to be kicked around, but that's history, brother.
Today we have good jobs, good pay, and we're lucky. Americans are proud to
say we send more of our kids to college than any other race. We're accepted.
We worked hard for it."[1] Lauren Yee's scathing satire is populated with characters who are seemingly like Tom and have thoroughly embraced their own
successful assimilation. In the program notes, Yee wrote that she first con-
templated the idea for *Ching Chong Chinaman* as a "play about white people":
"Way back before any of it was written, when I just had the kernel of the play
in mind (an American family adopts a Chinese indentured servant), I was dead
set on writing a play about white people." How this idea translates is that the

---

1. Frank Chin, *The Chickencoop Chinaman and the Year of the Dragon* (Seattle: University of
Washington Press, 2004), 59.

Illustration: Maria Kelly and Sherwin Resurreccion in *Ching Chong Chinaman.*
(Photograph used by permission of Michal Daniel.)

Wongs themselves have become thoroughly white, so much so that the humor relies on seeing them blithely enact the desperately materialist, deeply racist, or hopelessly clichéd vapidity of upper-middle-class success.

The play reminds us of the uncomfortable fact that the catchphrase for successful Asian Americans is the "model minority" rather than the "talented tenth." When their teenage son, Upton, brings J into the household to do his homework, each family member easily finds ways to benefit from this contemporary version of coolie labor, thus showing how much middle-class white American prosperity relies on the work of non-white people both in the United States and abroad. As the play progresses, elements of their American dream—suburban home, Ivy League schools, leisure activities, white-collar jobs—are increasingly exposed as fantasies of invisible labor. From a spectacular all-American tap-dancing number to Upton's success at World of Warcraft, the characters in the play reap the material rewards of a world enticed by globalism and fusion cuisine. But what doesn't translate is the deep anxiety felt by these model-minority characters, an anxiety that derails the straight line to assimilation. It is in this uncertainty that the true core of the play emerges and redeems them from both stereotype and their own happy endings.

———

ABOUT THE PLAY

Ching Chong Chinaman was selected for production through a call for submissions by Mu Performing Arts Emerging Writers of Color and was further developed and produced with funding from the Ford Foundation and the National Endowment for the Arts.

CHARACTERS (ORIGINAL CAST)

ED (Kurt Kwan): forties, Chinese American, a businessman; he has a nervous laugh

GRACE (Maria Kelly): forties, Chinese American, Ed's wife, a homemaker

DESDEMONA (Katie Bradley): seventeen, Chinese American, daughter of Ed and Grace, a vegan

UPTON (Eric Sharp): fifteen, Chinese American, son of Ed and Grace, a gamer

THE CHINESE MAN (Sherwin Resurreccion): twenties, Chinese, alias J, Jinqiang, or "Ching Chong"

THE CHINESE WOMAN (Erika Crane): all ages, Chinese; she plays a variety of roles, including Mrs. J, Kim Lee Park, Reporter, Asian Schoolgirl, and Little Chinese Girl.

TIME AND PLACE

The present; Palo Alto, California

SYNOPSIS

The ultra-assimilated Wong family is as Chinese American as apple pie: teen-age Upton dreams of World of Warcraft superstardom; his sister Desdemona dreams of early admission to Princeton. Unfortunately, Upton's chores and homework get in the way of his 24/7 videogaming, and Desi's math grades don't fit the Asian American stereotype. Then Upton comes up with a novel solution for both problems: He acquires a Chinese indentured servant, who harbors an American dream of his own.

Ching Chong Chinaman was a finalist for the 2008 Princess Grace Award and 2009 Jane Chambers Playwriting Award, and the winner of the 2007 Yale Playwrights Festival, Kumu Kahua Theatre's 2007 Pacific Rim Prize, and the 2010 Paula Vogel Award in Playwriting given by the Kennedy Center's American College Theater Festival. It received its professional world premiere in 2009 at Mu Performing Arts in Minneapolis. Other productions include the New York International Fringe Festival in 2007, Berkeley's Impact Theatre in 2008, and New York's Pan Asian Repertory Theatre and Seattle's SIS Productions in 2010.

SCENE 1

Family portrait. Any point in time. The Wongs, a Chinese American family composed of Ed, Grace, Desdemona, and Upton, sit for the annual family portrait. In the middle is a Chinese man in his twenties doing math homework. He would blend right in if he weren't wearing traditional Chinese clothing and a coolie hat.

ED: You know what I love about America?
DESDEMONA: Free speech?
UPTON: Free trade?
GRACE: Apple pie?
ED: Manifest Destiny.
GRACE: Many—what, darling?

(The family freezes in position. Camera flash.)

ED: The idea that we can conquer uncharted plains and retire to our homes and let other people with nothing better to do complete our dirty work.
DESDEMONA: Dad, that is SO not Manifest Destiny.
ED: It's just what Lincoln said about America, Desi.
DESDEMONA: Lincoln was an anti-Semite.
GRACE: "Semite" means "Jewish," Mona.
ED: Some of my best friends are Jewish.
GRACE: Didn't he free the slaves?
ED: Moses freed the slaves, Grace. Moses.

UPTON: Why do we need to do this now? Christmas isn't for another three months.

DESDEMONA: I think Christmas is kind of racist.

ED: The KKK is racist.

GRACE: I don't like the KKK. I don't know what it is about them.

DESDEMONA: Upton's making a face!

ED: One more shot for the Christmas card! Everyone open their eyes nice and wide now.

> *(Everyone stares wide-eyed at the camera. Briefly,*
> *they look pleasant. Flash.)*

GRACE: I love Christmas. It's so American.

SCENE 2

Kitchen. Late afternoon. The Chinese Man sits in the center of the room, working on homework. Grace enters and flips on the light. Distracted, she pats The Chinese Man on the head as she checks the answering machine.

GRACE: Hello, Upton. Don't work in the dark like that.

> *(No messages. Ed enters with his briefcase.)*

ED: Upton. Grace.

GRACE: How was work today?

ED: Same as usual.

GRACE: Mail came.

> *(Grace hands Ed an envelope, which has already been opened.*
> *Ed reads the contents.)*

ED: Thanks, boss.

GRACE: I think you should enter.

ED *(doubtful)*: Lots of guys in the company play golf.

GRACE: But nobody's as good as you. And I'm sure you could find a partner.

ED: Anything else?

GRACE: The doctor said she'd call soon.

ED: Great.

GRACE: Ed, do you think—

ED: Our lawn looked nice today.

> *(Desdemona enters.)*

GRACE: Hello, Mona.
DESDEMONA *(indicating The Chinese Man)*: Who's that?
ED: Who?
DESDEMONA: The Asian guy.
GRACE: Don't talk about your brother like that.
DESDEMONA: That's not Upton.
GRACE: Mona, of course that's—

(Grace and Ed stop to actually look at The Chinese Man.)

ED: Huh.
DESDEMONA: Hey, none of my friends are Asian.
GRACE: And I don't have any friends.
ED: Hello? Hello there? *(To Desdemona and Grace.)* Did it look like he comprehended anything I just said?

(Upton enters.)

UPTON. *(Indicates The Chinese Man.)* This yours?
UPTON: What about him?
GRACE *(whispering.)*: I don't think he speaks English, darling.
UPTON: Of course, he doesn't speak English.
GRACE: Then why do you know him?
UPTON: He's a refugee. He's staying in the laundry room. ⟩
GRACE: On top of the washing machine?
UPTON: Not when you're *doing* the laundry.
GRACE: Isn't there someone else he can stay with? Like someone who also doesn't speak English?
UPTON: He's fleeing persecution.
DESDEMONA: From who?
UPTON: From the Chinese government . . . and stuff.
ED: Ah HA! Knew he was a Chinaman.
DESDEMONA. I SO did not hear you say that.
ED: I can use it. It's like the N-word. *(To The Chinese Man.)* Hello, China-man.
UPTON: His name is Jinqiang.
ED: Come again?
UPTON *(deliberately)*: JIN-qiang.
ED: "Ching Chong"?
DESDEMONA: Omigod.
GRACE: Darling, that name sounds a little racist.
UPTON: "Jinqiang," spelled J-I-N-Q-I—A-N-G.
GRACE: And that's not how you spell Ching Chong, dear.

DESDEMONA: Mom, you can't say "Ching Chong." That's like the most offensive thing in the world.

ED: But if I called my fellow Asian Americans "Ching Chong"—

DESDEMONA: Racist.

ED: I didn't finish.

DESDEMONA: You *can't* say that.

ED: It's not like we're calling him "Chinky" or something.

GRACE *(to Desdemona)*: But if his name *is* Ching Chong, dear . . .

UPTON: Just call him J.

DESDEMONA: We need to return him to his natural environment. We don't know anything about his diet, his lifestyle, his basic wants. We don't even have the right sensitivity training to even begin to cater to his needs as a displaced person.

UPTON: Dad, if we send J away, who knows what kind of racism, oppression, and torture he'll face without our protection and benevolence. Plus, it's for school.

DESDEMONA: It is not for school!

ED: Well, we are benevolent.

DESDEMONA: Dad, housing a refugee can't be for school.

ED: Grace, you're the boss.

GRACE: I am?

ED: Do you have any problems with Ching Chong?

GRACE: Well, school *is* important.

UPTON: Great. It's settled.

DESDEMONA: Mom!

UPTON *(to The Chinese Man)*: Come on!

(Upton pulls The Chinese Man, now identified as J, out of the kitchen and up the stairs.)

GRACE: Wait, why is he here again?

ED *(shrugging)*: School?

DESDEMONA: This is ridiculous. How are we supposed to even communicate with him?

ED: If he doesn't know English and we don't know Chinese, as long as he's in America, that's his fault, not ours.

DESDEMONA: He's probably not even a real refugee anyway.

ED *(almost to himself)*: And what's wrong with "Ching Chong"?

GRACE: You know, you should really trust your brother a little more.

DESDEMONA: Why? He totally takes advantage of you guys. You buy him things he doesn't need. And then you buy him *more* things that he also doesn't need. I mean, where's my tuition money supposed to come from—hmm?—if he's buying everything?

GRACE: Should we not buy him things?

DESDEMONA: No! He's fifteen. He's never going to college. What could he possibly need?

ED: Now, now, there's plenty of money for everyone to buy lots of things they don't need.

DESDEMONA: He probably won't even graduate, failing everything.

GRACE: Mona, you're exaggerating: Ds are still passing. *(Produces Upton's report card.)* I think he's improving, Ed.

DESDEMONA: What is that?

GRACE: Your report cards came today.

DESDEMONA: Give it.

(Grace produces Desdemona's report card.)

You opened it?!

GRACE: You did well. You got a *[reads from report card]* "3.76."

DESDEMONA: That's not weighted!

GRACE: Isn't that a good grade? Ed . . . ? *(Shares the report card with Ed.)* Look: "A. A. A. A. A. C. A."

DESDEMONA: It was a C+!

ED: Very proud, Desi.

GRACE: That's a lot of As.

DESDEMONA: Mom, just shut up, OK?!

(Desdemona, tearful, grabs the report card from Grace.)

GRACE: You didn't fail anything, dear.

DESDEMONA: Not everyone's good at BC Calc.

GRACE: You even got all Es for citizenship.

DESDEMONA: Mom, no one *cares* about Es!

GRACE: I got all Es.

ED: I'm sure Princeton's not going to care.

DESDEMONA: DAD!

ED: And if you're applying early anyway, they may get your application even before you get a C or a D, right?

DESDEMONA: C+! And that's only the mid-semester report, OK?

GRACE: Well, I'm still very proud of you, Mona.

DESDEMONA: Omigod, Mom!

(Desdemona exits in despair. Pause. Desdemona pops her head back in, suddenly sweeter.)

Wait: Mom, can you drive me tomorrow?

GRACE: What time?

DESDEMONA: The interview's sometime in the evening. I'll check.

GRACE: All right, dear.

ED: Say hi to Princeton for me.

DESDEMONA: Dad, AAAARGH! You guys are stressing me out!

(Desdemona groans loudly and exits for good.)

GRACE: Do you think we put too much pressure on her?

ED: Don't worry about it. Probably her period.

GRACE: I suppose. *(Beat.)* It's my time of the month, too.

ED: That's nice.

(Grace comes closer to Ed.)

GRACE: Like, the other "time of the month." We could try—

ED: Maybe, maybe you should wait to hear from the doctor first. All that . . . movement . . . might jostle something out of place.

GRACE: I figure another try couldn't hurt.

ED: You know, dear, maybe it's too late. Menopause happens to a lot of women.

GRACE: Do you want carrots with the Cornish hen?

ED: Cornish hen. For dinner. Chicken.

GRACE: Is chicken not OK?

ED: Chicken's . . . OK, boss. It's just, I would've figured, with Ching Chong in the house . . .

GRACE: We shouldn't?

ED: Maybe we should order . . . I don't know, Chinese?

GRACE: We should order Chinese?

ED: Great. Order Chinese.

GRACE: Ed, you order.

ED: The number's on the fridge.

GRACE: Ed, I'm scared.

ED: What are you scared of? Just call the number and say it in English. They'll understand.

GRACE: Um. All right.

*(Ed hands Grace a menu and exits.
Grace picks up the phone.)*

(To the phone.) Hello there, do you have— *(Then more clearly.)* HELLO, I WOULD LIKE ONE ORDER OF SPRING ROLLS, ONE ORDER OF POTSTICKERS, ONE ORDER OF . . . *(To Ed offstage.)* Ed, what do you want?

ED *(offstage)*: The noodles?

GRACE: AND THE NOODLES— *(To Ed offstage.)* You'll have to be more specific.

ED *(offstage)*: The, uh, the noodles with the . . . beef.

GRACE: The flat ones?

ED *(offstage)*: The egg ones.

DESDEMONA *(offstage)*: No eggs. And vegetable Pad Thai, extra sprouts, no peanuts.

GRACE: FLAT NOODLES WITH EGGS, VEGETABLE PAD THAI— *(Stops, then to Desdemona offstage.)* What's Chinese for "Pad Thai?" *(To phone.)* The—uh . . . *(Stops, checks the menu.)* THE NUMBER FIVE, THE NUMBER FOURTEEN . . . THE NUMBER TWENTY. ALL RIGHT, uh, domo arigato. . . . Thank you.

(Grace hangs up the phone. She takes the tray of Cornish hens from the oven and sticks it in the refrigerator. She grabs her coat and exits.)

SCENE 3

Upton's room. Upton reads his essay to a microphone at his computer.

UPTON: Podcast for *Yankee Ingenuity*, an essay by Upton Sinclair Lewis Wong. Take one. *(Beat.)* Now say I am a fifteen-year-old male whose greatest ambition is to qualify for a coveted spot in the World of Warcraft international arena tournament. An objective that requires several months of diligent playing. Now I'm on this computer game, World of Warcraft, eight to ten hours a day. The rest of the time I am at school or I am asleep or I am doing homework/chores. In order to win my spot at the international arena tournament, I must play during nearly all of my waking hours. Yet there are also tasks in my life that must be fulfilled—education, family obligations, food, sleep, personal hygiene. But is there a way I can get both done?

SCENE 4

Kitchen. Ed and Desdemona sit at the kitchen table waiting for their food. Desdemona reads from her stack of papers. J sits across from them, looking unsure of what to do. Waiting.

ED: So, Ching Chong, what do you think of America?

DESDEMONA: Dad, stop it.

ED: You like the big cars? The highways?

DESDEMONA: If you don't speak his language, don't talk to him. It's insulting.

ED: What do you want me to do then?
DESDEMONA: Just sit there. Don't look at him; don't acknowledge him.

(Silence.)

ED: Nobody's called yet, right?
DESDEMONA: For who?
ED: For Mom.
DESDEMONA: Nobody ever calls Mom.
ED: The doctor.
DESDEMONA: No. The doctor hasn't called.
ED: Try to get it before she does.
DESDEMONA: Six and a half billion people in the world, millions starving below the poverty line. If she really wants a baby, she should go just go into Africa and sponsor a child.
ED: What about that little Korean girl of yours? She need a new home?
DESDEMONA: Kim is staying in Korea, her *natural* environment. And she is not mine; she is an independently sponsored child.
ED: But she's an orphan, right?

(The phone rings.)

Could be for one of us. Maybe Princeton on the phone.
DESDEMONA: Shut up. It's not them. I know.

(Nevertheless, Desdemona checks the Caller ID.)

DESDEMONA: Cripes.
ED: We don't know for sure what the results are.
DESDEMONA: *You* answer it then.
ED: We'll let the machine get it.

*(The phone rings several more times. Ed and Desdemona
wait uneasily. Then it stops.)*

DESDEMONA: You gonna tell her?
ED: We don't need to tell her anything. We'll just . . . leave a little note.

*(Ed gets out a pen and Post-It note and writes a message. He sticks the note
in plain view on the refrigerator. On second thought, he re-sticks it inside
the laundry basket. Silence.)*

We'll leave a note, and no one will say anything.

(Ed sends a meaningful glance at Desdemona and at J. Grace enters the kitchen with the takeout. She unpacks the takeout on the kitchen table.)

GRACE: Look! They even gave us chopsticks.
DESDEMONA: Mom, they always give out chopsticks.
GRACE: Yes, but now maybe Ching Ching can teach us how to use them.
ED *(to offstage)*: Upton! Dinner!

(Lights up on Upton in his bedroom, playing a computer game.)

DESDEMONA: I think you need to ban that game. He's gonna become a delinquent.
ED *(to offstage)*: Hurry up or no spring rolls for you!

(Upton enters the kitchen with his laptop still active. He reaches for a box of takeout. Ed stops him.)

UPTON: I've got a game in progress.
ED: Pause it.

(Upton in disbelief.)

UPTON: Dad, you can't *pause* World of Warcraft. *(No response from Ed.)* It's a *real-time* MMORPG [massively multiplayer online role-playing game]. *(No response.)* Real-time videogames don't pause.

(Nevertheless, Ed closes Upton's laptop.)

ED: Plenty of time later. And, Desi, put those away. Time to eat.
DESDEMONA: Dad— *(Referring to Upton's game.)* *That's* mindless, soul-sucking junk. This? *(Gestures to own papers.)* *This* is for school. *School* school.
GRACE: Your father's always right, darlings.
ED: Listen to the boss now. There're things more important than school.
DESDEMONA: There is nothing more important than school.
ED: Plenty of things more important than school. Togetherness, money . . .
UPTON: Guild rankings, power levels . . .
GRACE: Dental appointments. Children. Babies—
DESDEMONA: So, Mom, guess who called?
GRACE: Someone called—?
ED: Guess who called Upton a loser again?
UPTON: Hey, this does not make me a loser.
ED: Time to eat!
DESDEMONA: This has egg in it.

ED: Where?
DESDEMONA: Here.
UPTON: Des, it's egg foo young.
GRACE: Did someone call on the phone?
ED: So—company golf tournament. Family teams this year.
GRACE: I like golf.
ED: Desi?
DESDEMONA: Golf kills the earth.
ED: Upton?
UPTON: Is it outdoors?
ED: Probably.
UPTON: Can't do it.
GRACE: I used to play in high school.

(*Ed surveys the dinner table. He stops at J.*)

ED: Do they have golf in China?
UPTON: Um, I don't think J's gonna have time for that, Dad. Midterms're coming up.
ED (*to J*): You'll be a regular Tiger Woods in no time. Little known fact: He's Chinese, too.

(*The phone rings. Everyone pauses. Then the phone stops.*)

Wrong number, probably.
GRACE: Probably. (*Phone rings again. Grace jumps on the phone and answers.*) Yes?! (*Beat.*) What? (*To Upton.*) Did we order anything from Intel? (*As Upton shrugs.*) I'm sorry. (*Grace meekly returns to her seat.*)
ED: Ah, well. Time to eat!

(*Everyone collectively picks up their chopsticks. J breaks apart his chopsticks and rubs the sides against each other to sand off the splinters. Everyone follows suit. They then use them to eat with varying degrees of skill. J gags a little on the food. A frustrated silence.*)

GRACE: Anyone want a fork?

SCENE 5

Kitchen. Desdemona sits in the darkened kitchen with her papers. She opens a fortune cookie and reads it. The Chinese Woman materializes in traditional garb.

THE CHINESE WOMAN: "Success is a series of many tries and many failures."

(Unsatisfied, Desdemona opens another fortune cookie.)

"Even the greatest panda can fall from the trees."

(Desdemona reaches for another . . .)

"Princeton University rejects two-thirds of early applicants."

(Desdemona pushes the cookies aside. The Chinese Woman dematerializes. Desdemona picks up a document, reads . . .)

DESDEMONA: "Essay number 1: Tell us about a person who has influenced you in a significant way." *(Contemplates this, then . . .)* "Many years ago, my ancestors came from China in search of a better life. As much as I have enjoyed the fruits of their struggles, there still remain millions of children who seek adequate food and shelter. One such child is a young Korean girl by the name of Kim Lee Park. Seventeen years ago, Kim was born in Seoul, South Korea—"

(Lights up on Kim Lee Park, seventeen, a Korean schoolgirl. Desdemona copies down her words dutifully.)

KIM LEE PARK: "—at the mouth of a river, under the full moon of August. Abandoned by my mother, I was headed for a life of emptiness and sadness. I was a love child without love.

However, my salvation arrived when I became the sponsored child of Desdemona Wong, an American girl. With her first donation, I purchased a yak that soon became the sole source of my living. Its thick coat kept me warm during the winter, and I was able to use its milk to generate electricity. My yak also provided me with a sustainable source of food and transported me to school, where I began learning English.

Without Desdemona, I do not know where I would be. Her passion for academics and dedication to instigating community change have been the factors that prevented me from throwing myself into the river. Her high GPA, her near-perfect SAT score, her intense but rewarding AP and IB courses all encourage me to be greater."

(Pause.)

DESDEMONA: I need more words.
KIM LEE PARK: Desdemona, was that not enough?
DESDEMONA *(reading)*: " . . . a full page in length—about five hundred words."

KIM LEE PARK: I don't understand the question so good. I'm tired. And I need to milk the yak.

DESDEMONA: You can't be tired. It's only one o'clock in Seoul.

KIM LEE PARK: I'm not very well at English. I don't feel anymore like doing this.

(Kim Lee Park sighs. Desdemona grabs her roughly.)

DESDEMONA: Now listen, you stupid little girl: I need an essay and I can't wait 'til you FEEL like it!

(Desdemona slaps Kim Lee Park. Pause.)

KIM LEE PARK: I apologize. Do you want to start again?

DESDEMONA: "Seventeen years ago, Kim was born in Seoul, South Korea, at the mouth of a river, under the full moon of August. Abandoned by my mother—"

KIM LEE PARK: "Beaten by my mother?"

DESDEMONA: Oh, good. "—beaten by my mother, I was headed for a life of emptiness and sadness—" *(Stops.)* That just seems a little vague. What kind of emptiness?

KIM LEE PARK: Malnourishment?

DESDEMONA: " . . . malnourishment and . . . abuse . . . "

KIM LEE PARK: That sounds s<u>a</u>d.

DESDEMONA: Yeah, that's better. *(Pause.)* You're my best friend, Kim. I'm glad I didn't let you die.

KIM LEE PARK: Me, too, Desdemona.

(Desdemona and Kim Lee Park hug.)

SCENE 6

Upton's bedroom. Upton reads from his essay again.

UPTON: In 1865, in the midst of construction on the Transcontinental Railroad, building superintendent Charles Crocker was faced with a conundrum. Due to the harsh conditions and back-breaking labor, his workforce was hemorrhaging at an alarming rate. He needed able-bodied men, and fast. It was not until he finally started hiring Chinese workers—workers who could not have gained entry into America otherwise—that Crocker began to make progress. Four years later, thanks to Chinese sweat and Crocker's ingenuity, the railroad was completed, leading the country one step closer toward Manifest Destiny.

This example from yesteryear can provide us with ways to improve our own lives today. So say I want to progress in World of Warcraft AND lead a healthy, normal life. How can I achieve both? The answer can be found in Crocker's brilliant scheme from nearly 150 years ago: indentured servants. Workers from Third World countries whose time is worth far less than my own. I, hypothetically speaking, of course, buy them a one-way plane ticket to America and forge a student visa. They complete my homework, my chores, and my familial obligations. Like Crocker, I am able to achieve my goals painlessly, and they receive opportunities far beyond what they could get in their home countries. Cheaper than minimum-wage labor, indentured servants present a solution that is amenable to both sides.

Once my task is complete and his time is up, my indentured servant goes out into the world alone. Where does he go? What does he do? Beats me. So the next time you find yourself cursing the rise of the minimum wage and the deflation of your own wallet, think back to Charles Crocker and the—

(Lights up on Desdemona, who now holds Upton's essay.)

DESDEMONA: He's your indentured servant?!

UPTON: You know there are laws protecting my private property.

DESDEMONA: And how's he able to do your homework?

UPTON: I don't give him my *English* homework.

DESDEMONA: You need to send him back. You're exploiting him—with your little sweatshop den of vices.

UPTON: How is it a sweatshop? He takes out the trash, he does my homework—

DESDEMONA: You are cheating the system.

UPTON: Whether or not he's working for me, Des, doesn't change the fact that he's POOR. He's poor and he's oppressed. You say anything and he'll be poor and oppressed in China. Poorer. You gonna tell Mom and Dad?

DESDEMONA: Why wouldn't I?

UPTON: Because he's really good at calc, too.

DESDEMONA: I don't care.

UPTON: Like he wouldn't be getting Cs on midterm report cards.

DESDEMONA: It's *hard*, OK?

UPTON: *I* understand. I just don't know if Princeton will. So you gonna tell Mom and Dad?

DESDEMONA: Shut up. He stays. But he'd better be *really* good at graphing derivatives.

UPTON: I only work with the best.

SCENE 7

Kitchen. Ed enters with the newspaper, sans tie. Grace sidles up to Ed.

GRACE: Morning, Ed.

ED: Morning, boss.

GRACE: Anything interesting going on?

ED: More of our southern friends jumping the border.

GRACE: I think this time it worked.

ED: You know, two kids is a lot already.

GRACE: But newborns are different. They're so small. And they need constant attention.

ED: Constant feeding, constant crying.

GRACE: I like babies when they cry.

ED: You might be the only one. And you're good at that stuff, too.

GRACE: What else am I good at?

ED: Everything, dear. You're a tiger.

GRACE: No, really. What do I do well? Who needs me?

ED: Everyone needs you. Look: this coffee cup. It's empty. It needs you. You have the kids; they need you.

GRACE: Not for very much longer.

ED: You have to drive Desi to her thing today. That's probably very important. What you need . . . you need a hobby. Garden. Bake. Knit. No, wait, don't knit.

GRACE: Music. I love music. And dancing.

ED: Or crosswords. There's one of those every day.

GRACE: It takes two to tango.

ED: What about tap dancing? Takes two feet to tap. *(Beat.)* Wait. Wait a minute. You know what came this morning? *(Sings, as he retrieves a box.)* "I'm dreaming of a white Christmas." *(Ed hands Grace a large box of cards and a list. He pulls out a Christmas card.)* Someone's got a nice family, hmm?

GRACE *(Re the card)*: Our eyes *are* nice and wide.

ED: It's only November. Should give you plenty of time to stuff them all.

GRACE: I do like putting things in other things . . .

ED: That's the spirit.

GRACE: Do you need me to do anything else? Call the doctor?

ED: Hey, how about this: I'll let you help me pick out a tie.

GRACE: But which one am I supposed to pick?

ED: You get to decide.

GRACE: Ooh, I've never done that before.

ED: But first, I think there are some people who need you.

GRACE: Oh yes. *(To the upstairs.)* UPTON! DESDEMONA! WAKE UP, DAR-LINGS!

(Ed exits. Several alarm clocks go off. Desdemona stumbles in, brushing her teeth. Throughout the conversation, Desdemona goes through her morning routine, combing her hair, flossing, eating breakfast, drinking coffee, packing her backpack, etc. Grace tries to help Desdemona but is unsuccessful.)

DESDEMONA: Upton's gonna be late again.
GRACE: When was he late?
DESDEMONA: He's late one more time and he's gonna lose half a grade. Not that he cares.
GRACE *(to the upstairs)*: UPTON? UPTON, DEAR?
DESDEMONA: Mom, where're all the cans?
GRACE: For recycling?
DESDEMONA: For food. Canned food. We're having a food drive. I've gotta win.

(Grace indicates several cabinets. Desdemona rummages through and picks out several cans.)

GRACE: That's Sterno, dear.
DESDEMONA: Whatever. It's cans. Besides, homeless people need fire, too.

(Desdemona rips the labels off of the Sterno cans and continues emptying the cabinets.)

GRACE: That's a lot of cans, dear.
DESDEMONA: Mom, this is for the homeless. And *school.*
GRACE: Just leave the creamed corn for dinner tonight.

(Grace exits. Desdemona bags the creamed corn anyway. J enters the kitchen and sits at the kitchen table. Desdemona is uncomfortable in his presence. Pause.)

DESDEMONA *(to herself)*: Treat him with respect: Don't look at him; don't make eye contact. OK. *(Pause, then to J.)* I know you don't understand me, and I am really sorry I'm speaking in a language that automatically marginalizes your intelligence and capabilities, but hi. I'm Desdemona. And, um, Upton said that you might be able to help me. So . . . here it is.

(Cringing, Desdemona thrusts a math book at J.)

Pages 225 to 229, all the odd ones. I've marked them for you, just in case you can't understand, which you probably don't. If you could finish them by tonight, that would be great. Thanks. (*Adds.*) And just for the record, I really don't approve of how my brother's treating you. At all. Seriously.

(*Grace enters with two similarly colored ties.*)

GRACE: Mona?
DESDEMONA (*too suddenly*): I'm just getting cans!

(*Desdemona hurriedly retrieves more cans.*)

GRACE: Hello, Ping Pong.
ED (*offstage*): It's Ching Chong!

(*Grace holds out the two ties to Desdemona.*)

GRACE: Which one?
DESDEMONA: They're the same color.
GRACE: But Mona, I need to make a decision.
DESDEMONA: The left one.
GRACE: You're so good at this. (*Beat.*) You know, Mona, your father and I are always going to love you.
DESDEMONA: Uh huh.
GRACE: No matter what. Even if you get a C. Or if Princeton doesn't work out. I hear Stanford's a nice school.
DESDEMONA: Omigod, Mom, *you* go to Stanford then.
GRACE: What I'm saying is . . . you don't need to be perfect to get into Princeton. You just need to be yourself.
DESDEMONA: No. If I had cancer, if you disowned me, *then* I could be myself. *Then* I'd have a chance. *Then* I could say something interesting in my personal statement.
GRACE: I think you're very interesting.
DESDEMONA: Mom: I'm an Asian American female with a 2340 [a very high SAT score] and a 4.42 GPA at an elite public high school. That's like the worst thing in the world. Nobody's gonna want me.
GRACE: I'd want you.
DESDEMONA: Yeah, but that's you.

(*Desdemona surveys her bag of cans and looks around
for more cans. There are none.*)

DESDEMONA: *And* I'm gonna lose the food drive!
ED (*offstage*): Grace!

GRACE: Oh, wait. Which one was it?
DESDEMONA: The right.
GRACE: You're so good at this.

(Ed enters. Grace displays the chosen tie.)

GRACE: We like this one.

(Grace attempts to tie it on Ed. She does a poor job.)

ED: Get in the car!
GRACE *(to the upstairs)*: UPTON!
DESDEMONA: WAIT A MINUTE! Soda cans: Do these count as cans?

(Upton enters, groggy.)

UPTON: I need socks.
GRACE: I was going to do that today.

*(Grace goes over to the laundry basket. Ed and Desdemona
stop and eye Grace. Beat.)*

ED: Hurry up or you're walking.
DESDEMONA: Forget about the socks.
UPTON: But they're my socks!
ED: Time is money, not socks.

*(Ed gives Grace a peck on the cheek and shoves the box of Christmas
cards at her. Ed, Desdemona, and Upton exit. Grace surveys the half-eaten
breakfasts. Grace looks at J. J looks at Grace. Awkward silence. J hurriedly
exits. Grace then picks up the laundry basket and notices a Post-It note.)*

SCENE 8

*Kitchen. Grace is at the kitchen table, stuffing Christmas cards as she listens
to the voicemail. The laundry basket of dirty clothes has been very obviously
rifled through. Beep. Lights up on The Chinese Woman as Grace's Doctor,
who speaks perfect, unaccented English.*

DOCTOR: . . . Mrs. Wong, the procedure only had a 20 percent chance, and
there are a lot of variables that affect its success. Your husband's sperm
count was not the only factor. The age of you and your husband, the
state of your eggs—these are all possible causes.

GRACE *(to audience)*: I can never understand these doctors. Such thick accents. If they're going to treat patients, they should learn how to speak English better. *(To The Chinese Woman.)* I don't know what you're saying!

DOCTOR: If you have any questions, you have my number. But I do hope you will agree with me that perhaps it was for the best.

GRACE: Delete delete delete.

> *(Grace pushes delete and hangs up. She continues stuffing Christmas cards. Then stops. Sigh.)*

SCENE 9

Kitchen. J sits on the phone.

RECORDED VOICE: Thank you for calling Intel. For information on Intel boxed and retail products, please press or say one—

> *(J presses one. The Chinese Woman answers. She speaks with a Midwestern accent. She wears a headset.)*

THE CHINESE WOMAN: Intel Customer Service. This is Lurleen. How may I be of service?

J: It's me.

THE CHINESE WOMAN: I am sorry, sir, but I did not catch that.

J: Ma. It is me.

> *(The Chinese Woman—Mrs. J—drops the accent.)*

MRS. J: Oh. Jinqiang. Hold on.

J: Are you busy?

MRS. J: No. Today has not been busy. So do you like the food?

J: No.

MRS. J: What did you eat?

J: They served this American . . . I don't know what it was. They eat their food with this sweet and sour stuff. Only not sour.

MRS. J: Sweet sauce?

J: "Duck" sauce.

MRS. J: Does it have duck in it?

J: No, it is *for* fried chicken. Like a dip.

MRS. J: Plum sauce . . . ?

J: You'd think so. But no. "Duck" sauce.

MRS. J: That is stupid. It *must* have duck in it. What kind of family is this?

J: They wear shoes . . . *indoors.*

MRS. J: Why?

J: To track in the dirt.

MRS. J: That is silly.

J: And they don't even have a rice cooker.

MRS. J: How do they cook their rice then?

(As J shrugs.)

Are you sure they're Chinese?

J: Maybe. I can't tell. And we do not talk. It is not like everyone speaks Chinese.

MRS. J: They should. Shame on them. Once you become famous, you will never have to see this family again.

J: Like that is going to happen anytime soon.

MRS. J: You cannot expect fame to fall into your lap. You are auditioning for things, yes?

J: It is a little hard talking to people when you only speak Chinese.

MRS. J: I have always said, dance is the universal language. You go in there and you dance. You could speak Martian and they would hire you. Look at the Russians.

J: I cannot dance right if I am always hungry.

MRS. J: Just wait, Jinqiang. Keep practicing. It will come. So what did you call about?

J: So, Mom, you know, if I just felt like finding the integral of one plus e to the x—

MRS. J: This doesn't sound like dancing. Why are you doing math?

J: Why do you think they wanted me here?

MRS. J: You are terrible at math.

J: I know! But apparently, that does not matter.

(Out of the corner of her eye, Mrs. J sees her boss coming around and readopts the Midwestern accent.)

MRS. J: I understand your difficulty, sir, but Intel is just not responsible—

J: Can I call you tomorrow?

MRS. J: We do not cover burns, cuts, or maim-ment of any sort—

J: On the other line?

MRS. J: Yes, I highly suggest you notify your insurance provider just as soon as humanly possible. And sir?

J: Yes?

MRS. J: I will remind you that what you have is not a round-trip but a one-way ticket.

J: I know. I miss you. I miss rice.

MRS. J: Yes, indeed, sir, miss you, too.

SCENE 10

Kitchen. Upton plays on his laptop in the corner. Lights up on Desdemona, who reads from her essay.

DESDEMONA: As I look toward my future at Princeton University, I cannot help but look back at the generations of Wongs who believed in something greater than themselves—namely, me getting into Princeton.

(Upton exits. Desdemona continues to read.)

Which is why I have also sought to take the time to care for others, particularly my newfound friend, a Korean orphan. Although our lives are vastly different, she has helped me to see that—

(Lights up another part of the stage. Desdemona looks in that direction expectantly. It is not Kim Lee Park, but Upton, who reads from a new essay.)

UPTON: —Third World child sponsorships that reached record highs in the latter half of the twentieth century, as more and more Americans inserted themselves into the lives of the poor—
DESDEMONA: Shut up.
UPTON: —forcing these young children to become dependent on strangers thousands of miles away— *(Stops.)* You don't really think Princeton's going to want to hear that.
DESDEMONA: You're not even going to college. *(Beat.)* Wait, why not?
UPTON: *(Reads from paper.)* "Tell us about a major struggle in *your* life."

(Desdemona grabs the paper from Upton.)

DESDEMONA: I am answering the question. I just . . . I think it'll be a refreshing change for them. To hear about how good my life is.
UPTON: Suit yourself.

(Ed enters with his golf clubs and J in tow.)

What're you doing with J?
ED: Just thought I'd take him out for a spin . . . practice for the old golf tournament.
UPTON: Um, I don't know about that. . . . I think J's going to be a little busy.
ED: Oh?
UPTON: Yeah. I was gonna teach him . . . about my physics project.
DESDEMONA: And I've got calc homework . . . that I thought he might find interesting.

ED: Won't be a minute. Just a little practice.

UPTON: Doesn't Mom need help with the Christmas cards?

DESDEMONA: And Dad, nobody's gonna believe he's family. He doesn't even look like you.

ED: I don't know . . . I think we all kind of look alike.

(Desdemona and Upton look at J; they don't see the resemblance.)

Couple hours won't hurt.

(Grudgingly, Upton pulls out his whistle and hands it to Ed. Ed tries it out. J follows Ed closely.)

Hit the road then! Sayonara, folks! *(Stops.)* Hah, "sayonara."

DESDEMONA: I need a ride to the interview.

ED: I thought your mother was taking you.

DESDEMONA: Yeah, but then she's gonna cry, and that's gonna freak out my interviewer.

UPTON: Why's she gonna cry?

DESDEMONA: You know why. Again. *(To Ed.)* You told her, right?

ED: Um . . . oh . . . I thought maybe, maybe one of you would like to talk to her.

UPTON: Don't look at me.

DESDEMONA: The interview's in half an hour.

ED: Get in the car with Ching Chong. I'll be there.

(Desdemona and Upton exit with J. Ed looks at audience.)

My wife, she's just not very good at anything. She can't work, she can't turn on a computer, she can't cook—we're always ordering take-out—but there it is. That's the job of the daddies, so that's what I want: I want to make everyone happy.

(Grace, Desdemona, and Upton materialize for a family portrait. Grace looks morose. Ed holds up a camera.)

(To family.) Everyone, be happy. *(To Grace.)* Can we see a smile?

(In response, Grace just sobs. Ed holds up a squeaky toy and tries to distract her. He hands Grace a Slinky to play with.)

Come on! Come on, boss. You want some money? Money'd make you happy?

UPTON: I want some money.

ED: Come on, dear. Just play with the Slinky.

GRACE: I broke it, Ed. It won't slink.

ED: Don't worry, we'll get Ching Chong to fix it. OK, smiles, right here.

(Grace sobs. Ed takes the picture anyway.
He evaluates his shot. It's horrible.)

Great, great. That was, uh, not so bad.

(The family dematerializes.)

(To the audience.) This is my job. I love it, I do.

(Grace, in real life, enters with a Kleenex box, the box
of Christmas cards. Her eyes are red.)

Oh! Hey, Tiger. We're just leaving.

GRACE: I was going to make pork tonight. And corn.

ED: Don't worry, dear. Just order out.

(Grace looks around for the cans of creamed corn.)

GRACE: Where did all the cans of corn go?

ED: We'll be back soon. I've just got to take Desi to her interview thing.

GRACE: I thought I was going to take her.

ED: Yes. I know, but, uh, no problem, it's on the way.

GRACE: I didn't finish the cards. You want to know why?

ED: No, not really.

GRACE: I was doing the laundry.

ED: Not to worry, we'll just get Ching Chong to help you.

(Ed exits hastily. Grace sobs loudly. Upton enters the room and sees
Grace. He has a look of horror and quickly exits.)

(Grace grabs one of Ed's golf clubs and whacks it
against a wall.)

GRACE *(calling out)*: Something happened to your golf clubs, Ed!

(J pops into the kitchen. He stares at Grace and the golf club. She stares
at J. Beat. Grace puts the golf club back in the bag. J takes the golf clubs.
A tacit understanding. Both of them back out of the room, with opposite
exits.)

SCENE 11

A café. Desdemona sits with Princeton Alum, played by The Chinese Woman.

PRINCETON ALUM: So, Desdemona Wong. Classic Chinese last name, huh?

DESDEMONA: Oh. Yeah. Classic. *(Beat.)* "Wong."

PRINCETON ALUM: I know this is supposed to be an alumni interview, but it's really more for you. Do you have any questions about the school?

DESDEMONA: Princeton? Nooo. I've done all my research.

PRINCETON ALUM: We don't have to take the full hour.

DESDEMONA: No! I mean . . . of course, I have questions. *(Looks through her notes.)* Um, what do you think it was that got you into Princeton?

PRINCETON ALUM *(full of herself)*: Oh, God, here we go. Honestly?—no idea. I'm sorry, that's probably not the answer you're looking for. Um, really, I don't know. It must be so different now. You kids are so smart these days. APs?

DESDEMONA: Yeah.

PRINCETON ALUM: IBs?

DESDEMONA: Guilty!

PRINCETON ALUM: You're so lucky. Back when I was your age, at my school, we didn't even do APs or IBs or . . . *(Consults Desdemona's résumé.)* "Future Business Leaders of America, National Forensics League, Mock Trial." I can't even imagine trying to get into Princeton today. Boy, if I were you, I would've never gotten in.

(Princeton Alum laughs. Desdemona tries to laugh.)

DESDEMONA: Yes. I am lucky.

PRINCETON ALUM: And all the pressure your parents must be putting on you.

DESDEMONA: Yep. It's tough.

PRINCETON ALUM: Traditional Chinese parents, huh?

(Beat. Desdemona gives a delayed response.)

DESDEMONA: Oh. Yeah. We're big on Chinese traditions.

PRINCETON ALUM: My parents were the same way: "Be a doctor! Be a lawyer!" Really doesn't change, huh? But you know, Desdemona, in the end, you've just got to do what you want to do.

DESDEMONA: Thanks. That's really . . . helpful.

(That was not helpful at all.)

PRINCETON ALUM: I see it all the time with girls your age. It's difficult being a Chinese American woman.

(Desdemona pauses in genuine surprise.)

DESDEMONA: It is?

PRINCETON ALUM: Our suffering may not be as acknowledged as it is with other minority groups, but Chinese Americans have faced so many hardships.

DESDEMONA: *Yeah.* Like— *(Tries, stops.)*

PRINCETON ALUM: Like *Joy Luck Club.*

DESDEMONA: *Joy Luck Club* . . . ?

PRINCETON ALUM: Every time I see it, I still cry.

DESDEMONA: Oh. Me, too. Wait. *(Furtively takes notes.)* Why do you cry?

PRINCETON ALUM: God, so many reasons. Those women, you think they're the model minority. On the surface, they lead these glossy, perfect, over-achieving lives. But then below, you discover the unspeakable tragedy.

(Fireworks go off in Desdemona's eyes.)

DESDEMONA: Tragedy?

PRINCETON ALUM: You can't watch that movie without feeling such sympathy for those women.

DESDEMONA: Yes. Those Chinese American women . . .

PRINCETON ALUM: I'm sorry, is this boring you?

DESDEMONA: No. It's fascinating. I should watch it . . . again.

SCENE 12

Golf course. Ed leads J to the first hole of the golf course.

ED: Some people say golf is a white man's sport. I say, if you're gonna have that attitude, you might as well call America a white man's country. But look at all the Chinese Americans excelling athletically. Michelle Kwan. Yao Ming. Kristi Yamaguchi. Makes you think.

Now, in the business world, golf is of the utmost importance. During those games, lives are changed. Men are made. The stakes are enormous. So when you play golf, you need to be aware. Of your grip. Of your stance. And every time you tee off, you want to ask yourself some questions. Such as:

Does my swing feel natural?
Do I commit with my follow-through?
What club should I be using?

Am I hitting it at the right spot?
Did I wash my balls today?
And most importantly: can I get it in the hole?

And the answer is no. NEVER. And you can't just upgrade your equipment, because it's the only club God gave you, and sometimes I just want to say, "Shut up: keep your head down, and spread your legs wider and maybe it'd go in for once!" *(Stops, then . . .)* But that's just because you always want to aim for perfection. And practice your golf swing.

(Ed pulls a club out of his bag. It is the same one
that Grace bent earlier. He turns to J.)

How about you give it a try?

(J takes out a different club and tees off. Ed watches J sink a hole in one.)

Well. This one's only a par-three anyway.

SCENE 13

Kitchen. Grace enters, looks around, bored. She sits at the kitchen table next to a package and the Christmas cards. She tries to stuff Christmas cards, but even this proves to be boring. She stares at the package and finally opens it.

Grace wades through bags of dried squid and other Asian foods. She is puzzled. Finally, she takes out a pair of men's tap shoes. She looks around. No one. She puts them on. They are too big.

Still, she closes up the box and takes a couple steps. Tap. Tap. Although her movements are halfhearted at first, she picks up speed. Tap tap tap.

Somewhere else in the house, someone else is also tap dancing. Tap tap tap.

Grace hears the noise and stops. She does a tap step. The other person answers. They continue conversing through tap dance, the steps and rhythms growing more complex.

J enters, tapping. He is the other dancer. Pause. They look at each other. Grace offers a step, J returns it. They tap dance their way out of the kitchen.

SCENE 14

Kitchen. Desdemona listens to her iPod. Introductory music plays. Chinese Lesson, voiced by The Chinese Woman, begins slowly but increases in speed.

CHINESE LESSON: *Ni hao.*
DESDEMONA: *Ni hao.*
CHINESE LESSON: *Zaijian.*
DESDEMONA: *Zaijian.*
CHINESE LESSON: *Jintian tianqi hen hao.*
DESDEMONA: *Jintian tianqi hen hao.*
CHINESE LESSON: *Duibuqi, wo dei zou le, zaijian.*
DESDEMONA: *Duibuqi, wo dei—*
CHINESE LESSON: *Yi.*

(Desdemona tries to rewind—but she is unsuccessful.)

CHINESE LESSON: *Er.*
DESDEMONA: *Er.*
CHINESE LESSON: *San. / Si. Wu—*
DESDEMONA: *San . . .*
CHINESE LESSON: *Liu, liu—*

(Desdemona hits the iPod, which then begins to skip.)

DESDEMONA: Stupid motherfu—
CHINESE LESSON: *Liu, liu . . . (Sudden break.)* Can't even count to ten, you piece of shit.

(Desdemona, startled, looks at the iPod, which resumes the lesson at a normal pace.)

CHINESE LESSON: *Liu. Qi.*

(Desdemona shuts off the iPod and returns to her essay, voiced by The Chinese Woman.)

DESDEMONA: "Essay Number *Yi,* Version *Er*-point-*Yi.*"
ESSAY: Tips for prospective applicants: Be specific in your choice of topic and details.
DESDEMONA: "As a member of the . . . Wong village dynasty in the main part of China, I've learned so much since our family immigrated to America in . . . "

ESSAY: Be specific.

DESDEMONA: "Since my great-great . . . ancestor came here X number of years ago."

ESSAY: Be specific!

DESDEMONA: I'll fill it in later, OK?!

(Desdemona crumples up her essay violently. The Chinese Woman wheezes in pain. Desdemona, disturbed, tries to smooth it out. The Chinese Woman slowly dematerializes, but not before handing Desdemona a flier and gesturing to the package still on the kitchen table.)

THE CHINESE WOMAN: All my good intentions . . .

(Desdemona reads the flier with growing interest and grabs the box.)

SCENE 15

Upton's bedroom. Upton reads from another essay.

UPTON: There are many cultural differences between the East and the West. For instance, gaming in America is often considered an anti-social activity, leaving gamers friendless and— . . . something something whatever. Yet in more technologically developed countries such as South Korea, gaming is considered an active social sport.

Skilled gamers do not play alone but gather in large rooms, better known as "PC bongs," to exhibit their videogame mastery. National competitions are played in stadiums before tens of thousands of adoring, teenage fans—

(Asian Schoolgirl materializes. She sees Upton and shrieks.)

ASIAN SCHOOLGIRL: OH MY GOD, OH MY GOD, OH MY GOD!

*(Asian Schoolgirl barrels into Upton, and they make out
as he plays his computer game.)*

Is that Frostmourne? The runeblade of the Lich King himself?

UPTON: Yep.

ASIAN SCHOOLGIRL: That is SO hot.

UPTON: I just picked up some epic items, too.

ASIAN SCHOOLGIRL: Your armor is so strong and recently upgraded!

UPTON: Americans may find it difficult to believe the superstar status that Korea's most accomplished and popular gamers enjoy. Yet, in Korea—

(Grace materializes at the door.)

GRACE: Upton, dear, don't you think you should get out once in a while?
UPTON: Uh huh . . .

(Ed materializes at the door.)

ED: Upton, you know we're kicking you out of the house once you hit eighteen.
UPTON: OK . . .

(Desdemona materializes at the door.)

DESDEMONA: I just don't think Koreans would find you attractive as an American unless you were white. I'm just saying!
UPTON: All right, thank you and good-bye!

(Upton slams the door on his family and turns back to Asian Schoolgirl.)

I have something for you.

(Upton hands Asian Schoolgirl a fancy box. She opens it, gasps.)

ASIAN SCHOOLGIRL: Not the Rimetooth Pendant! It must've taken you days to kill the raid boss Sindragosa.

(A tender moment between Upton and Asian Schoolgirl.)

Did they release the rankings yet?
UPTON: I'll make the tournament. I passed the qualifier top of my battle-group.
ASIAN SCHOOLGIRL: But that was only the initial ladder phase. And don't you think two healers would be better for the finals? I've always had a thing for Holy Paladins.
UPTON: There is no one better at PvP [player-versus-player] combat than yours truly. Just a couple more weeks and soon I'll be at your side.
ASIAN SCHOOLGIRL: Yes, it will be beautiful when you get to Korea. I can't wait for all my friends to meet my big white American boyfriend.
UPTON: Yes. Um.
ASIAN SCHOOLGIRL: And when you come to Seoul, there is something I want to give you—

(Asian Schoolgirl loosens her clothing and is about to pounce on Upton. Desdemona enters with a DVD and a large package. Struggling to set

down the package, Desdemona closes Upton's laptop. Asian Schoolgirl dematerializes.)

UPTON: WHAT?!

(Upton immediately pushes Desdemona aside and reopens his computer.)

DESDEMONA: How do you work the DVD player?
UPTON: Use the remote.
DESDEMONA: There are, like, three remotes downstairs.
UPTON: The big one.
DESDEMONA: OK. *(Re the package.)* This yours?
UPTON: No. Go away.
DESDEMONA: *(Re the writing on the package.)* What does that look like to you?
UPTON: Well, it's not Japanese.

(Beat.)

DESDEMONA: You ever thought about being Chinese?
UPTON: We already are.
DESDEMONA: No. Like what that might mean about us. Or all the challenges we've had to endure.
UPTON: What challenges?
DESDEMONA: You know, as— *(Consults her notes.)* —"people of color."
UPTON: No.
DESDEMONA: OK.

(Computer restarts. Asian Schoolgirl reappears. Upton sighs in relief. Desdemona rolls her eyes and exits.)

ASIAN SCHOOLGIRL: Ohhh, you have sooo many dragon kill points!

(Upton makes out more with Asian Schoolgirl.)

SCENE 16

Kitchen. Desdemona watches The Joy Luck Club, *taking notes. She has opened the large package and strewn the contents of the box all over the room—all kinds of Asian snacks.*

JOY LUCK CLUB WOMAN: I will tell them this feather may look worthless, but it comes from afar and carries with it all my good intentions.

(Ed enters.)

DESDEMONA: Dad, why didn't you tell me?
ED: Hmm?

(Desdemona gestures to the movie.)

Oh, Joy Luck Club.
DESDEMONA *(reading from her notes)*: Teen marriage, drug abuse, adultery, concubine suicide, disfigurement, drowning.
ED *(re the movie)*: Is this the one who throws away the babies or cuts her arm off?
DESDEMONA: Why didn't you ever tell me? This is exactly what I need for my application. *(Beat.)* So, tell me about our family.
ED: About what?
DESDEMONA: Like about us being Chinese. *(Stops, refers to notes, corrects herself.)* "Chinese *American*." I just need some basics. OK: Where are you from?
ED: Here.
DESDEMONA: Like where were you born?
ED: San Francisco.
DESDEMONA: No. *(Deliberately.)* Where are you *really* from?

(Blankness.)

Did we have any relatives who died?
ED: Think so.
DESDEMONA: I mean, like significantly.
ED: I think we know all we want to about your heritage.
DESDEMONA *(almost to herself)*: Amy Tan's family was so much better. Figures. Bet I don't even have a Chinese name.
ED: Sure, you do. It's— *(Stops, then . . .)* Lu . . . cy . . . Liu.

(Desdemona eyes Ed suspiciously.)

DESDEMONA: How do you spell that?

*(Desdemona gestures for Ed to write it down. Ed tries,
comes up at a loss.)*

ED: You know, there're a lot of Chinese things that you never had.
DESDEMONA: Like what?
ED: Like Chinese New Year. A red egg and ginger party.
DESDEMONA: What's that?

ED: Chinese people have them. It doesn't make a huge difference, really. You know we're not *that* Chinese.
DESDEMONA: My app's due in on Tuesday. I need something.

(Ed peers inside the package, takes out a rice cooker.)

ED: We used to have one of these.
DESDEMONA: What is that?
ED: It's a rice cooker.
DESDEMONA: For . . . ?
ED: Rice?
DESDEMONA: Just rice?
ED: Most Chinese people eat rice for dinner.
DESDEMONA: This is exactly what I need.

(Desdemona grabs the package and almost exits.)

What's your credit card number?
ED: Hmm?

(Desdemona flashes the flier she received earlier.)

InstantHeritage.com—

(Brief lights up on The Chinese Woman.)

THE CHINESE WOMAN: Your source for all things heritage-related! Only $159 for the first four generations!
DESDEMONA: If you don't tell me, I'm going to need to get it from somewhere.

(Desdemona exits menacingly.)

SCENE 17

Not in the kitchen. A tape player in the center of the room. Grace races in, turns on the tape player, and hurries out. "Gimme Some Lovin'" or any upbeat oldies song plays. J enters. Grace then enters from the other side. They dance around the kitchen. Their dance is over the top but heartfelt. They are not half bad. The song ends. J and Grace plop down together on the floor, exhausted and tangled up.

GRACE: Ohhf! You're good.
J: Thanks. You, too.

(*Beat.*)

GRACE: Did you just say something?

J: Yes?

GRACE: You speak English!

J: No.

GRACE: Am I speaking Chinese?

J: No.

GRACE: Then how are we talking?

J: Body language.

GRACE: Oh. Well, that makes sense. You *do* dance well, Ching Ching.

J: It's Jinqiang.

GRACE: Ching Chong?

J: You can just call me J.

GRACE: So then, J, what are you doing here?

J: Finishing your son's homework.

GRACE: His grades have been better lately. No, really. What are you doing here? In America, I mean.

J: You're gonna laugh.

GRACE: I won't!

J: You're gonna tell.

GRACE: Who would I tell? No one ever listens to me anyway.

J: Well . . . OK. So, what does every Chinese boy want to be when he grows up, more than anything else in the world?

GRACE: A doctor?

J: A dancer!

GRACE: A math dancer?

J: A *dancer* dancer.

GRACE: Do Chinese people dance? I mean, since all the songs are in English?

J: Of course. I mean, dancing *is* the universal language.

GRACE: But aren't you dancing here already? What else do you want?

J: This is nice, but you're one person. Now I'm thinking, millions.

(*J takes a flier from his pocket and hands it to Grace.*)

GRACE: "America's Next Top Dancer: open call for talented young dancers to star on our show and win a $100,000 dance contract." Could you? Wouldn't you be "China's Next Top Dancer?"

J: Small technicality. The real issue's getting on the show first. And my audition tape. And the knowing English part.

GRACE: I could help. Read the forms, send it in.

J: You would? You wouldn't tell?

GRACE: Who'd believe me?

J: True. *(Beat.)* So what about you? What do you want to do?

GRACE: Oh, well, I've got everything I want. A house. A husband. Children. No one asks me for anything, I don't have to do anything. I just sit around all day, bored. It's wonderful! *(Awkward pause.)* You dance well!

J: Likewise.

(Desdemona enters the room with the envelope from the previous scene.)

DESDEMONA: Mom, guess what?

GRACE *(too loudly)*: We were just being friends!

DESDEMONA: Come on, guess what?

GRACE: Another time, dear.

DESDEMONA: I wasn't asking. It's called a rhetorical question.

GRACE: Mona, Jing Jing and I're busy. Isn't that right?

DESDEMONA: Don't talk to him; it's insulting. *(Beat.)* And J can't be busy. He's busy . . . with his own stuff.

(Desdemona makes eye contact with J and tries to gesture to her calculus textbook. Ed enters with his golf clubs.)

ED: Ah, there he is! Big day at the links, right, Ching Chong?

DESDEMONA: See, Mom, you have nothing to do.

ED: C'mon, son.

(Ed tugs at J. Desdemona tugs at Grace. Grace gestures to J. J grabs the tape player and scuttles out of the room with Grace. Ed and Desdemona exchange a look.)

DESDEMONA: What are we supposed to do now?

(Ed and Desdemona simultaneously stare at the box of unfinished Christmas cards.)

SCENE 18

Laundry room. A tripod and camcorder are set up in one corner. Grace and J are in the middle of a dance. A joyful, extended dance sequence. They finish, beaming. Grace hurries over to the camcorder.

GRACE *(to video)*: And that was America's Next Top Dancer audition tape, J . . . something. Take one!

(Grace shuts off the camcorder and embraces J.)

Oh! You were wonderful!

J: And you! You, too!
GRACE: You're just—you're exaggerating.
J: No, Grace, really—
GRACE: We should probably get to work.
J: I've got your son's homework to do.
GRACE: And I've got his laundry.
J: We should, uh, get to that then.

(Grace and J go off in opposite directions. They stop and exchange a glance. Music. They dance. Then they make out. More making out. They fall into a pile of laundry.)

SCENE 19

Kitchen. Desdemona and Ed sit at the kitchen table, silently stuffing Christmas cards. Sound of music and dancing coming from the laundry room. Desdemona stops.

DESDEMONA: I have homework.
ED: Only three hundred–something more to go.
DESDEMONA: Isn't this Mom's job? Or can't you make Upton do this?
ED: Now, Desi, in this family, we don't make anyone do anything they don't want to do.
DESDEMONA: I don't want to do this.
ED: Nobody wants to go to the family golf tournament; nobody wants to go.

(Sounds from the laundry room.)

DESDEMONA: Um. So, the results came back.
ED: Um hm.
DESDEMONA: About our, heritage. And apparently, we're Cantonese speakers. From the Toisan region. And we're—or, rather, *I'm* fourth-generation Chinese American.
ED: American, through and through.
DESDEMONA: But you wanna know the most interesting thing?— We're not exactly "Chinese American."
ED: You know, about that, Desi—
DESDEMONA: So, the interesting thing is, we're Mexican.
ED: That's one thing we're not.
DESDEMONA: Hear me out. According to all this, my great-grandfather, *your* grandfather, was the first of the family to immigrate in the United States.

ED: And?

DESDEMONA: But *before* that, before Great-Grandfather Wong immigrated to America, we should be asking ourselves where he immigrated from. His father—Great-Great-Grandfather Wong—apparently sailed from China to America, failed to get in, and eventually settled in Mexicali, Mexico, where he worked as a cook. Not saying we're fully Mexican, but for a while your family could have been considered Chinese Mexican.

ED: But Mexicans are so poor. And noisy.

DESDEMONA: Dad, those are *totally* not the right adjectives for your ancestors.

ED: Mexicans don't even speak English. (*Contemplates this news.*) Sorry it turned out like that, Desi. Hope you're not disappointed.

DESDEMONA: About being Latino? Are you kidding? This is SO much better. I've researched it: Hispanic girls like me face *huge* obstacles in their lives. Discrimination, lack of access to education and contraception, machismo—

ED: Machismo?

DESDEMONA: It's a huge problem in Mexican culture. According to Wikipedia. The stereotype that Mexican men are masculine and powerful and uber-sexual and dominant over women—you know, ridiculous.

ED: Yeah, ridiculous.

DESDEMONA: I've always thought: There must be something wrong with me. And now, here it is!

ED: My father did slap my mother around from time to time . . .

DESDEMONA: You see! It's in our blood.

ED: I always liked Mexican food—all this time, I never knew why.

DESDEMONA: I knew there was something holding me back from achieving my potential. I am more at-risk than I ever imagined.

(*Ed and Desdemona share a mutual sigh of content.*)

ED: You want to get a burrito?

DESDEMONA: Sure, Dad.

SCENE 20

Upton's bedroom. Lights up on Upton, intently playing his computer game. Reporter appears.

REPORTER: And today I am here in Palo Alto, where in just a few moments Upton Wong is poised to be the first to break a twenty-four hundred rating for his three-versus-three team and catapult himself to the top of his battlegroup, securing his spot at the international arena tournament this December—

CROWD: FIVE . . . FOUR . . . THREE . . . TWO . . .

(New Year's–type celebration noises. Streamers, noisemakers. Reporter rips off her jacket to reveal herself as Asian Schoolgirl. She hands Upton his Korean airplane ticket and proceeds to make out with him.)

SCENE 21

Kitchen. Desdemona and Ed play a tequila-drinking game. They imbibe and bang their shot glasses on the table.

ED: **Una mas!**

(The game is over. Desdemona and Ed sigh, contented.)

DESDEMONA: I like being Mexican. *(Re the tequila bottle.)* It's so much easier to read.

(Ed caps the tequila bottle.)

ED: We'll save the rest for later. You're not eighteen yet.

DESDEMONA: Eighteen. I'm gonna be SO old. When you got me, did you ever think I'd be that smart?

ED: Always!

DESDEMONA: I mean, like THAT smart.

ED: You were my perfect little Chiquita banana. I remember the first time your mother got pregnant.

*(From offstage, a very pregnant Grace screams.
Her cries grow increasingly loud.)*

We were so excited. Your mother especially. *(To offstage.)* Hang in there, Tiger!

(However, it becomes clear that Grace's screams are the sound of J and Grace making out noisily.)

And then we got you. Those were nice days. Right, Grace?

(Pause. Grace enters, a little sore and distracted.)

GRACE: Hm?

ED: And we never realized how lucky we were.

GRACE: Well, in a way, I guess.

DESDEMONA: Mom, guess what we're doing for Christmas?

GRACE: Is that another rhetorical question, dear?

DESDEMONA: OK, where do I want to go more than anywhere else in the world?

GRACE: Princeton . . . ?

ED: Mexico!

(Ed brandishes four plane tickets.)

DESDEMONA: We're going to Mexico. For my *quinceañera*.

GRACE: Was that in *Joy Luck Club*?

DESDEMONA: "*Quinceañera*: a celebration of a young girl's maturation into a woman on her fifteenth birthday." It's like the most important thing in my life. And we're already three years late.

GRACE: Weren't we Chinese yesterday?

DESDEMONA: According to InstantHeritage.com, "Wing Ack Wong and Josefina Enriquez Wong gave birth to a son: Romero Wong."

ED: Romero, *my* great-grandfather. Born in Mexicali, Mexico.

DESDEMONA: Which is where we're going. Dad just picked up the tickets.

ED *(counting each ticket)*: Uno! Dos! Tres!

DESDEMONA *(finishing)*: Cinco!

(Grace silently counts the tickets.)

GRACE: What about J?

DESDEMONA: There're plenty of problem sets he can do at home. You know, only if he really wanted to.

GRACE: I might need him. To hold bags. And things. Or maybe I should stay home, wait for the Princeton letter?

DESDEMONA: The Princeton thing'll come when it comes.

GRACE: Though Mexico would be nice . . . I repeated Introductory Spanish in high school.

DESDEMONA: Mom, *everyone* takes Spanish.

ED: If you really want J to come, he can use Upton's ticket.

GRACE: Oh, but we couldn't do that to Upton . . .

(Upton barrels into the room, waving his plane ticket.)

UPTON: Mom! Dad! I'm going to Korea! I'm going to Seoul for Christmas!

DESDEMONA: See? He won't even be here. Four tickets, no problems.

ED: All settled then!

GRACE: I guess.

DESDEMONA *(to Ed)*: Let's get some guacamole.

> *(Grace spies J. Everyone except Upton exits the room in different directions. Upton speaks to the empty room.)*

UPTON: I made the tournament! I'm going to Korea . . .

> *(Pause. Upton waits.)*

SCENE 22

Kitchen. J is on the phone.

RECORDED VOICE: Welcome to 1-900-GIRL-SEX. Home of 901 sexy, sexy girls. For Olga, press one. For Irina, press two. For big mama love, press zero.

> *(J presses zero. Mrs. J answers the phone, sporting an imitation Eastern European accent. Heavy breathing.)*

MRS. J: In Bulgaria mountain, where I hot and bloated, I want reach big, thick American—

J: Ma—

MRS. J *(drops accent)*: Oh, hey. Jinqiang.

J: What is happening?

MRS. J: I thought you would tell me that. It has been a while.

J: Sorry. I have been busy. We filmed the video last week.

MRS. J: We?

J: Grace was wonderful.

MRS. J: Why does she help you?

J: Ma, reading the instructions is hard if you cannot speak English.

MRS. J: You can use a dictionary. You can look at the pictures.

J: Ma—

MRS. J: What does she want from you?

J: Nothing. We are just having fun.

MRS. J: If she helps you, she must want something. Everyone wants something, Jinqiang.

J: She is a good dancer. That is all.

MRS. J: I do not want you to lose sight of your goal. Do I have to come over there and *(with accent)* "give you big Bulgarian man-slap?"

> *(Grace peeks into the room.)*

J: I will call you back, Ma.

MRS. J: Jinqiang, do not get distracted. This is your calling.

(A noise. Grace and J exchange a look and run out of the room. J leaves the phone off the hook. Ed enters, eating a chimichanga, and picks up the phone.)

RECORDED VOICE: You have reached an unassigned number at 1-900-GIRL-SEX. To find steamy bunny love, press four. To return to Vulva Mountain, please press five.

SCENE 23

Kitchen. Several suitcases. Dressed in World of Warcraft gear, Upton sits on his suitcase and clutches his Korean Air ticket. Ed enters in a sombrero.

ED: Merry night before night before Christmas, Upton. *(Ed blows the whistle and waits for J to enter. Nothing.)* J? *(Ed leans over to pick up the suitcases himself.)* Well, nothing like carrying heavy objects to assert your manhood. *(Knocks on laundry room door.)* Grace, you OK in there?

GRACE *(from inside)*: I've got cramps, dear. I'm just resting.

ED: Oh, OK. What about J?

GRACE: I don't think J's feeling well either. I think it's contagious.

ED: You gonna be OK on the plane?

GRACE: We'll be fine.

ED: Can I get your keys?

GRACE: What about your keys?

ED: Can't find 'em.

GRACE: They're on the counter!

ED: I don't see 'em.

GRACE: They're there.

ED: Where?

GRACE: The drawer in the counter. It's . . . to the left, left, down, down, down, down, down . . .

(Ed knocks on the door again.)

ED: Couldn't find 'em.

(From inside the room, Grace pitches keys at Ed.)

Thanks. You gonna be OK?

GRACE: *Yes.* Yes yes yes yes yessssssss . . .

ED: All right, I'll be back.

*(Lights up on Little Chinese Girl, who peeks through the keyhole
of the laundry room door. She looks at Ed.)*

LITTLE CHINESE GIRL: Shhhh! I'm being conceived.
ED *(to no one)*: Well, hasta la vista, Tiger. *(To Little Chinese Girl.)* And I don't
know who you are, but scram before I call INS.

*(Little Chinese Girl waves and dematerializes. Ed starts taking the
suitcases out to the car. Desdemona enters and crosses the stage to exit.)*

UPTON *(too quickly)*: Des, Des! You want anything from Korea? I could—
Or maybe, maybe if your letter comes while I'm still here . . . ?
DESDEMONA: What letter?
UPTON: The Princeton letter.
DESDEMONA: Oh. I don't know.
UPTON: You could let me know where you're staying—
DESDEMONA *(confused)*: You're not coming with us.
UPTON: I know, but—
DESDEMONA: Whatever. Call. Or whatever.

(Desdemona exits. Grace enters from the laundry room.)

UPTON: Hey, Mom, you done with the laundry?
GRACE: Laundry?
UPTON: I need some more socks for the trip.
GRACE: I thought you weren't going to Mexico.
UPTON: No. To Seoul. I'm going to Korea.
GRACE: Oh, you kids go to so many places. Your socks are in that pile . . .
on the floor. *(Stops.)* You know, maybe you should buy new socks. I
don't know if those are clean anymore.

(J enters from the laundry room.)

UPTON: And I was thinking, my flight doesn't leave until later tonight, so
maybe I could—
GRACE: Hm? Oh. OK.

(Grace and J exit.)

UPTON: Bye, J!

(Ed enters for the last suitcase.)

ED: Have fun at your thing. See you in a week.
UPTON: A week?
ED: Oh, and before you go—

(*Upton prepares for a hug. Ed hands him some money.*)

Say hi to Kim Jong Il for me. (*To those outside.*) Vamonos, mucha-chos! Andale to Mexico!

(*Ed exits. Door slams. Upton sits. Time passes.*)

SCENE 24

Mexican hotel room. Desdemona in a hideous quinceañera dress. She hums "Feliz Navidad" as she applies sunscreen.

Kim Lee Park, looking emaciated and desperate, enters.

KIM LEE PARK: Desdemona . . . Desdemona . . . I am so hungry.
DESDEMONA: Go eat your yak.

(*Ed enters with a Corona, a piñata, and piñata bat, which he leaves on the bed. Desdemona appeals to him and points to Kim Lee Park.*)

Dad!

(*Ed shoos Kim Lee Park out.*)

ED: All right, nothing to see here. You can make the room up in half an hour. (*Ed lays himself out on the bed.*) Smell that? Mexican air.
DESDEMONA: Smells like a taco.
ED: Yeah . . . Mexican air.
DESDEMONA: Ready for my *quinceañera*?
ED: Almost. But first, where's your mother?

(*Desdemona gestures to the adjacent bathroom.
Ed knocks on the door.*)

How's it going in there, boss? Bad huevos rancheros?
GRACE: I'm fine!
ED: She's basically in the room.
DESDEMONA: What is it?

ED: Well, Desi, now that you're a woman. Or will be at midnight. Or became one three years ago. Well, now that you're of age, I thought I'd
give you something that your mother and I got eighteen years ago—

(Desdemona's cell phone rings.)

DESDEMONA: Oh, wait, hold on.

*(Desdemona answers her cell phone. Lights up on Upton, somewhere else,
eating a bag of Korean snacks. He holds a stack of mail.)*

Hello?

UPTON: Des! Des! Merry Christmas!

DESDEMONA: It's not Christmas yet. We've still got three hours.

UPTON: I know, but I am in Korea. And it's Christmas! I'm just . . . waiting
between rounds. I made it to the finals—

DESDEMONA: Upton, stop talking, this is long distance.

UPTON: Wait wait wait wait wait—I got the mail before I left.

DESDEMONA *(intense)*: What does it say?

UPTON: You know, Des, no matter what Princeton says, just remember that
I'll always look up to you—

DESDEMONA: READ IT.

UPTON: OK. *(Opens the envelope, reads.)* "Dear Desdemona Wong, Princeton University is pleased to offer you admission into the class of—"
(Stops.) Do you want me to keep going?

*(Desdemona screams and embraces Ed. Desdemona hangs up on Upton.
Mariachi music plays, seemingly from nowhere.)*

DESDEMONA: I'm going to Princeton! I'm going to Princeton!

ED: *(Knocks on the bathroom door.)* Did you hear that, boss?

GRACE: Where's that music coming from?

(The light begins to fade out on Upton.)

UPTON: Hello . . . ? Hello . . . ? Did we get disconnected? Des?

ED: Knew you could do it, Desi.

DESDEMONA: I'm going to Princeton! I'm an interesting, worthwhile person. I'm going to Princeton!

ED *(to Grace, in bathroom)*: Hear that, Tiger?

(Desdemona's enthusiasm finally subsides.)

DESDEMONA: So what was it you wanted to give me?

(Ed takes out a bracelet.)

ED: This is something your mother always wanted you to have.

DESDEMONA: Mom, that's kinda ugly.

ED: Not your *mother* mother. This is from your Korean mother. They gave this to us when we went over to Korea to get you. See? Now it's yours.

(Ed attaches the bracelet to Desdemona's wrist. Pause.)

DESDEMONA: I'm adopted?! *(Beat.)* And I'm *Korean*?!

ED: Aren't you happy? You were so excited about the Chinese thing. And the Mexican thing. Look! You get to discover more now!

DESDEMONA: Eighteen years, you never told me.

ED: We never told Upton either.

DESDEMONA: So what's he?

ED: Japanese. I think. *(Thinks.)* Honey, what's Upton?

DESDEMONA: You lied to me.

ED: It's not like we're sending you back. *(Laughs, stops.)* Grace? Grace, you coming out soon?

DESDEMONA: I'm *Korean.*

ED: I like Koreans. I do. They're very peaceful. Hyundai . . . Samsung . . .

(Kim Lee Park materializes.)

KIM LEE PARK: Dear Desdemona: Mother Superior told me the wonderful news. I cannot wait until you come to visit me at the orphanage, where we will become best friends.

DESDEMONA: Shut up, you are not me!

KIM LEE PARK: I am also working on my application to Princeton for next year. Thanks to you, I am inspired to write about deep and tragic things. *(Reads from essay.)* "Eighteen years ago, Desdemona Wong was born in Seoul, South Korea—at the mouth of a river, under the full moon of December. Abandoned by her mother—"

(Desdemona tackles Kim Lee Park and beats her up.)

DESDEMONA: YOU LITTLE CHINK! I'LL CUT YOU SO BAD YOU RE-ALLY WILL HAVE DOUBLE LIDS!

ED: That's enough now, Desi. Come on.

DESDEMONA: I KNOW WHERE YOU LIVE! KOREA'S NOT THAT BIG!

ED: You can discuss it with your therapist on Monday. Now say good-bye to your little Asian friend.

(Ed rips Desdemona off Kim Lee Park, who remains bashed on the floor for a moment. They wait awkwardly.)

We'll just wait until she, uh, goes away.

(Kim Lee Park dematerializes.)

Ah, there we are.
DESDEMONA: You said you were excited when Mom first got pregnant.
ED: Yes, that's true, and—
DESDEMONA: *Well?*

(The sound of Grace, offstage, in labor. This time, the baby's cries turn into Grace wailing in despair. Kim Lee Park, as the nurse, enters with a cold-looking bundle and hands it to Ed.)

(Ed is extremely uncomfortable holding the bundled dead baby. He hands it off to Desdemona but then rethinks this and takes the baby back. He discretely dumps or hides it somewhere.)

ED: And then we got you. You know, in the grand scheme of things, you and Upton are very lucky those babies died.
DESDEMONA: So is my birth mother dead or alive?
ED: What'll make you feel better? *(Stops.)* Korea's VERY close to China, you know.
DESDEMONA: So I'm not Chinese?
ED: No.
DESDEMONA: Or Mexican?
ED: No.
DESDEMONA: Not even un poco?

(Ed shakes his head. Desdemona makes a sob.)

ED: But look! Look! Princeton! You got in!
DESDEMONA: I can't go to Princeton: I'm Korean.
ED: Of course, you can.
DESDEMONA: They think I'm a person of color!
ED: Yellow is a color.
DESDEMONA: Like "color" color.
ED: Desi, nobody really thought you were Mexican.
DESDEMONA: Why didn't you tell me before?
ED: But you got in!
DESDEMONA: That's not the point!
ED: It isn't?
DESDEMONA: I *liked* being Mexican.
ED: Chinese, Japanese, Korean . . . Mexican. They're basically the same country.

DESDEMONA: The Chinese killed Koreans.
ED: The Japanese killed Koreans! Koreans killed Koreans! WE killed Koreans! No one'll know the difference. Chinese, Japanese, Indian chief—nowadays everyone's Asian. So come on, celebrate your *quinceañera* like a good little girl.
DESDEMONA: I don't want it. I'm not Mexican! And I'm not even fifteen!

> *(Desdemona grabs the Corona from Ed,
> takes a swig, and runs off.)*

ED: Desi! Come back! Or at least put the Corona down!

> *(Ed glances at the bathroom door.
> He pursues Desdemona.)*

(Pause. Flushing noise. Grace enters from the bathroom. She looks at the pregnancy test in one hand and then tries to read the box. The Chinese Woman appears as Pregnancy Test.)

PREGNANCY TEST *(specifically to Grace)*: Usted está embarazada.
GRACE: ¿Embarazada?
PREGNANCY TEST: Embarazada. Encinta.
GRACE: ¿Encinta? ¿Quién, yo?
PREGNANCY TEST: Sí.

> *(Grace embraces Pregnancy Test.)*

GRACE: Gracias! Gracias, señora, prueba de embarazo! *(For good measure.)* Danke schön!

> *(J enters. Pregnancy Test dematerializes.)*

> *(To J.) Estoy embarazada!*
J: What?
GRACE: Oh, sorry. I forget you don't speak Spanish. Or English!
J: Good news?
GRACE: You, too?
J: I think so! But you go first.
GRACE: No, you!
J: Your cell phone—

(J thrusts the cell phone at Grace. She listens. Upton appears, eating a different Korean snack. The wrapper for the first is somewhere nearby. Upton's message starts off slowly.)

UPTON: Hey, Mom, nothing much is happening over here. I bought some socks—

J: Skip the first one.

(Grace skips the message. Lights flicker over Upton, who tries to get in his message before it's too late.)

UPTON *(speedily)*: And just wanted to let you know I'm going into the championship round soon, so if you call and I don't answer, or if you call and I do answer and I'm busy or you're busy, just leave a message so I can call you back when you're—

(Beep. Upton's lights are snuffed. Next message. Ambitious Asian Intern materializes.)

AMBITIOUS ASIAN INTERN: Hi, this is Betty Nguyen, here at America's Next Top Dancer. Hollywood. Congratulations, Mr. . . . uh, Jin *(Mumbles his name.)* You've qualified for the next round. To stay in the running, you must be at our studios for the semifinalist round by the twenty-sixth. Repeat, you *must* be down here, day after Christmas. No exceptions. You have our number. Hope your day's super! Bye-bye.

(Click. Ambitious Asian Intern dematerializes.)

J: Well?

(Grace nods. J and Grace scream and embrace each other.)

We're going to be famous! The next nine months're gonna be grueling, but it'll be worth it. When we're in Hollywood together— Wait, what was your news?

GRACE: Nothing. It's nothing.

J: What was it?

GRACE: You go. To Hollywood.

J: With you. I need you, Grace.

GRACE: Yes, but other people need me now, too. Sorry.

(Ed enters, winded.)

Jinqiang needs a ride to the border, dear.

ED: Oh?

GRACE: Just drop him over the American side.

ED: Can do, boss. *(Ed's cell phone rings. He answers and stands off from Grace and J.)* Hello?

(Lights up on Upton again, this time eating a cup of ramen, next to his two empty bags of Korean snacks.)

UPTON: Is Mom's phone dead?
ED: No, no, it's fine. Everything's fine. Everything's totally functional.
J *(in parting)*: I couldn't have done it without you.
GRACE: Likewise.
UPTON: I wanted to leave my hotel number—

(J gratefully embraces Grace. They share a moment. Ed watches from afar.)

ED: Oho, need to give J a ride now.
UPTON: —you know, so that if my phone dies or your phone dies or Desi's dies or I die, just—just so you can reach me.
ED: All right! Keep up the good work!

(Ed hangs up and joins in on J and Grace's hug, somewhat awkwardly. The light lingers on Upton, who looks around for something to do. He eats some ramen.)

All right then. *(As J exits, to Grace.)* And if you see Desi, you might want to talk to her. Think she's having some female problems. Or something.

(Ed picks up the pregnancy test, which has fallen on the floor. He hands it to Grace, but not before taking a quick peek.)

"Hecho en China." Hm. Who would've known! Be back soon, Tiger. *(Beat.)* Congratulations.
GRACE: Thanks, Ed.

SCENE 25

In the car. Ed is in the driver's seat. J sits shotgun. Ed speaks to J.

ED: Machismo was probably the one thing about Mexican culture that I never understood. I mean: sombreros, chimichangas, Speedy Gonzales, I could relate to that. But the whole Mexican male-dominated culture thing, I mean, it just seemed a little unbelievable to me, honestly. But I've come to realize that machismo is not so much about hitting women as it is embracing who you are and what life has given you. "You're a man! Be a man! Do man things! Stand your ground!"

It's the same as one's culture. You're Chinese; you're Mexican—do Chinese Mexican things. "Use chopsticks! Make tortillas! Build low-cost automobiles!"

Americans, we're always trying to blend in. Be part of the melting pot. Meltmeltmelt. But let's be honest: That's never going to work, because at the end of the day, I'm still going to look different than them. And the best I can do is embrace my machismo, my culture, my life. Because once we know exactly who we are and what life has given us, then we can be happy.

My daughter may not be the exact person she wants to be at this moment, but in the end she's going to be much happier because she now knows exactly who she is.

(*Lights up on Desdemona, nursing a Corona grimly.*)

Or Upton. He knows what he wants in life, and he doesn't need me there to hold his hand.

(*Lights up on Upton, eating a Korean snack—or several snacks. He waits for his cell phone to ring.*)

As for Grace and me, we accept the way our lives are. Our limitations, our faults.

(*Lights up on Grace, examining the pregnancy test.*)

Celebrities divorce all the time. Why? Because they've forgotten that marriages, above all, are hard. But even when you fall out of love with someone, it's no reason to divorce them. If you divorced someone as soon as you didn't love them anymore—well! There wouldn't be any married people, now would there? (*Laughs.*) Sometimes I think my wife's silly. Sometimes I think her demands are stupid. "Take out the trash." "Mow the lawn." "Make me a baby." What does she want me to make it out of? Money?

But I don't divorce her. When she complains it's MY fault our kids are OTHER PEOPLE's kids, I say, "No! Next best thing in the world." Because as long as I embrace who I am and my children know who they are and we all love what we've got, which is, well, each other, then that's the most important thing. Right, Grace?

GRACE: No, Ed.

(*Ed looks at Grace.*)

That's not enough.

(Somewhere, a tap. Another tap. Grace looks off into the distance. She takes a step in that direction.)

ED: She'll be back.

(Grace disappears. Ed parks the car; gestures for J to get out.)

Well, it's a clear shot from here to wherever you want to go in America. Just as long as you don't get shot on the way!

(Ed hands J a wad of cash. J pockets some and tries to return the rest.)

Take it all.

J: Thanks. You're all very lucky.

ED: Don't I know it. *(Beat.)* You're still illiterate, right? Like you don't actually speak English?

J: Nope.

ED: Just checking.

(Ed shuts the door and drives off.)

SCENE 26

Mexican hotel room. Grace packs her bags. Desdemona enters, frustrated. She tries to get the bracelet off her wrist. She sees Grace.

DESDEMONA: Help me. *(Waits.)* MOM, help me.

GRACE: Just hold it straight.

DESDEMONA: No. You do it.

(Desdemona bangs the bracelet against a table.)

GRACE: You're going to break it.

DESDEMONA: I don't like it. It's stupid and it won't come off. I don't want it anymore.

GRACE: It's your mother's.

DESDEMONA: *You're* my mother. Mom, come on!

GRACE: I'm busy.

DESDEMONA: You never have anything to do. *(Gestures to bracelet.)* This is something to do.

(*Grace finishes packing. The sound of tap dancing, not too far away. Little Chinese Girl arrives, tap dancing.*)

You need to help me. Mom!
GRACE: You'll be fine, dear. You always have been.

(*Grace returns the steps. The mother and daughter dance more deeply into Mexico.*)

DESDEMONA: Mom, will you stop that? You need to come here. I can't do this myself!

(*Grace and Little Chinese Girl dematerialize.*)

(*To no one.*) I can't do this myself.

(*Beat. Desdemona tries one last time to wrench the bracelet from her wrist. Pitiful. Unsuccessful, Desdemona looks around for something to destroy.*)

(*She grabs the bat and mashes the piñata into pieces. She ends up on the floor with the piñata, sobbing. She starts eating the Mexican candy—all the candy.*)

(*Her cell phone rings. Beat. With her mouth full, Desdemona answers.*)

What.

(*Lights up on Upton, eating kimchee, now engulfed by Korean snack food wrappers. He clutches a large trophy.*)

UPTON: Hey, Des. I think you got cut off last time, so I just thought I'd check. You busy?
DESDEMONA: No. No, just . . . sitting around.
UPTON: How're Mom and Dad?
DESDEMONA: Oh, they're fine. (*Pause.*) How's the, uh, World Warcar thing going?
UPTON: I won.
DESDEMONA: Oh, yeah?
UPTON: The whole tournament.
DESDEMONA: You got a trophy?
UPTON: Yeah.
DESDEMONA: I want to see.

UPTON: Oh. OK. Well, when I get back. Next week. I wanted to celebrate. So I bought some kimchee. For Christmas.

DESDEMONA: How is Korea?

UPTON: Good. Though not as many yaks as I thought there'd be.

DESDEMONA: Really?

UPTON: And you! Princeton! Boy, we're having a great month. *(Beat.)* We got a Christmas card.

DESDEMONA: From who?

UPTON: From us.

DESDEMONA: How is it?

(Upton looks at the card.)

(Lights up on Ed and Grace posing for the picture. J and Little Chinese Girl stand where Desdemona and Upton should be. Upton and Desdemona look at the family portrait warmly.)

UPTON: It's nice.

DESDEMONA: Yeah. We do look happy.

(Flashbulb. The family portrait dematerializes.)

UPTON: What time is it there?

DESDEMONA: Right about midnight.

(The clock strikes twelve. A snowflake. Another. It's unclear whether we are in Korea or Mexico. Upton and Desdemona watch the snow fall.)

UPTON: The snow sure is pretty, huh?

DESDEMONA: Yeah.

UPTON: Merry Christmas, Des.

DESDEMONA: Merry Christmas.

UPTON: See you at home.

DESDEMONA: OK.

(Desdemona and Upton don't hang up but stay on the line as they watch the snow. We perhaps hear "Feliz Navidad" in the background.)

END OF PLAY

Afterword

R. A. SHIOMI

卞   汐

M u Performing Arts participated in the development and produced
the world premieres of all but one of the plays in this anthology.
The question that comes to mind is "How on earth did this happen?"
The answer is a story that blends my own personal and artistic journey with
the emergence here of a new community of Asian American theater artists.

My career in theater began in San Francisco with the Asian American Theater Company (AATC), where I wrote my first play, *Yellow Fever*, in 1982. It was
a hit there, receiving a "Bernie" and a Bay Area Theater Circle Critics Award.
Later that year, it was produced in New York by Pan Asian Repertory Theatre,
where it received rave reviews from Mel Gussow of the *New York Times* and
Edith Oliver of the *New Yorker*. Those productions essentially launched me as
a playwright, and over the next decade I had more plays produced at the AATC
and Pan Asian Repertory Theatre, as well as at East West Players in Los Angeles and at other theaters in Seattle, Vancouver, and Toronto.

In developing *Yellow Fever* in the Bay Area, I was blessed to know and
work with such major artists in the making as David Hwang, Philip Gotanda,
Marc Hayashi, Amy Hill, Lane Nishikawa, Dennis Dun, and many more. It
was Philip who had steered me to work with the AATC, and it was a time of
tremendous artistic energy there; in fact, this period is now looked on as the
"Golden Age" of the AATC. And with all the productions by other companies,
I had the opportunity to see how theater companies operated—the good, the
bad, and the ugly. I was able to watch and learn about directing from different artists, such as Lane Nishikawa in San Francisco and Raul Aranas in

New York. I saw many actors develop their talent in this wave of emerging artists and participated in the artistic decision-making process at AATC. So the 1980s was the time for not only my primary writing as a playwright but also my general education in theater.

During that first cycle of my theater life, I had heard of David Mura as a prominent poet buried deep in the hinterland of the Midwest, and I wondered how he could survive without an Asian American community. A second incident was an actual visit I made to Minneapolis in 1985 in support of a tour of my play *Rosie's Café*. I gave a short talk for about five people, among whom were Jack Reuler, the artistic director of Mixed Blood Theatre, and David Moore Jr., then the executive director of the Playwrights' Center. All I can remember from that visit, besides their congeniality, is that it confirmed my opinion that Minnesota would be the last place in the world I'd want to end up. In fact, around that time there was an interesting story about Philip Gotanda, who had received a grant to work on a new play with the Playwrights' Center. He left after staying only a few days because there were no Asian American actors to work with. Such are the ironies of my own journey—that realities I believed so remote from my own existence became the very framework for two decades of my life in theater.

By 1990, I was based back in Toronto and working in Canadian television as a staff writer for the series *ENG*. Eric Hayashi asked me to speak at a session of the annual conference of the Association for Theatre in Higher Education (I knew Eric from the AATC days.) I accepted and, you might say, "the rest is history." At the conference, I met both Dong-il Lee, a graduate student at the University of Minnesota, and Martha Johnson, a theater professor at Augsburg College. From that encounter, I began to visit the Twin Cities and get to know the local theater community. I was not thinking of working or staying in that community, so I was more of a tourist than an artist with intentions to relocate there. But the thought did occur to me that it would be a challenge to survive there as a theater artist.

On one of my visits in 1992, Dong-il Lee asked me to help him start a theater company in the Twin Cities. I was initially quite skeptical but wanted to support him in his dreams. Knowing that two artists running a company is a dicey proposition, especially since I was still transient, I insisted on finding a managing director before we started. We found that person in Diane Espaldon, who had recently relocated from New York with a master's degree in international diplomacy from Columbia University. The other key members at this time were Martha Johnson, whom I later married; her friend, Donna Gustafson, a local lawyer who set up the official status of the company and became the first board chair; and Andrew Kim, a recent graduate of Carleton College. The founding members of Theater Mu were set up in 1992, with Dong-il as the artistic director, Diane as the managing director, and Martha, Andrew, and me as artistic associates. The five of us became the Core Artistic Group, which formed the leadership of the company.

This Core Artistic Group became a key factor in the development of the company over its whole journey. Diane had insisted that the managing director be involved in all major artistic discussions and decisions to maintain the financial and organizational balance of the company. She was right and set us all off on a path that would match growing artistic development with successful financial and organizational systems. The Core Artistic Group was the place where all the tough decisions were hashed out among the members, and we usually arrived at a consensus on them that moved Mu forward.

We immediately began working on the development of new theater actors and writers. Among the young people we worked with, we found many Korean adoptees, and their powerful stories became the source for Mu's first mainstage production, *Masked Dance*. The play, which I wrote, told their stories through Western drama and Korean mask dance and drumming. As fate would have it, Dong-il Lee was finishing his graduate work and moved on to teach on the East Coast in 1993. He is now working back in Korea. I became the interim artistic director in 1993. As with many new companies, personnel changes occurred. Andrew Kim shifted his theater work more to In the Heart of the Beast Puppet and Mask Theatre, and Diane moved on to work as an arts consultant with a national firm, and she has since become a prominent consultant in the field. So by 1996, the "interim" tag was removed from my title, and Martha, Sandy Agustin (a local Filipino American dancer, choreographer, and performance artist), and Zaraawar Mistry, were the artistic associates. And as a novice artistic director, I treasured the work of the Core Artistic Group for guidance in the making of critical decisions.

Through the first decade of work, Mu focused on blending traditional Asian performance forms and contemporary Asian American stories. This became the signature style of our company and resulted in the development of new plays, such as *Temple of Dreams,* by Marcus Quiniones; *Legend of the White Snake Lady,* by Shen Pei; and my plays *Song of the Pipa* and *Tale of the Dancing Crane.* We felt we had created a style quite distinctive from the generally more naturalistic approaches of the major Asian American companies. *Walleye Kid: The Musical* was perhaps the most recent embodiment of this style, but the blending was not to remain our primary focus for much longer.

In the early 2000s, Mu made a significant shift to more contemporary plays as the Twin Cities Asian American community matured and demanded works reflecting their experiences. This shift had already begun with our productions of plays such as *Song for a Nisei Fisherman,* by Philip Gotanda, in 2001; *Falling Flowers,* by Jeany Park, in 2003; and *99 Histories,* by Julia Cho, in 2004. With a more directed focus, Mu started to canvas for scripts from around the country and soon produced *Happy Valley,* by Aurorae Khoo, and *Bahala Na,* by Clarence Coo. As with all Mu productions, there is clearly a powerful issue at the heart of each of these plays. In *Happy Valley*, it's the emigration crisis in Hong Kong at the turn of the twenty-first century. In *Bahala Na*, it's the need for acceptance of a gay grandson by a resistant grandmother. And each of these plays has an interesting story of discovery. With *Happy Valley*, it was how the play took me back to the world of Hong Kong when I lived there in the early 1970s. Even then I felt the mounting anxiety among the Chinese about the upcoming transfer of Hong Kong to Mainland China. I passed the script on to Jennifer Weir, and she immediately embraced the play, which Mu produced in 2005. With *Bahala Na*, it was hard to find someone to direct a reading because the lyrical writing style seemed unsuited for the stage. But as soon as we heard it at the reading in our New Eyes Festival, everyone agreed it should be produced, and in 2007 it was.

As we moved down this road of developing new contemporary work, our path broadened to include new variations. One was *Walleye Kid: The Musical*, for which Sundraya Kase and I wrote the book and Kurt Miyashiro composed the music and wrote the lyrics. It was a story meant for families about Korean adoption, told through a contemporary folktale style. We produced it twice, in 2005 and 2008. In 2007, I was interviewed by Farrell Foreman about new play development for a report he wrote for the Ford Foundation. Out of that report came the Ford Foundation's initiative to encourage emerging playwrights of color. Mu received funding that resulted in the world premiere of *Bahala Na* in 2007 and the world premiere of *Ching Chong Chinaman* by Lauren Yee in 2009. About the same time, we created Mu's Jerome New Performance Program funded by the Jerome Foundation, in which Mu worked with artists from related writing and performance fields, such as performance art, poetry, spoken word, and prose. The first round of this program produced *Q & A*, by Julianna Pegues, in May 2008; *Asiamnesia*, by Sun Mee Chomet; and *Sia(b)*, by May Lee-Yang, which premiered under the title *Under the Porcelain Mask* in the fall of 2008.

The one exception in this anthology is *Indian Cowboy*, a play that was created and performed independently by Zaraawar Mistry; however, Zaraawar is based in the Twin Cities and worked with Mu before he started the Center for Independent Artists and, later, Dreamland Arts in St. Paul, which he now runs with his wife, Leslye Orr. And the careers of a few other local Asian American theater artists, including Aditi Kapil, Dipankar Mukherjee, Masa Kawahara, Aamera Siddiqui, and Lia Rivamonte, have developed mainly outside of Mu.

Mu has had tremendous success with these various new play development initiatives. *Asiamnesia* was chosen as best new play in the Twin Cities in 2008 by the *Star Tribune*, and *Ching Chong Chinaman* has been subsequently and successfully produced in New York and Seattle. What's more, another play developed and produced by Mu in 2006, *Cowboy versus Samurai*, by Michael Golamco, has received successful productions around the country. So suddenly a whole new wave of plays and playwrights has been developed by Mu Performing Arts.

I believe that the explanation for the phenomenal development of Mu is a combination of my previous experience and understanding of the Asian American theater movement, the key input of cofounder Martha Johnson and the rest of the Core Artistic Group, and the coming of age of a whole community of Asian American theater artists in the Twin Cities. Having worked at all of the major Asian American theater companies and with many of the best artists of those communities, I always measured Mu's work against that national standard. And it was always a thrill to discover new young talent, because I knew that any hope of future success rested on their abilities. In fact, there are more than a hundred theater artists on my local contact list, and that number is growing.

Now, looking back over the past two decades, I feel that we are in a "Golden Age" for Mu. This anthology reflects the long road that brought us here through the successful selection of plays and playwrights from across the country and the development of a new and exciting wave of theater artists locally. Mu Performing Arts has already had a significant impact on the Asian American theater community, and I truly believe it will become an important part of the American theater landscape.

Contributors

Sun Mee Chomet is an actor, dancer, and playwright based in St. Paul. As an actor, she has worked with many local and national theaters, including the Guthrie Theater and Mu Performing Arts. She holds a bachelor of arts degree in sociology and anthropology from Earlham College and a master of fine arts) degree in acting from the Tisch School of the Arts at New York University.

Clarence Coo's work has been developed, presented, and produced by the Kennedy Center, the Mark Taper Forum, the New York International Fringe Festival, East West Players, Round House Theatre, and the Inkwell Inkubator Festival. In the master of fine arts playwriting program at Columbia University, he studied under Charles Mee.

Don Eitel is a musician, composer, actor, director, and arts administrator. Currently the managing director of Mu Performing Arts, he was also a founding artistic director of Starting Gate Productions and has worked as the development associate and assistant to the artistic director at Park Square Theatre, a mid-sized company based in St. Paul.

Sundraya Kase is a Korean adoptee who grew up in St. Paul. In her professional career, she is a community organizer who brings people together around issues of social justice and racial equality. She is also a writer, artist, daughter,) sister, and mother of four sons.

Aurorae Khoo, whose plays have been produced and developed around the country, has had commissions from the Gerbode Foundation, South Coast Repertory, and the Statue of Liberty–Ellis Island Foundation. Currently, she is a writer for the Fox television show *Running Wilde*. Khoo was a Fellow at Harvard University's Radcliffe Institute. She holds a bachelor of arts degree from Brown University and a master of fine arts degree from New York University.

Josephine Lee is professor of English and Asian American studies at the University of Minnesota, Twin Cities. She is currently the president of the Association for Asian American Studies. Her most recent book is *The Japan of Pure Invention: Gilbert and Sullivan's* The Mikado (2010). She is also the author of *Performing Asian America: Race and Ethnicity on the Contemporary Stage* (1997) and co-editor of *Re/collecting Early Asian America: Essays in Cultural History* (2002).

May Lee-Yang is a first-generation Hmong American writer and performance artist. Her plays include *Confessions of a Lazy Hmong Woman, Ten Reasons Why I'd Be a Bad Porn Star, Sia(b), Stir-Fried Pop Culture,* and *The Child's House.* She has won grants from the Playwrights' Center, the Midwestern Voices and Visions Residency Award, and the National Performance Network.

Zaraawar Mistry has written and performed three solo shows: *Sohrab and Rustum* (City Pages Ten Best in 2002), *Indian Cowboy* (Star Tribune Outstanding Experimental Show in 2006), and *Children's Stories from India.* He is the co-owner of Dreamland Arts, a forty-seat theater attached to his home in St. Paul. Mistry holds a bachelor of arts degree from Bennington College and a master of fine arts degree from the University of California, San Diego.

Kurt Miyashiro is a professor of music at Southeastern Illinois College and a graduate of the University of Minnesota. His primary compositions have been for musical theater. He and his wife, Beth, have three children—Tori (age twelve) and twins Madeleine and Andrew (age five). When he is not teaching or composing, he enjoys long-distance running and working with horses.

R. A. Shiomi has been a leader in the Asian American theater movement since the 1980s, as a playwright, a director, and an artistic director. His plays include *Yellow Fever, Rosie's Café, Play Ball, Mask Dance,* and *Journey of the Drum.* He has directed at Mu Performing Arts, the Asian American Theater Company in San Francisco, and Interact Theater in Philadelphia. He is one of the founders of Mu Performing Arts and has been its artistic director since 1983. In 2007, Shiomi received the Sally Irvine Ordway Award for "Vision" for his work with Mu Performing Arts.

Lauren Yee has been a MacDowell Colony Fellow, a Dramatists Guild Fellow, and a member of the Public Theater Emerging Writers Group. Her play *Ching Chong Chinaman* was a finalist for the Jane Chambers and Princess Grace Awards and was produced by Impact Theatre, Mu Performing Arts, Pan Asian Repertory Theatre, and SIS Productions. Originally from San Francisco, Yee holds a bachelor of arts degree from Yale University and a master of fine arts degree from the University of California, San Diego.